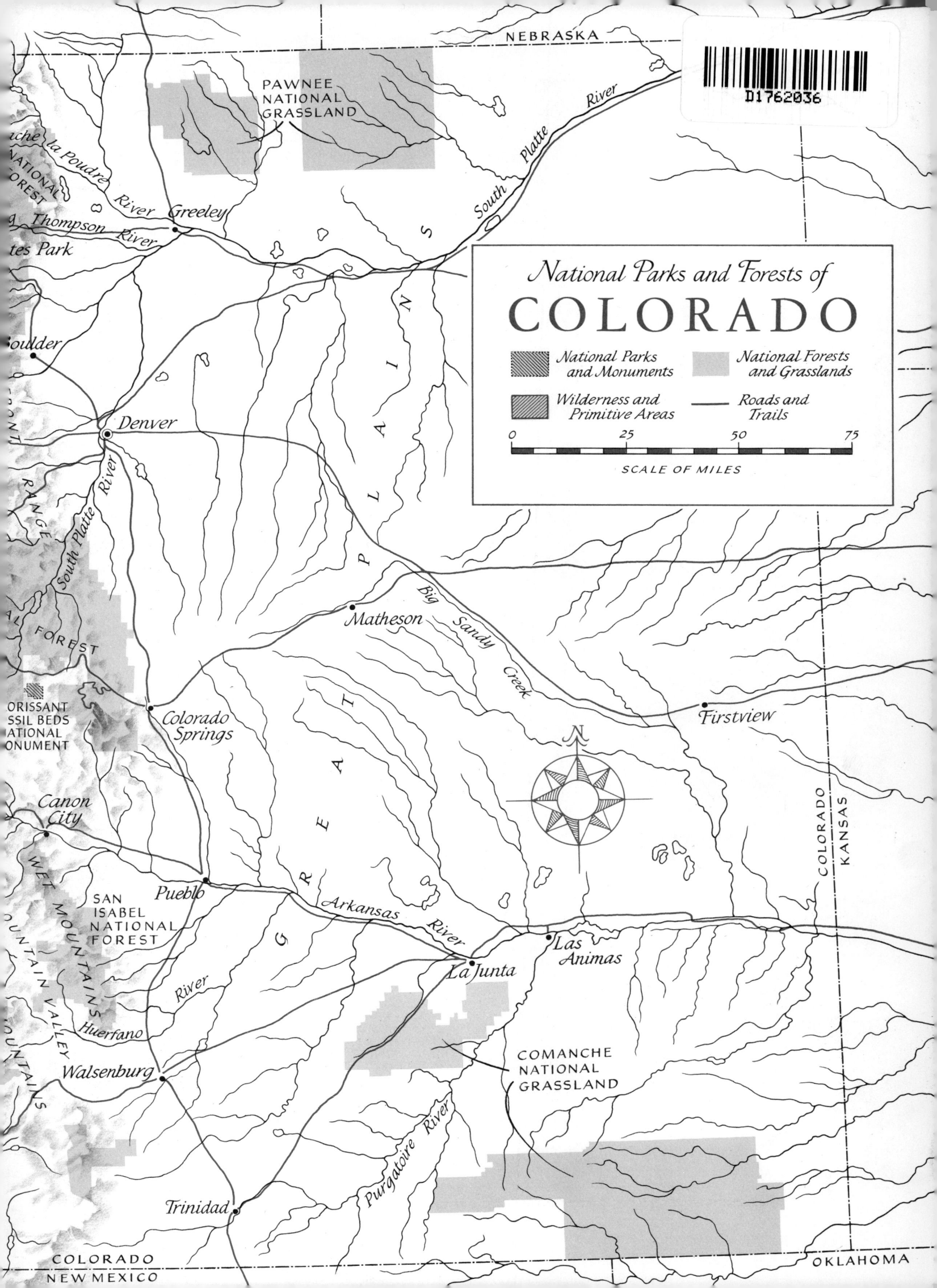

#  DAVID LAVENDER'S COLORADO

## BOOKS BY DAVID LAVENDER

David Lavender's Colorado
Nothing Seemed Impossible: William Ralston and Early San Francisco
California: A Bicentennial History
California, Land of New Beginnings
The Great Persuader
The Rockies
The American Heritage History of the Great West
Climax at Buena Vista: American Campaigns in Northeastern Mexico, 1846-47
The Fist in the Wilderness
Westward Vision: The Story of the Oregon Trail
The Story of Cyprus Mines Corporation
Land of Giants
Bent's Fort
The Big Divide
One Man's West

FICTION

Red Mountain
Andy Claybourne

JUVENILES

The Story of California
The Trail to Santa Fe
Golden Trek
Mike Maroney, Raider
Trouble at Tamarack

*David Lavender's*
# COLORADO

by DAVID LAVENDER

WITH 105 PHOTOGRAPHS IN COLOR
BY THE AUTHOR AND LEE BOLTIN

DOUBLEDAY & COMPANY, INC., GARDEN CITY, NEW YORK
1976

COPYRIGHT © 1976 BY LEE BOLTIN AND DAVID LAVENDER
ALL RIGHTS RESERVED

*Library of Congress Cataloging in Publication Data*

Lavender, David Sievert, 1910–
David Lavender's Colorado.

Bibliography
Includes index.
1. Colorado—Description and travel—1951–
2. Lavender, David Sievert, 1910–   I. Boltin, Lee.
II. Title.
F781.2.L38       917.88'04'3
ISBN 0-385-06337-7
Library of Congress Catalog Card Number 75-32013

PRINTED IN THE UNITED STATES OF AMERICA

FIRST EDITION

# TO MILDRED

for being the main part of all of it

*Maps by John V. Morris*

## PHOTO CREDITS

**BY DAVID LAVENDER:**

5, 11, 12, 13, 14, 15, 17, 18, 21, 36, 41, 42, 43, 44, 46, 47, 48, 52, 54, 56, 58, 59, 60, 61, 62, 63, 64, 65, 67, 68, 71, 75, 78, 79, 82, 83, 84, 85, 86, 87, 88, 90, 91, 92, 93, 95, 97, 98, 101, 104, 105

**BY LEE BOLTIN:**

1, 2, 3, 4, 6, 7, 8, 9, 10, 16, 19, 20, 22, 23, 24, 25, 26, 27, 28, 29, 30, 31, 32, 33, 34, 35, 37, 38, 39, 40, 45, 49, 50, 51, 53, 55, 57, 66, 69, 70, 72, 73, 74, 76, 77, 80, 81, 89, 94, 96, 99, 100, 102, 103

# CONTENTS

Preface     *ix*

Acknowledgments     *xi*

### *Part One*    *THE SEASONS: EXCURSIONS UP AND DOWN*

1. The Verities and Varieties of Winter     *3*
   *Into a White-Out . . . The Implacable Powers of Wind and Snow . . . Snow Sports . . . An Overview at Last*

2. A Thunder of Waters     *16*
   *Riding the Snow Melt . . . Rafting in Dinosaur National Monument . . . Outward Bound . . . Meeting the Yampa River . . . The Warm Springs Maelstrom . . . Defending the Wilderness*

3. Unexpected Bounties     *28*
   *The Laggard Season . . . Weather Hang-Ups . . . Learning to See*

4. Full Color     *37*
   *The Summons . . . First Snow . . . The Italian Cowboy . . . New Looks at Old Vistas*

### *Part Two*    *THE WAY THE LAND LIES*

5. The Plains     *49*
   *The Nimble Creatures of the Plains . . . Bringing Moisture to Dryness . . . The National Grasslands . . . Ecological Ranching*

6. Transitions     *59*
   *The Urban Strip . . . The Warped Earth . . . The Impact of Altitude . . . The Topmost Life Zones . . . Timberline Struggles*

7. The Main Ranges     72
   *Relics of the Mining Rush . . . The Tortured Mountains . . . The Varied Faces of the Front Range . . . Intramountain Flatlands . . . The Winding Divide . . . River Patterns . . . Ice Carvings . . . High-Country Driving . . . Climbing the Fourteeners*

8. Breakaway Country: The Plateaus     86
   *Colorado's Rugged Western Slope . . . Exclamation Marks in Granite . . . The Marvelous Plateaus . . . The Long Valleys . . . Colorado River Country . . . The First Residents . . . A Hard Way to Make a Dollar*

## Part Three     THE THIRSTY LAND

9. The Ancient Ones: Vistas in Time and Space     101
   *The Culture of the Ancient Ones . . . The Long View from Lowry . . . Altering Nature's Rhythms . . . Persistent Patterns . . . Prehistoric Urbanization . . . The Great Towers . . . The Mysteries of Mesa Verde*

10. Dog Town     115
    *Random Death . . . Warring on Predators . . . The Problems of Poison . . . A Dog's Life, Prairie Style*

11. Farewell to a River     125
    *The Dam Syndrome . . . Preparations . . . White Water . . . Climbing Out*

12. The Salts of Paradox: Serendipity in Reverse     135

## Part Four     BYWAYS

13. Marmots and Marble     145

14. The Arkansas Mixing Bowl     153

15. Fads in Mountaintops     164

## Part Five     WILDERNESS

16. Triumph in the Flat Tops     177
    *Seedbed of the Wilderness Movement . . . Arthur Carhart's Private Revolution . . . . Clashing Interests*

17. Solo     186
    *Reluctant Wayfaring . . . The Old San Juan Primitive Area . . . What Is Wilderness? . . . Toward Snowmass . . . Over the Top . . . The Crowded Wildlands*

*Epilogue   A DIFFERENT WORLD*

18. The Sneffels Range: Halfway Between Yesterday and Tomorrow    *203*
    *Mountaineering on Mount Sneffels . . . A Woman in Marlboro Country . . . The Changing San Juans . . . A Mountain Dilemma . . . Over the Hill to Resurgent Telluride . . . A Most Uncertain Prospect*

Glossary of Terms    *218*

Bibliography    *221*

Index    *223*

*Maps    12–15*

# PREFACE

This is a book about some of the surprises, delights, and occasional shocks that anyone exploring Colorado's outdoor country is likely to encounter. Neither the words nor the pictures concern themselves, except incidentally, with the state's burgeoning cities or even with the small towns of the mountains and plains.

Of necessity the presentation is mostly personal. I was born and grew up in a remote area of southwestern Colorado, less school years in Denver. Although the exigencies of making a living took me away from the state when I was twenty-eight, I have returned year after year, abrim with chauvinism (not male, just patriotic), to visit old haunts and explore new areas. The sentimental entanglements are so strong that I never even considered trying to be detached when presenting the descriptions of season, place, and events that follow—with this tempering. Accompanying me on all the trips and balancing my prejudices (I called them enthusiasms) was my wife Mildred, a non-Coloradoan with a cool sense of proportion.

The pictures, too, represent personal points of view. Scenes were chosen not primarily to illustrate, though at times they do that, but to convey essential qualities. I found it very exciting to learn, from Lee Boltin's example, how to search for character rather than panorama in landscape. Because of that fundamental lesson even the pictures that Boltin did not take bear his touch.

To me the chief element in the Colorado landscape is contrast, seasonal as well as topographic. Thus the account begins with a telling of four outdoor experiences designed to show the impact of changing weather patterns both on the countryside and on the recreationists who are abroad in the land during the four seasons. That section is followed by another unit of four chapters that present a broad overview of the state's major physiographic units, each sharply different from the others—the plains, the abrupt rising of the eastern slope of the mountains, the moisture-catching main ranges, and, lastly, the plateaus and canyons of the Western Slope.

In the second half of the book the focus narrows onto smaller areas that for me have a special significance of one sort or another. Again that significance emerges in part through personal narratives telling of delight and not infrequently of alarm.

Colorado's superb attractions, like those of every other beautiful area in the world, are beset with threats brought on by economic demands, increased population, and overpowering technology. In one sense this book compounds the problem by calling attention to spots that might flourish better by being overlooked by tourists. In justification I plead my belief that ultimately even the most isolated parts of the back country, to say nothing of the muddy-aired cities, will survive only if everyone, not just environmental freaks, learns respect for them.

If one person who might otherwise carelessly turn a four-wheel-drive vehicle across untracked tundra or thoughtlessly pick a bouquet of wildflowers or indifferently leave his refuse where he picnicked—if such a reader afterward checks himself before the damage is done, then there has been purpose to the writing. Better yet, if people who are quite content to see the outdoors from the windows of resort hotels like the Broadmoor in Colorado Springs—if such people, instead of shrugging when they hear of environmental controversies in the back country, will take the trouble to ask what the stakes really are, then the angels will rejoice. Conversely, if these words and these pictures merely whet today's appetite for enjoyment at the cost of an unsullied tomorrow, then I owe a profound apology to the land that gave me my roots.

# ACKNOWLEDGMENTS

The backbone of this book is the many friends, old and new, who helped us reach all parts of the state and, after we were there, shared with us their knowledge and enthusiasm. Particularly indefatigable were Mel and Barbara Griffiths of Denver and Ouray, Bert and Becky Tucker of Paonia, Duane Vandenbusche and Chuck and Mary Jean Cliggitt of Gunnison.

Other patient guides to locales for which they have special attachments include Marshall and Edna Jane Sprague of Colorado Springs, rancher Tom Lasater of Matheson, mining expert Duane Smith of Durango, Buckie Shuler of Telluride, Ned Blair and Charles Marshall of Leadville, and John C. Johnson, Jr., of Gothic. James A. Michener and his research assistant Leslie Laird took us on a memorable tour of that part of the high plains country that furnishes the setting for Michener's novel *Centennial*. The Roundup Riders of the Rockies cordially let me accompany one of their excursions part way along Main Range Trail on the eastern side of the Sawatch Mountains, high above the Arkansas Valley. Joe Nold, director of Colorado Outward Bound School, and his assistant, Gary Templin, cleared the way for a memorable trip down the Yampa River with a group of young river rats from Englewood High School headed by Don Loptien, the results of which are told in Chapter 2. Larry and Pat Weinberger, summer residents of Crested Butte, not only housed us in that area but also lent me photographic equipment at a time of need.

Government agencies responded generously to calls for aid. For help ranging from informal discussions to lengthy excursions in the field, I am grateful to the following:

*United States Forest Service:* Allen H. Mullen, Assistant Regional Forester, and Dick Hauff of the Denver office; District Ranger Dale Harthan and Marshall Steen of Meeker; District Ranger Jim Ficke, Dick Crozier, and Helen Epperson of Leadville; District Ranger Dick Shafer and Chip Mehring of Dillon; District Ranger Bill Conklin, Jim Webb, Harvey Fluke, and Ted Greathouse of Steamboat Springs; District Ranger Ed Browning, Fred Trevey, and Frank Eherberger of Minturn; Forest Supervisor H. Peter Wingle of Durango; and Jim Hollenbach of La Junta.

*National Park Service:* Acting Superintendent Wayne B. Cone and Steve Hickman of Rocky Mountain National Park; Superintendent Ronald Switzer and Ann Marie Rasor of Mesa Verde; Superintendent Richard S. Tousley of Dinosaur National Monument; and Jim Crown of Hovenweep.

*Bureau of Land Management:* Kip Hinton, Chief, Public Affairs, of the Denver office and District Manager Marlyn Jones of Montrose. Chip Marlow of the Montrose office shared with us the frustrations of a low-water raft trip through Dolores Canyon and then, with BLM archaeologist Floyd Emmons of Durango, toured the Anasazi country with us.

Essential in helping me draw the greatest possible yield from all this formidable assistance was my wife Mildred, who in addition typed the manuscript.

PART ONE

*The Seasons:
Excursions Up and Down*

# 1
# THE VERITIES AND VARIETIES OF WINTER

The snow cat in front of the main field station of Colorado's Institute of Arctic and Alpine Research, 9,600 feet high in the Front Range of the Rockies, looked irresistible. Its squat body rested on broad tracks of cleated steel. The cab, large enough to encase an operator and four or five passengers, was constructed of rigid bars and thick glass. Even in the gloomy light that leaked through the low clouds its bright red and shiny aluminum paint made it defiantly visible against the dark evergreens.

*Anyway,* I thought, *we won't end up stranded this time.*

We—photographer Lee Boltin and I—had been frustrated all winter by weather which, for desert-girt Colorado, was abnormally severe. Our idea had been to gain perspective for this book by flying twice, once in winter and again in summer, over the main physiographic regions of the state in a light plane. In that way we could perhaps find coherent patterns in Colorado's infinite richness of detail and multiude of contrasts. We would gain a comprehensive idea of how winter weather arranged and rearranged snowfall on the plains and in the broad interior parks, in the forests of aspen, pine, and juniper. We could note how drifts piled up in above-timberline cirques and how cornices curled over the lee sides of the ridgetops. A follow-up flight in the summer would enable us to relate our discoveries, so we hoped, to the occurrence of grass and trees. We could discern on a grand scale how streams gather in the high valleys and why they slit their giant canyons where they do. We could glimpse the relationship of plateau to lowland. Most of all, we might obtain a broader understanding of what man is achieving—or not achieving—in his efforts to adapt this diversity of forces to his own vision of what the land should be.

Alas for plans. In December 1972, the month we picked for our first excursion, a long cold spell dragged temperatures so low that engine oil no longer functioned properly. Mel Griffiths, professor of geography at the University of Denver, who had volunteered to be both our pilot and mentor, declined to go aloft until conditions improved.

They didn't. Throughout January and February storm after storm swept across the Continental Divide from the west, piling snow to unprecedented depths. As March opened there was a letup, but by the time we had assembled in Denver, weather reports were pessimistic again. But at least Mel was able to produce a substitute through INSTAAR, the Institute of Arctic and Alpine Research, whose staff members have been studying the complexities of high-altitude ecology for the past two decades. INSTAAR also monitors data sent by radio impulse from an earth resources satellite circling the globe in a polar orbit. The stations that receive the data—meanwhile automatically recording the climatic happenings in their vicinities—are scattered just below and just above treeline on Niwot Ridge. These stations have to be serviced at intervals, and Mel arranged for us to catch a ride with the snow-cat operator assigned to the task.

*Into a White-Out*

Niwot is a broad ridge of boulders that spears out toward the plains from the striking cone of Navajo Peak. Thirteen thousand four hundred feet high, Navajo is the dominant summit of the Indian Peak section of the Front Range of the Rockies. These peaks (Ogalalla, Paiute, Shoshoni, Apache, Arapaho, Arikaree, Navajo, and so on) are the teeth of a serrated ridge lying directly south of Rocky Mountain National Park. Their sharp edges and steep sides present fine views to travelers driving north from Denver. More scenery is still being created among them, very slowly, by the small glaciers remaining in their cirques, a geologic term for amphitheaters of rock gouged by ice out of the flanks of most of the world's high peaks. Since glaciers are rare in Colorado, we hoped for a glimpse of the one nearest Navajo. And if that failed because of weather—the morning we drove to INSTAAR's green central station was overcast—we would at least have a close-up view of storm activity.

Off we clattered along a rough opening in dense ranks of tall, thin lodgepole pines—John Clark, the snow cat's black-bearded young operator, Mel Griffiths, Lee Boltin, my wife Mildred (a mainstay on all these excursions), and I. Hard pellets of snow rattled against the windshield. Now and then we passed white meadows. Leafless willow branches and the tips of last year's pale tan grass showed above the undulant surface of the snow. Puffs of wind now and then snatched up handfuls of the covering and sent it flying through the murky air.

As the growling cat climbed higher, the wind puffs coalesced into a gale. The lodge poles gave way to Engelmann spruce and alpine fir. They are sturdy trees, and it was alarming to see how easily the wind set them to thrashing in wide arcs above our heads and to remember the splintered stumps and prostrate giants we had clambered past during summer walks through similar high-country forests.

Through the mottled clearings opened by the windshield wipers we glimpsed unique events—the formation of banner trees. A banner tree has branches on one side of its trunk only. The rest are kept stripped away by strong winds. In the snow-filled hurricane they looked like flags on a buffeted rampart—a frantic flowing with the wind in a situation where resistance meant disaster.

The cat lurched on. The trees became miniatures, bent and tortured, and then disappeared entirely as we climbed above timberline. John's guides were colored stakes set 15 feet apart along the edges of the road. Then they too vanished in the blizzard and we were imprisoned in nothingness.

The cat stopped. We stared—at nothing. We could discern no ground, no sky, no rocks, no shape of any sort. "White-out," John said. The wind shrieked, the cab shook. An eerie sense of disembodiment, of floating, turned my senses topsy-turvy. I could not tell up or down, north or south. We had lost our inner ears, John explained.

Obviously it would be folly to try to reach the high stations. John turned the cat around—cautiously, for how was it possible to tell when the turn was completed?—and crawled outside to search for a guiding stake. Thinking to sample the storm with him, the rest of us started out through the rear door of the passenger compartment. Mel went first. Inadequately braced, he was toppled from his feet by the wind. Warned thus, the rest of us dug in firmly but even so were almost upset. Our breath was wrenched out of our mouths. A directionless roar bore down from everywhere. We lost all desire to follow John, barely discernible 10 feet away.

He found a stake. We all got back inside, eager to leave, but John moved only when brief lulls made it possible for him to glimpse the next stake ahead. Snow driving through tiny door and window cracks filled the cab with a ghostly mist. As we shivered, John reassured us with figures. Though they were only estimates, we liked the sound of them, as though their concreteness somehow provided anchors of familiarity in the white blankness. We were 11,300 feet high, he said. The speed of the wind was approximately 60 miles an hour. The temperature, counting wind chill, was probably 20° or 25° below zero.

"It was worse earlier in the year," he finished casually and eased ahead to another stake. Once we had gained the shelter of the trees—their thrashing no longer seemed so alarming—we picked up speed. As we relaxed, John grew apologetic. "I'm afraid you didn't see much," he said.

*The Implacable Powers of Wind and Snow*

He was wrong. Through luck we had experienced a phase of the mountain winter that no amount of reading could have prepared us for. We understood, in part, the paramount role played by wind in the shaping of high-altitude environments. Wind and not cold, except as wind creates its own chill, sets the upper limits to tree growth. Tongues and islands of evergreens will extend beyond the average cutoff line not because there is protection from low temperatures but because there is shelter from the gales that blow with increasing destructiveness at elevations in excess of 11,000 feet.

Wind redistributes enormous tonnages of snow. The process goes on even when skies are brilliantly clear, as is readily apparent to anyone basking, say, in the lower reaches of Rocky Mountain National Park while watching long snow plumes feathering off the flat-topped stretch of the Continental Divide between Hallett and Taylor peaks. The snowdrifts arranged by the wind determine which of the mountain streams will receives the most water. Government agencies are now taking advantage of that fact by setting up long lines of slatted fence on strategic ridges. These fences create arbitrary drifts called, in the aggregate, snow reservoirs. The captured snow melts into creeks where it is most wanted and during the summer helps fill the more familiar water reservoirs in the lower valleys. A noticeable example is the snow fences lining many of the ridgetops near the Independence Pass road leading to the town of Aspen.

The snow that falls on the high slopes during the coldest months of winter blows away promptly because it is generally a light, dry, fluffy mass termed powder. To make the first sweeping ski tracks on new powder is an intoxication to skiers familiar with its special characteristics. By contrast, skiers intent on speed, on the flash and dash of twisting slalom runs prefer slopes where the snow has been pressed into shiny compactness.

The phenomenon of snow continued to rule our actions after we had returned from Niwot. Unable still to fly a light plane across the Continental Divide because of weather conditions, we decided to split from Mel Griffiths for the time being and drive by car to the Western Slope, as Coloradoans call that part of the state whose waters drain down the Colorado River to the Gulf of California. The route we chose was Monarch Pass, 11,312 feet high, the same elevation at which we had been turned back on Niwot.

The snow was different, however. The flakes were wet and heavy, the kind that often begin falling as March wanes and then continue sometimes until mid-May. Unlike powder snow, these moist blankets are not so likely to be skimmed off the ridgetops. When there is no wind—and there was none as we slipped and slid around the banked curves leading to the top of the pass —the flakes come down in gentle spirals, clinging to and bending down the boughs of the evergreens. The three-dimensional shapes of rocks and cliffs grow blurred, and travelers are wrapped in a depthless, elemental world of gray and white.

We did not escape from this soft, sifting, insistent monotone until after we had dropped down the far side of Monarch Pass into the broad expanses of the Gunnison country. There the snow stopped. After so much of it we felt as if we were leaving a cocoon. We expanded as the view expanded. The clouds were lifting slowly, a gray topping still, but just above the horizon were deep slits of silver. A steely glow that turned into a lemon-colored radiance suffused the snowy fields where livestock stood huddled around their feeding stations.

*Snow Sports*

The next morning the sun leaped into a flawless sky, reminding us that Colorado lies in the semiarid western third of the nation and that most of its days really are dry and bright. Eagerly we joined the line of cars moving north from Gunnison to the ski lifts outside Crested Butte.

Crested Butte was once a coal-mining town. Other Colorado ski areas have picked more glamorous historical settings. Aspen, the most famous, was once an old silver-mining camp; Telluride, the newest, was a gold-mining center. Other resorts have been manufactured from scratch, each with its own distinctive architecture, environmental problems, and hedonistic clientele. Vail, Snowmass, Copper Mountain, Mount Werner—the list grows steadily. The ambiance is much the same everywhere: shifting, colorful costumes, instructors and their charges on the bunny slopes, long lines at the lifts, the strong rise of tower-borne cables, curling runs hacked through clots of spruce and aspen trees. The euphoria: relaxed crowds on the sundecks, the easy gossip and mild horseplay at the après-ski gatherings. Otto Schniebs, one of the early promoters of Aspen, spoke truly when he declared many years ago, "Schkiing is not a schport; it iss a vay of life."

Other activities abound on the peripheries. Most noticeable among them is snowmobiling. It is easy to fault the grotesque machines. Their heavy engine housing, staring headlights, and the extended tails on which the driver and perhaps a passenger sit give them the appearance of monstrous insects. They buzz like chain saws. Driving them full tilt on flat stretches or charging up and down challenging banks interests many addicts much more than does the look of the land through which they speed. Purists, despising them, accuse them of bringing smog and litter to the crystalline outdoors, of damaging vegetation by compacting the snow that covers it, of chasing wild animals until they die of exhaustion.

Defenders of the sport insist that the charges are unfairly exaggerated. Manufacturers are working with some success to reduce noise. And, like the machines or not, they do offer many people an irreplaceable way of sharing in the joys of a mountain winter.

A quieter way is Nordic, or cross-country, skiing. (Downhill skiing is often called Alpine skiing.) The equipment, including narrow touring skis, is relatively cheap. There are no lift tickets to buy or lift lines to wait out. (During the winter of 1972–73 Colorado's lifts elevated Alpine skiers a total of 36,000 vertical miles, roughly one sixth of the way to the moon, at costs almost as astronomical.) Families can share ski-touring as a unit, whereas downhill skiing is pretty much a solo trip, as least as far as the bottom of the run.

As we learned from friends at Crested Butte, it is possible during the waning months of the season to combine the splendid loneliness of ski-touring with the excitement of downhill runs. This particular March we left the sleeping town just as a full moon was setting and it was impossible to tell whether its light or the paleness of the new dawn was giving the most glimmer to the snow. We watched two coyotes, fluffy in their winter fur, loping among the pallid boles of a leafless aspen grove. It was cold, perhaps zero, and the snow squeaked underfoot as we stepped from the car.

We struck directly uphill, walking—not skiing—on a strong crust formed by the nighttime freezing of yesterday's partially thawed surface. Such travel is not possible earlier in the winter, for powder does not crust and if you wish to go uphill you have to rely on special waxes to grip the snow, or on animal skins buckled to the bottoms of your skis. Today, however, we dispensed with all that and moved steadily upward afoot with our skis—Alpine-style skis—on our shoulders.

The rising sun flushed the white peaktops behind us with a golden pink. As it cleared the horizon its slanting rays turned the hillside up which we were walking into pure light. Our eyes watered even behind dark glasses. Soon we began shedding parkas and sweaters on tree branches, to be picked up on our return.

When altitude and lack of conditioning began to tell, Mildred and I dropped behind, content just to enjoy the brightness of the morning. Our younger companions pressed on up the steepening slope, hopeful of reaching the top of the peak, Mount Emmons, 12,392 feet high. After they had disappeared from sight among the trees, the long white valley became utterly silent. For the next two hours or more we did not see a soul, though we knew that by then the ski runs at Crested Butte, only a few miles away, were thronged.

As the sun grew fiercer on the snow, a thread of uneasiness raveled out of our contentment. Avalanches are likely to thunder down sunny, south-facing slopes if temperatures rise rapidly following a heavy snowfall. (In midwinter north-facing hills are more dangerous.) Leeward slopes where wind-crusted snow has compressed into hard, hollow-sounding slabs are also treacherous.

Most avalanche victims trigger their own slides by unsettling, with their weight, the uneasy balances that prevail in the steep gullies and on the open hillsides above the treeline. But our companions, who must have been nearing the summit, knew how to read snow. They'd have no trouble . . . and, sure enough, we soon heard a ringing shout, looked up, and saw them hurtling downward in swishing curves. They cut across a level bench, launched themselves half a dozen feet into the air as they left its lip, and then braked to a slithering halt right at our noses. "Fantastic!" was their description of their morning. It's an abused word, but this time it was right.

*An Overview at Last*

The fantasy continued throughout the next day. The weatherman's promise of continued sunshine had led us to telephone Mel Griffiths at Denver the night before, and he had agreed to pick us up at Montrose, 70 miles from Gunnison, for an aerial tour of the rugged San Juan range. Luxuriously tired, we drove through the twilight to the rendezvous. The balm of false spring was in the air—false because snow could, and that year did, keep falling well into May. But the streams sparkled free of ice between the white scallops on their banks, and the tips of the cottonwood trees showed red where the leaf buds were swelling.

Scores upon scores of deer fed on bare patches of low brush and brown grass near the highway. Winter must be bewildering for them. Snow and instinct drive them to ancient grazing lands in the wide valley bottoms, but those old havens shrink steadily, laced with concrete and filled with reservoirs. At night automobiles hurrying along behind glittering headlights are deadly. Every few miles we passed a shattered carcass, and some of the joy went from the day.

The flight over the San Juans brought it back. Until then we had been bit players in the drama of winter, feeling its moods, and smelling its fragrances, for fresh snow, no less than a sun-warmed fir bough, had its evocative odors. Now we became spectators, aloof and apart, yet overwhelmed by the pageant spread before us. We saw surrealistic patterns of pastel aspen groves and black spruce against undulant meadows of silver. We brushed the faces of the peaks, wrinkled monoliths rising timelessly from their ragged bases. We saw the splitting of great waters. The Animas Canyon, gathering veins into its great black artery, flowed crookedly south; the Uncompahgre, born in deep cirques filled with blue shadows, created a crashing counterpoint as it drove in the opposite direction out through stratified foothills into a broad and naked valley. But the most awesome sight was the high-country snow, rolling, dipping, swelling, slit by chasms and punctured by giant fists of rock. There indeed was the ultimate truth of the mountain winter: almost incalculable amounts of future water, captured by altitude in the midst of a thirsty land.

During the white-out on Niwot Ridge, winter had been fearful with its threat of extinction. Here, under blue skies, it shone like a guarantee of life. Already the snowfields were shrinking. Soon only patches would be visible. But the creeks would sing, the underground tables would be full. Fields of wild flowers would burnish the moist slopes. Lower down, cattle would eat hay grown in irrigated fields; peaches and apples would glow on branches coaxed to fruitfulness by these liquids born of tumult. Southern California would drink part of that water; the plains communities in the dry eastern half of Colorado would draw similarly on mountaintop storehouses farther to the north. Summer rains would freshen the land periodically, but it was winter that sustained it.

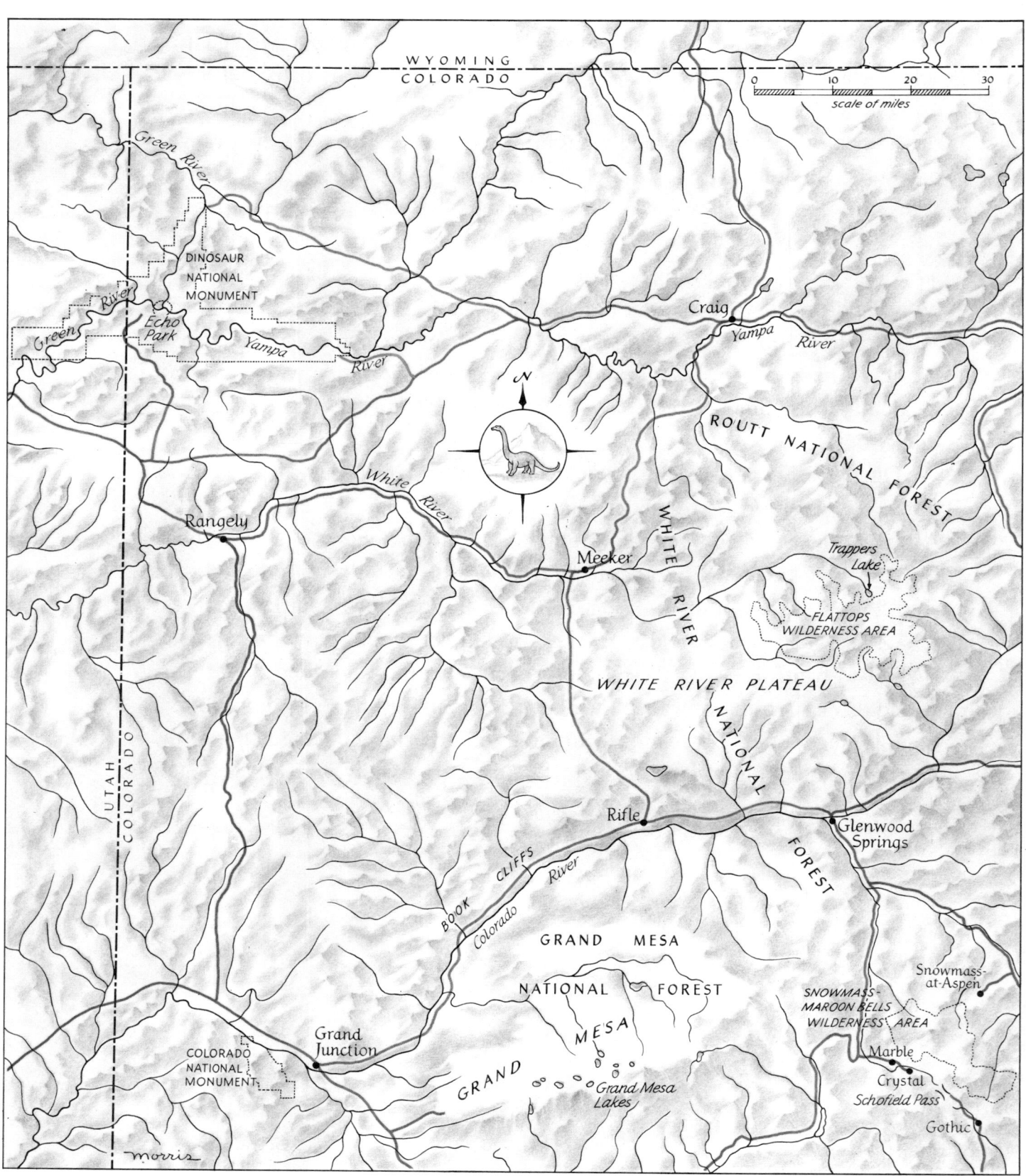

Northwest Colorado

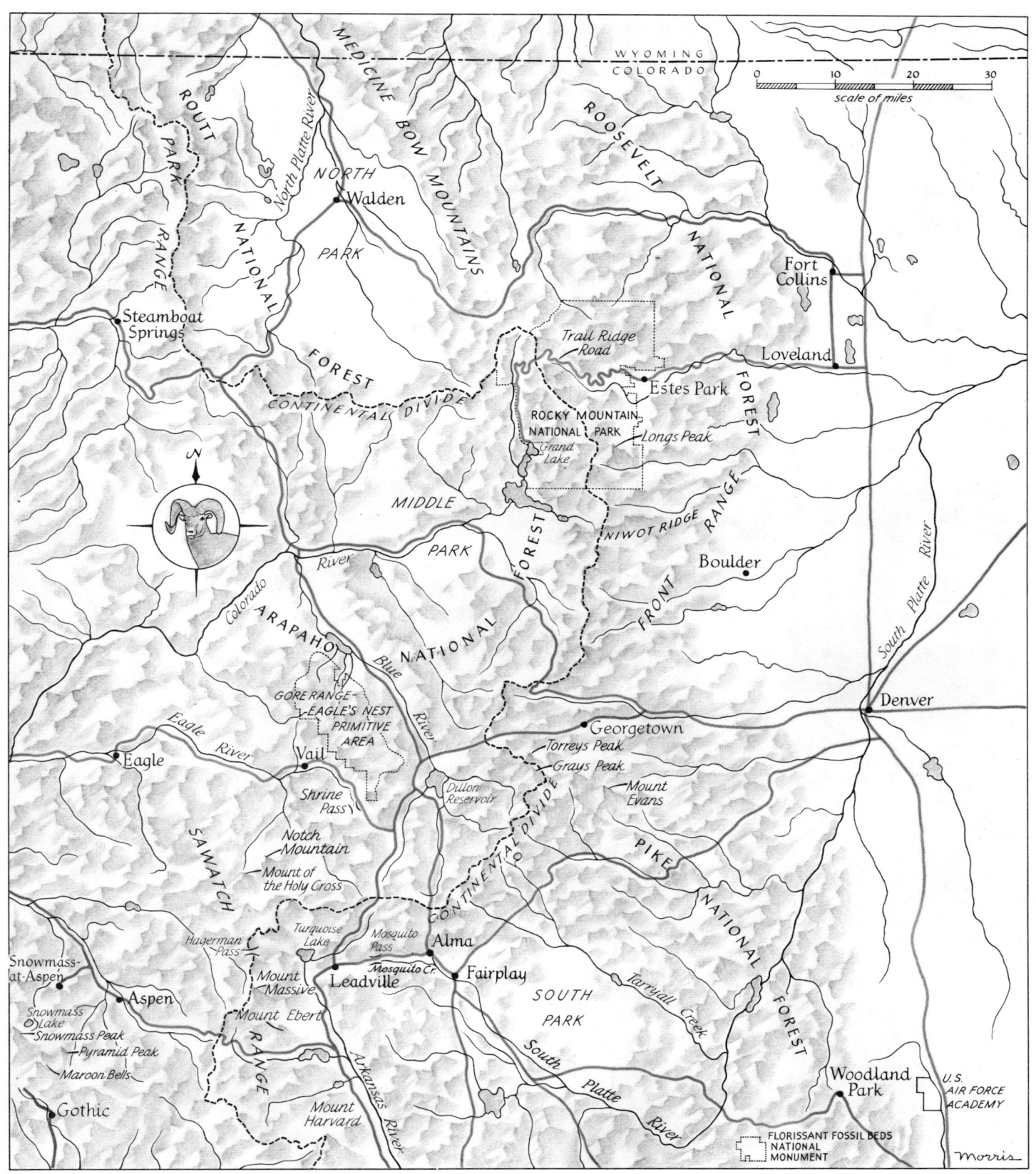

North central Colorado

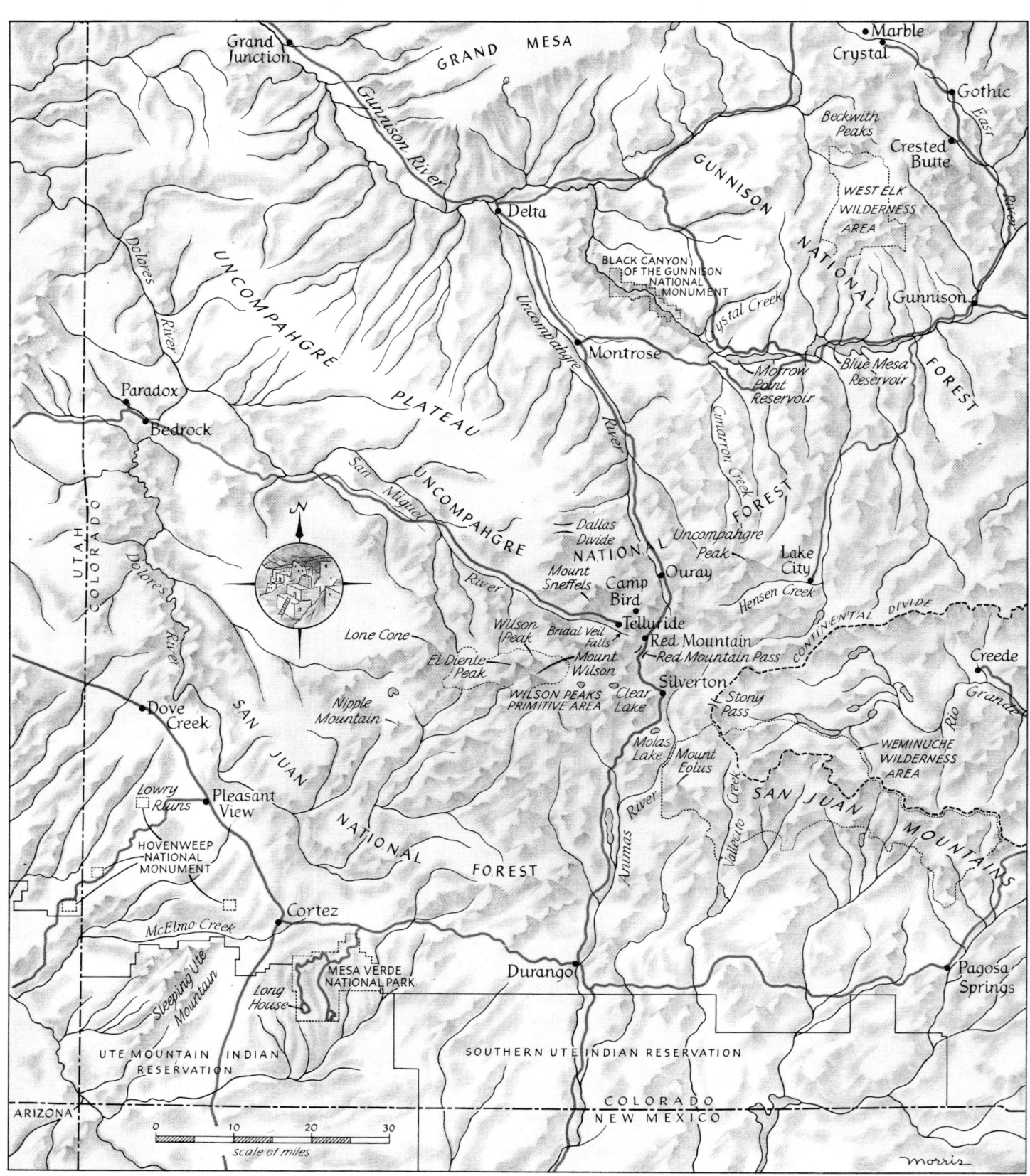

Southwest Colorado

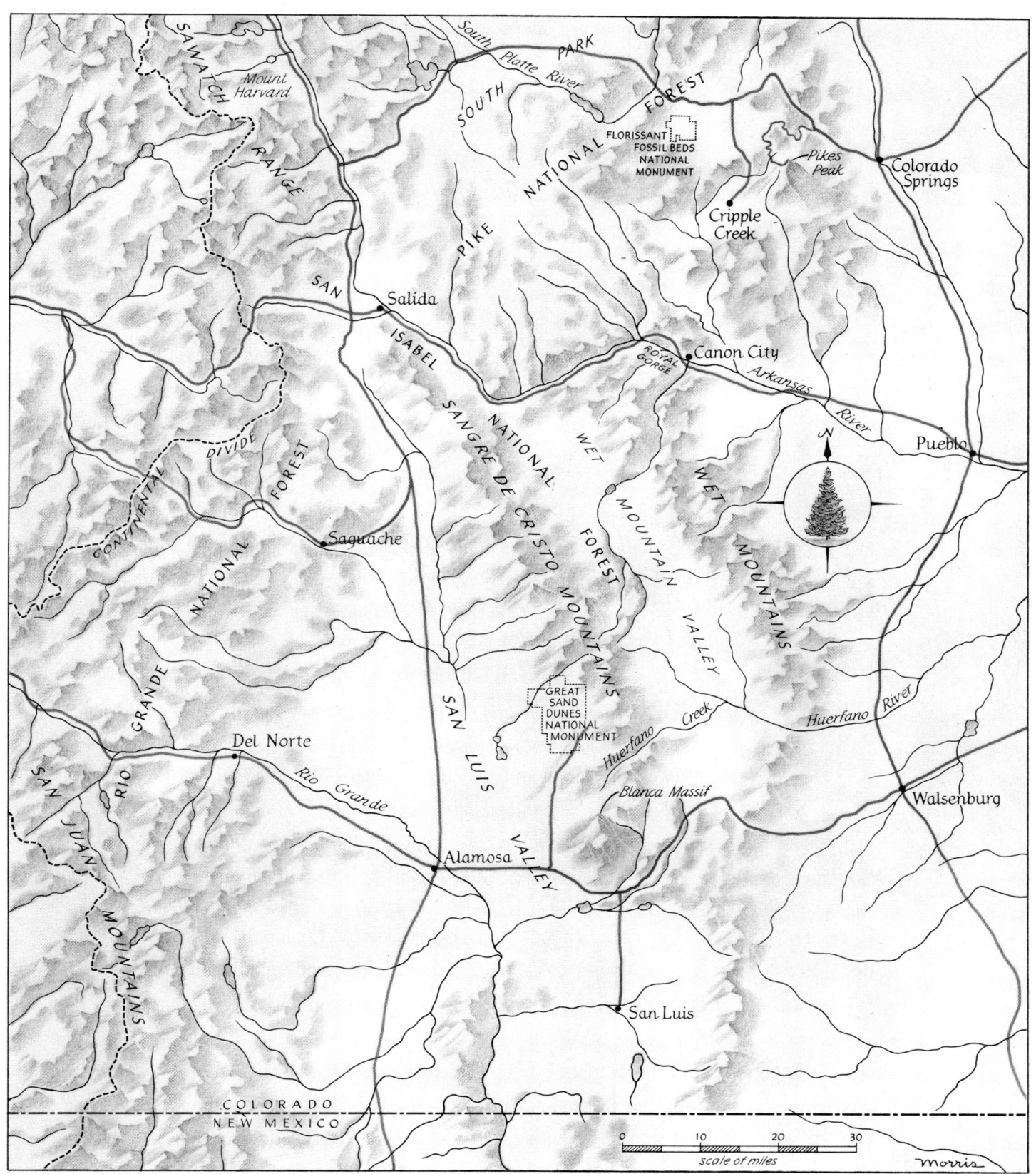

South central Colorado

# 2
# A THUNDER OF WATERS

*Riding the Snow Melt*

The cascades of spring bring forth swarms of a new kind of outdoors-oriented people—river runners, eager to share with the water the release from winter. For many the venture is a spectator sport staged by commercial firms utilizing neoprene rafts ranging from 22 to 33 feet in length and capable of carrying from nine to fourteen fare-paying passengers each, depending on size. The center sections of these aquatic pachyderms are fitted with heavy wooden frames holding rowlocks. The locks in turn support a pair of long sweep oars manipulated by an extraordinarily agile, hard-muscled, carefully trained boatman.

The boatman's main function is to keep maneuvering his craft into such a position that the boisterous spring currents will do most of the work of propulsion. Meanwhile the clients sit or lean on the blubberlike roll of inflated air chambers that circle the raft, and cling for support to handy ropes. Though they are not working at the sport, they are not passive either. Waves tower high in the newly invigorated rapids. Hard slaps of cold spray bring out gasps and squeals, and it is always possible for the raft to jam immovably against a midstream boulder or even be flipped upside down in some raging hole.

In between cataracts, travel is a silent glide over cliff-girt stretches of glassy water. The occupants soak up sunshine (and occasionally rain) while watching the ever-shifting panorama of the canyon's welcome to spring. If the idyll grows monotonous, it is easily enlivened by starting a water fight with the people in a companion boat. The clean air invigorates; the sense of adventure releases spirits crimped by routine; and nippy evenings of yarning and singing beside the campfire become part of a reservoir of strength on which one can draw for years afterward.

Some people want to add to the joy by managing their own craft. For them pontoon rafts are too big and expensive to be practical, yet ordinary canoes are too unstable and ordinary rowboats too inflexible to stand the repeated shocks of the rapids. Fortunately modern technology has provided a popular substitute: streamlined fiber glass versions of the old Eskimo kayak.

Although tandem kayaks exist, most hold only a single individual. He or she—women are as adept at the sport as men—sits in the bottom of the craft, legs extended and lower body buttoned in tight by a water-repellent apron. The operator propels the long, slim craft—it is pointed at both ends and is generally painted bright yellow—by wielding alternately to the left side and then to the right a single paddle with a blade at either extremity. Light of weight, kayaks can survive in only inches of water, a marked advantage on rivers whose levels drop rapidly after the thunderous spring runoffs. In addition, the gay craft are highly maneuverable among boulders and easily portaged around whatever rapids seem unduly fearsome. They are not foolproof toys, however, as is evidenced by the crash helmets and life jackets worn by most kayakers when they take to white water.

A swiftly moving line of kayaks makes a fine sight as it sweeps around a sparkling curve backed by fresh green meadow grass or a bank of Colorado blue spruce, with russet cliffs rising overhead. Favorite streams include Waterton Canyon on the South Platte not far from Denver, the limpid Taylor River north of Gunnison, the turbulent Colorado above Glenwood Springs, and the aptly named Roaring Fork below Aspen. Most exciting of all, in the minds of many enthusiasts, is one of the classic kayaking streams of the West, the Arkansas River both above and below the hamlet of Buena Vista. Farther south, below Salida, the Arkansas flows through a swift stretch of white water studded with pink granite boulders. This is the scene each year of downriver and slalom races, events well worth watching from the edges of Highway 50, which parallels the course.

*Rafting in Dinosaur National Monument*

Kayaking is largely an individual sport. Teamwork calls for rafts. Though made of heavy neoprene like commercial boats, these rafts are smaller and unframed. Propulsion comes not from sweep oars managed by a single boatman but from paddles wielded by each occupant. The rafts are lineal descendants of landing boats used during World War II. Indeed, some World War II vintage rafts are still in use, though most have been replaced by Green River boats developed especially for the sport. What the Army called ten-man rafts will hold only six vacationists, plus lean supplies for a four- or five-day trip. Green River rafts hold eight travelers.

A strong head of water is needed for pleasant voyaging. (How well we learned that truth one spring of meager runoff in deep, remote, gorgeously terraced Dolores Canyon in the southwestern part of the state; we spent as much time overboard in the icy current, manhandling the raft across boulders, as we did floating the navigable stretches.) Because of these water requirements, the two most satisfactory rivers in the state—good for kayaking, too—are the Green and the Yampa, which come together in the heart of Dinosaur National Monument in Colorado's northwestern corner.

For an overview of this magnificent site, turn north from Monument headquarters on Highway 40 and drive across the treeless swells of Blue Mountain to the end of the only paved road that enters the reserve. From there follow a foot trail a mile through a scattering of desert evergreens to a vantage point overlooking the two streams and their handiwork.

At first the vista seems chaotic—a random jumble of buttes and beneath the buttes great whorls of sandstone strata laid down by ancient seas. Mixed with the whorls are long, whitish cliffs streaked here and there by desert varnish. In places the cliffs have collapsed, making way for long slides of rock that afford precarious footing for occasional trees. Downstream, the prevailing horizontal alignment is wrenched into folds by pinnacle-crested Mitten Park Fault. Everywhere are wrinkles created in petrified sand by aeons of scouring winds. The chocolate-colored rivers seem almost at your toes, the Green coming from the north, the Yampa from the east. Joining at the base of elongated Steamboat Rock, they swing around its prow in a full 180-degree turn before striking west into Utah.

The remorseless power of grinding water!—inevitably you want to get down to the rivers themselves to experience their surge and gain new perspective by seeing their work close at hand. Another attraction is the moonlike remoteness and apparent solitude of the area.

Actually the solitude is an illusion. One learns with shock that during the few months of 1971 when the rivers were navigable, a total of 10,300 boaters spent at least one night camping somewhere in the canyons. This population explosion in the midst of a seemingly primeval world resulted in the Park Service's imposing the following year a ceiling on the amount of human use the rivers are permitted to receive. Commercial operations were frozen roughly at 1971 levels, and the privilege of stopping at the campgrounds was granted to applicants on a first-come, first-served basis.

Rules that accompany the issuing of permits are strict. They specify the kinds of boats that may be used ("Conventional rowboats and canoes are unsafe on these waters and will not be considered.") and the maximum number of people that may be carried in each. Safety rules are enforced. ("Each passenger and boatman MUST wear a Coast-Guard approved life preserver. . . . NO EXCEPTIONS. Each party must be in charge of a competent, responsible, and experienced leader.") The strongest emphasis is given to cleanliness. ("Combustible trash shall be burned. CANS, BOTTLES, TINFOIL, AND ALL OTHER NON-COMBUSTIBLE MATERIALS OF ANY KIND SHALL EITHER BE TRANSPORTED TO DISPOSAL FACILITIES AT ECHO PARK OR SPLIT MOUNTAIN OR REMOVED FROM THE MONUMENT. . . . Camping and fires are permitted at designated, reserved campsites only.")

Do these limitations interfere seriously with the sense of freedom that one hopes to find during a wilderness vacation? Can ten thousand people travel through a constricted area without damaging its social capacity?—social capacity being a subjective term for the number of people one can see during an outing without feeling that the experience has been spoiled.

### Outward Bound

My wife and I were given an opportunity to explore the problem when we were invited to visit the Monument with a group from Colorado Outward Bound School. Outward Bound is a worldwide institution made up of nearly thirty "schools" on five continents. The Colorado unit has no campus as such —just an office and extensive warehouse facilities in Denver and Spartan bases in half a dozen of the state's remote mountain areas.

The goal of the program is to lead teen-age boys and girls, many of them from disadvantaged urban areas, toward self-sufficiency by helping them overcome outdoor challenges that at first seem beyond their capacities. Emotional and psychological hurdles are often harder to surmount than physical ones. Confidence comes from the rigorous training and self-discipline that eventually enable the participant to draw on strengths he did not know he possessed. Thereafter, in theory at least, no frustration, outdoors or in, will ever look quite as hopeless as before.

In 1967 Colorado Outward Bound expanded its activities to include team situations as well as predominantly individual challenges. River running with rafts was chosen as a medium because of the tight social cohesion demanded from groups of paddlers if they hoped to take their boats safely through difficult water. Along with this physical activity go opportunities for experiential learning. How are canyons formed? How do the laws of physics relate to disturbed water currents? What happens to local ecosystems when great numbers of people invade them? Who traveled these rivers first and why? What social functions are served by National Monuments? Can the language in which these questions are answered be made clearer and more forceful?

Unable and unwilling to establish formal classrooms in the open air, Outward Bound decided to take its river-running programs to whatever high schools were interested. Outward Bound professionals would train selected students and teachers in the mechanics of river running, suggest ways of grafting academic subjects onto the preparations being made for the trips, and then let the staff of each school carry on the program as part of its curriculum.

We were attached to a pilot group of faculty and students from a high school in Englewood, a suburb south of Denver. There were three raftsful of them, eleven boys and girls, nine teachers, and three Outward Bound instructors. One of the instructors, Susan Rittenhouse, was there to show that successful raft handling is not a male prerogative. Another, wiry Al Brown, was the captain of the fleet. Our tag-along boat, a weary ten-man raft of World War II days, held six people. In addition to Mildred and me there were two observers from Outward Bound, Bill McCabe and mountaineer John Evans, who has climbed in both the Himalayas and Russia, John's wife Loie (pronounced Low-ie, for Laura), and Barbara George. The two young women were about to apply for certification as licensed—well, the word is still boatmen—and were using this opportunity to brush up on techniques. Most of our crew's orders during the next five days would come from one or the other of them.

Our river was to be the Yampa. The rapids on the Green between the Gates of Lodore and Steamboat Rock, where the streams unite, are more taxing. The Yampa's scenery is more varied, however, and its greater length inside the Monument allows for a fuller camping experience.

*Meeting the Yampa River*

We assembled one twilight in May at Deer Lodge Park, where the canyon walls, slacking off into hills, leave room beside the river for a sizable flat. The branches of scattered cottonwood trees, still bare of leaves, drew a shifting black tracery across the enormous yellow disc of the rising moon. Wind fluttered our nylon shelters. A deep-throated murmur came from the river, swollen from bank to bank with melt from the high country.

We were up at dawn, preparing breakfast with cold hands and then tediously pumping air into the rafts which had been hauled to Deer Lodge by truck. We learned how to lace our personal gear into rubber dunnage sacks and then lash the sacks, the food boxes, and the plastic jugs of drinking water into the bottom of the boat firmly enough so that even an upset would not dislodge them.

Before departing we gathered in a semicircle beside the river for a lecture on camp manners, water safety, and hypothermia. Hypothermia is the result of prolonged exposure and fatigue. Body heat drains from the flesh, particularly the flesh of arms and legs, faster than normal biological functions can replace it. It is an insidious thing. Struggling too long in cold water or in any other exposed situation can reduce a victim to uncontrollable shivering and even unconsciousness before either he or his companions are fully aware of what is happening. In extreme cases life can be saved only by stripping the sufferer and sandwiching him between two other naked bodies that will provide the natural heat the skin demands.

As the lecturer talked, we eyed the river. It was thick with sediment and burdened, we knew, with sewage dumped into it from towns upstream. The lecturer said that phalanxes of Cadillacs as wide as the stream and racing by at the rate of one thousand per minute could not generate equal energy. Unconsciously we pulled the ties of our life jackets tighter around our throats and waists.

We learned the basic commands for turning and holding, and as we descended the initial gentle stretches of the spring-swollen stream we practiced the various maneuvers until our arms and shoulders protested. Sunlight bouncing off the encompassing walls of red, brown, and yellowish-white sandstone grew oppressive. It was a relief to relax with horseplay, sousing the occupants of a neighboring boat—and being soused in return—with water dashed up by paddle blades or hurled out of bailing buckets.

We camped that night at the head of our first big rapid, Tepee, named for tepee-like shapes in the rock wall across from the campground. The next morning we walked downstream to a point from which we could study the furious water. We analyzed the reflex waves set up by currents bouncing off impervious barricades. We learned what sleepers are—boulders hidden just beneath the frothing surface. We examined holes, a sort of vertical eddy created when a big head of water, pouring hard over an obstruction, digs out a pit at its base. After tumbling into the excavation with a deafening roar, the water piles up the steep far side until gravity overtakes it and it curls back on itself in a boil of spray.

As soon as each crew thought it knew the water, its members squatted together beside a bare piece of ground. Our group used a chip to represent the raft and drew diagrams with twigs as we discussed the best way of meeting every foot of the cataract. The instructor, in our case John Evans, offered and explained amendments, and then Loie was assigned the task of taking our raft through. The other crews were directed by teen-age neophytes whose throats, if mine was any indication, must have been pretty dry.

We donned slicker suits, for the spray was going to be thick. The setup was gay—yellow slickers, yellow paddle blades, red lifejackets, silver-gray rafts. We sat on the round edges of our boat with one foot hooked for security under the lashed dunnage in the middle. It's an awkward position for paddling, but the day before, we had grown used to it.

We eased into the stream at an angle to the current. Normally you don't want to risk getting caught crosswise to the thrust, yet you do want to present the current with enough surface so that you can utilize the force of the water in reaching the position you desire.

"Right!" Loie called, and the paddlers on the opposite sides of the raft swung their blades contrary to each other, one half driving ahead, the others back-paddling. "Forward—hard! HARD!" We dug the blades deep and skinned past a seething rock into the slot she wanted. "Hold!" We sat frozen and breathless while the water hurled us toward a wave towering over our heads. The flexible craft curled ponderously over it and came down with a bang that nearly shook me from my perch. "Right—hard!" Loie yelled and after one more nearly suffocating splash we were through.

So it went, occasional uproars of water separated by long stretches of quiet. The variegated cliffs were a succession of vast concavities, prows, and buttresses, broken here and there by creases carved by sidestreams, dry except after rare, hard rains. Each day the sun seemed to grow stronger. On the bank maple trees and box elders were leafing out. Downy goslings were hatching; two even wandered with complete aplomb into one of our camps. In the half-light of dawn and evening adult Canadian geese flew by close to the water, gabbling as they went. High on one of the red side walls a doe took fright at our appearance and bounded off along a narrow terrace. Eagles appeared during midday, coasting the air beside the cliff faces, their shadows trailing them with dazzling speed across the sheer rock.

We entered a series of horseshoe curves cramped between thousand-foot cliffs of dun-colored sandstone. In places the awesome rock rose perpendicularly out of the water. Here and there desert varnish—manganese oxide leached from the overlying soil by rain and snow—has drawn strong black stripes down the fronts of the precipices. (Desert varnish also stains red cliffs with streaks and blotches of black, but on them the contrast is less pronounced.) One wall, whose vast brow curves out over the water, is marked by such vivid stripes that it is called Tiger Wall.

The water is quiet there. We paddled close to the rock, hearing only the lapping of ripples. Setting the boat to revolving, we lay back. The wall, not we, seemed to be turning, a psychedelic color wheel of cosmic proportions winding hypnotically against a spring sky of electric blue.


*The Warm Springs Maelstrom*

Midway through the third day we faced the wildest of the Yampa rapids, Warm Springs. It is a new cataract. In 1965 a wedge-shaped mass of rock broke loose from the high red cliff on the south side of the river and dropped with what must have been an indescribable crash into the canyon. Shortly thereafter a cloudburst sent a flood rampaging out of the north, down Warm Springs draw. This flood created a delta of huge boulders near the debris of the rock fall and forced the river to thrash and leap ever higher as it searched for a way through the obstructions.

We had been preparing for this ever since Deer Lodge and considered ourselves ready. Two minutes of wet violence—no big deal. Several rafts had gone through already that month. Dozens would follow. Just the same, Mildred and I were nervous as we crawled, overwhelmed by the din, out onto a flat rock with the rest of our crew to study the water and watch Al Brown take the first boat through.

The problem was a wedge of rock thrusting from the bank into the stream and then, a little way below it, an enormous hole—a 4-foot drop of chocolate-yellow water ending in a wild backlash that would inevitably flip any raft unfortunate enough to be trapped there. The solution was to swing far out around the upper wedge, pick up the reflex waves from a line of boulders, and ride them into a relatively smooth tongue of water between the bank and the maelstrom.

Al's crew skinned by shrouded in spray and tossed like a chip but fully in control. Reassured somewhat, we trudged back to our own raft to do likewise, if we could. My station was on the hole side; Mildred's was on the land side, where fangs of rock discouraged any idea of crowding too close to the bank in order to give wide berth to the hole. As we picked up our paddles and settled into place on the rubber roll of the raft, jamming our feet under the lashed duffel for added security, we bantered about which side was the worst.

Then there was no time for talk. We paddled hard around the corner and with John bawling directions caught the reflex wave we wanted. Suddenly a black boulder loomed up from I don't know where. But John evidently did. "Left! Left! Now back-paddle! Hard!" We missed the boulder but hit something else that toppled me off my seat—into the boat, fortunately, and not out. As I struggled back I looked straight up at a sky composed entirely of waves waiting to crash on me and everyone else, which they did. Drenched, we paddled furiously on as John directed, the boat climbing, dropping, climbing again. Then, with startling abruptness, everything was behind. No big deal. Just the same, when you look back at the yellow spume you remember that there was a moment when you'd rather have backed out and walked around. But you didn't, and that of course is one of the main points of the exercise.

As we rounded yet another bend the next noon, we saw dead ahead the long, white, red-tinged face of Steamboat Rock, with the chocolate-colored Green River sliding in from the right. John and Loie Evans, accomplished yodelers, sang out their exhilaration and we listened enthralled as the echoes flooded back across the water. The huge sounding board gives part of the name—Echo—to the area. The rest—Park—comes from the way the walls opposite Steamboat Rock curve back to form a roomy flat. You can drive a car to Echo Park if the weather is dry and if you don't mind steep, unpaved roads. It's a good trip.

### Defending the Wilderness

A multitude of final impressions pulled together at Echo Park, even though we weren't yet through with the river—a river doubled in volume now that the Green had absorbed the Yampa. We would camp this night at Jones Hole just inside Utah, and those of us with fishing licenses would try our luck with the big rainbow trout that lurk in the hole's clear sidestream. We'd thread the intricate channels of Island Park, where ducks and geese nest and tall-legged herons stand as still as stumps in the marshes. We'd encounter more brisk rapids as we pushed through Split Mountain to the boat ramp where the trip would end. But that would be a winding down. The heart of the matter, so it occurred to me later, revealed itself here at Echo Park.

Landing, we walked past cottonwood trees to sprawl out on the green mat of cheat grass. After lunch, Al Brown read to us from Aldo Leopold's *A Sand County Almanac*. The *Almanac* was a passion of Al's. Throughout the trip he read snatches of it to us whenever he could, even tying the four rafts together as we drifted along a slow current and then standing on the gray rim of one so that all could hear. Today he chose Leopold's passage about cheat grass, a meretriciously beautiful invader from the outside that has caused great harm to the once-balanced natural environment of the mountain West.

During the reading my mind wandered to the most relentless outsider of all, urban man—and also to man's paradoxical efforts to protect choice bits of landscape from destruction at his own hands.

Dinosaur National Monument came into being in 1915 as an 80-acre preserve designed to guard a rich deposit of petrified dinosaur bones on the flank of Split Mountain in Utah. Twenty-three years later Franklin Roosevelt extended the Monument boundaries to include the scenic canyons of the Green and Yampa rivers. He acted just in time. During World War II another governmental agency, the Bureau of Reclamation, decided that Split Mountain and Echo Park would provide magnificent sites for reservoirs.

Years of controversy followed. Were National Parks and Monuments to be inviolate, or should more utilitarian values take precedence? Conservationists won the battle in 1956 when Congress inserted into the Colorado River Storage Project bill a clause decreeing that "no dam or reservoir constructed under the authorization of this Act shall be within any National Park or Monument."

But now another invasion is under way, inspired in part by the publicity given the Dinosaur area by the debates. Bearing it irresistibly ahead are the innovations of modern sports technology. Its shock troops are we, ten thousand strong each year.

True, we are trying to preserve the values of the land we are invading. To that end we have surrendered some of the vaunted freedoms of the wilderness; we have consented to regimentation, camping when, how, and where we are told. In return the Monument rangers have worked skillfully to reduce annoyances. Thanks to the reservation system, none of the limited number of campgrounds was overcrowded. When two groups occupied the same flat, as happened, they were kept out of each other's hair by means of effective natural screening and mutual respect. Under such circumstances regimentation is better than competition.

Our own group of twenty-nine persons were united by a common purpose. As a consequence the number did not seem excessive, as it might have during a backpacking hike to a solitary mountain lake. Camp cleanliness was notable. We held a treasure hunt one evening during the course of which each member was required to produce, in addition to such things as box-elder bugs and deer droppings, waste pieces of plastic, metal, and tinfoil. Even in the heart of the campground other people's litter proved to be the hardest items to find.

Gentle, cooperative, regimented invaders—we were proud of the ten thousand. And yet, as we sat there in Echo Park, talking about incursions of cheat grass, it became evident that our noses had been much too close to the ground. We weren't seeing mankind's really massive invasions. Because the river sliding along the base of Steamboat Rock was thick with natural sediments, we tended to ignore, even as we drank stale water out of plastic jugs, the distasteful knowledge that it also carried the sediments of raw sewage. Because the effluents in the air above Echo Park were still so sparse as to be invisible, we forgot them, too, except when a high-flying jet drew white contrails across the sky.

We were jarred back to awareness by three hard shocks. The earth jumped under the cheat grass—bang! bang! bang! *Earthquake,* I thought and expected debris to rain from the cliffs. Not a stone fell. As we relaxed, we realized the cause of the disturbance—atomic blasts set off in a mile-deep well near Rangely, 30 or more miles away, in the hope of creating a huge underground cavity for the collection of natural gas.

Another invasion. They come from everywhere—in the air, down the rivers, through the earth itself.

Like natural gas, the American outdoors is a resource. As supplies shrink, increasingly sophisticated methods will be necessary if we are to exploit fully what we have. Yet to work under the assumption that, whether in the field of energy or recreation, areas and problems can be treated in isolation is a mere treading of water. We need to face whole challenges, not bits.

One help in getting over the waves, and this is perhaps the fundamental lesson of Echo Park, is to shift attitudes—to act not as temporary invaders, however gentle, but as concerned inhabitants of an interdependent whole. We'll see then that the greenness our hearts need should begin in the darkest parts of the cities and from there ripple out indivisibly to places like Dinosaur, places that will truly be lost if we keep thinking of them as apart and isolated. Our world is so interlocked now that no single area can ever be really fresh with spring again until all areas are.

# 3
# UNEXPECTED BOUNTIES

*The Laggard Season*

Spring is not a transitional season in the Rockies. It's a sudden letting go. You don't think of nymphs; you think of shaggy dogs coming in out of the snow and shaking themselves.

You can see that the days are getting longer and that at noon the sun stands nearer the zenith than it did a month ago. You can hear the roar of released water in the canyons. But snow squalls still sweep across the peaks and raw winds still torment the valleys. Farmers coming into the small towns for supplies invariably say to whoever is pumping gas into the tanks of their pickups, "Summer sure is a long time coming this year."

Perhaps one reason it seems so laggard is that nature apparently is making ready but then keeps postponing. As early as March leaf and flower buds begin swelling on the branches of the cottonwood trees beside the streams and on the aspens patterning the slopes above. The buds' protective red membranes, designed to keep the tender growth from freezing or being dried out by the wind, bring a warm tinge to the cold-looking trees. On rare noons when the wind is quiet and the sun strong, you think the shields should break open, freeing the fuzzy catkins and tiny new leaves. But they don't. The cold air stirs again, the clouds roll in, the branches rattle. You blow on your hands and settle down to wait some more. Indeed, some mountain people take their vacations in April. They need to see spring somewhere, but they can't do it here.

Then abruptly one day the ponderosa pines—foothills ranchers generally call them yellow pines—smell warm. Their pungence is noticeable the year around, of course. But when the resinous odor becomes emphatic, when it takes on what I can describe only as a rich, full roundness, then summer is at hand, even though spats of snow may freckle the needle-strewn ground the very next day.

Pasqueflowers pop out of nowhere. Their big chalices, white inside, purplish out, stand atop short stems that are leafless still and jacketed in down as if the plants are distrustful of the weather but can't wait any longer to be about their business. Tiny brownish leaves mist the dense stands of twisted Gambel oak—scrub oak, the local people call it, or oak brush. As the notched leaves grow, they turn chartreuse and then a deep, lush green. As soon as green shoots appear in the tan grass clustered around the bases of the thin, gnarled trunks, the ranchers in the valleys relax. They have been running short of hay in their fields, ajump now with new colts, new calves, and new lambs, and it's a relief to know that they can soon start edging their herds up through the oaks to the luxuriant grass of the high country.

By the end of May only the highest of the deciduous trees keep the cold, pale look of winter. Snowbanks linger only on north-facing slopes or under the dense canopies of Engelmann spruce and alpine fir. The aspen groves, shimmering with the tenderest of greens, are alive with the songs of wrens and the hammerings of redheaded woodpeckers.

*Weather Hang-Ups*

June is a month for drying out. As a rule, little rain falls. South-facing slopes turn dusty. As the boggy flats drain off, a vivid mantle of green appears—sedge, scrub willow, grass. Early flowers riot, notably dandelions. Pests in the cities, they bring a dazzle of gold to mountain hillsides. Thin cataracts that have been falling like silver ribbons down wrinkles in the cliffs disappear. The main streams retreat to the shelter of their banks, and the water that sings between the rocks is as clear as polished crystal. Reservoirs fill. Trout that have been fattening on grubs and larvae awash in the roily currents now take to jumping high after hovering flights of midges and newly hatched mayflies.

Vacationists pour up the winding roads. Most are sight-seers, content with leaving their cars only at scenic overlooks, where they take pictures and shiver in the unexpectedly cool air. Meanwhile the children, shrill with delight, feed the golden-mantled ground squirrels that have learned to hang around such places waiting for handouts. Often these sunny little animals are called chipmunks. Chipmunks, however, are a different, smaller species. The stripes on a chipmunk are more numerous and extend onto the animal's head. A ground squirrel's color is a richer gold. The white stripe on his sides stands out sharply. The white line that circles each eye makes him look as alert and perky as he is.

Fishermen—and just plain travelers, too—jam the waterside campgrounds with their tent trailers, camper coaches, and motor homes. Sailboats dip and wheel on the big lakes and reservoirs. Trail bikes growl through the spruce; the operators of four-wheel-drive vehicles hunt out the steepest, roughest old mine roads they can find. Backpackers, scorning all forms of motorized recreation, head for the wilderness areas. Patient wives drive day hikers to the trailhead on one side of a range and then drive 50 or 60 miles around it to pick up the weary walkers when they emerge on the other side. Guests at dude ranches gallop joyously across the flower-strewn meadows and through the dappled shade of the aspen groves.

A myriad of glorious settings, activities to suit nearly every taste—it is easy to forget, when trying to embrace as much as is possible in a limited time, that the mountains can be enjoyed fully only when you accept them on their own terms.

I remember one August when Mildred and I had only four days available. We laid plans carefully. Our fellow plotters were Bert Tucker, one time National Forest supervisor, now a fruit grower near the little town of Paonia, and his wife, Becky. After deciding to concentrate on trout, we pinpointed our sites. We would rent a four-wheel-drive car in Silverton, in the southwestern part of the state, and on the first morning drive to Highland Mary Lake, a sapphire gem in a glacial cirque near the head of Cunningham Gulch. We would fish at Highland Mary until noon on the second day. We would then break camp and follow a difficult old wagon road over Cinnamon Pass to Cottonwood Creek, dancing between tawny cliffs on its way down from the Continental Divide to the Lake Fork of the Gunnison River. After a day and a half at Cottonwood, we would return the car to its stable. Variety calculated with precision—what could be better?

A drizzle dampened our twilight entry into the old mining town of Silverton, but the dawn sky turned out to be a flawless blue. Energetic in the crisp, thin air—Silverton stands 9,300 feet high in a county that reputedly does not contain a single tillable acre—we rented a bright red station wagon, loaded in our gear, and started up the road that follows the Animas River toward its source.

The Animas is a boisterous, handsome stream. Below the town it has carved its way through a magnificent gorge. Threading the gorge is one of the nation's last narrow-gauge railways, operated now as a tourist attraction. Above the town the stream flows through a broad, U-shaped trough. On either side rise rows of huge peaks, 13,000 feet high and shaped like volcanoes, their shoulders steep but not rugged.

We were hardly under way when we saw gray cloudcaps beginning to form around the summits. Afternoon showers ahead, I told myself. Such rains are common during the latter part of July and most of August. As the air at the base of the mountains warms during the morning, it flows upward. The moisture in it condenses, forming clouds right in front of your eyes. If patterns are suitable, the condensation becomes a storm. Drops swirl inside the gray veil; lightning crackles; puffs of rain or even sleet send you scurrying for shelter. Such storms generally do not last long. The cloud cover breaks into giant, shifting cauliflowers. Rocks and trees sparkle. Alpenglow suffuses the mountaintops, and as shadows creep across the lakes the fish sometimes feed as if frenzied.

Not every rain is a shower, however. Big-muscled storms from the outside occasionally sweep across the land. The peaks catch them in a lover's embrace. Rain pours and then the storm tries to leave. It ravels. The sun bursts through the small openings in what photographers call Jesus rays. Sometimes at dawn there is a complete clearing. But the peaks are seductive. Back the clouds come, purple and swollen, either sluicing the ground with repeated rains or blanketing it under shadow until finally, out of exhaustion it seems, the clinging ends and the storm rolls sullenly on with its diminishing thunders.

According to the man in the garage store at Silverton, this storm had been trying to break loose for several days. So perhaps the cloudcaps taking shape ahead of us were merely early precursors of normal afternoon showers. On we went, pretending not to notice how black their centers were.

We turned east into Cunningham Gulch. Like the rest of the upper

Animas country, its deep valley and steep sides had once been the scene of intense mining activity. The remnants of old silver mills sagged beside the stream. A thousand or more feet above them were the mines, their tunnel entrances marked by colorful dumps of waste rock, piles of old boards, and the tangled traces of the cable-borne tramways whose lurching buckets had once carried ore down the precipitous hillside to the mills.

As the gulch began to pinch off, the road steepened. Bert shifted into four-wheel drive. We followed tire tracks across a tilted, ancient plank-and-log bridge. We wound through the debris gathered around a cluster of abandoned buildings and goat-leaped up a series of rock ledges. By risking the brink of space, we managed to twist around the roots of a toppled spruce tree.

"That's the worst of it!" Bert exulted and then came to an abrupt halt. The road ahead was covered by a mudslide.

We got out to investigate the obvious. We had only one short-handled shovel. The slide was 40 feet wide, as much as 3 feet deep in places, and filled with boulders. But, as Bert pointed out, the tire tracks we had been following reappeared on the far side. Somebody was up yonder, either fishermen or miners who had been lured back to the region by the soaring prices of silver.

"The county road department will have to get them out," Bert said. "Let's go back to Silverton and learn when the dozer is coming up."

"We'd be shooting what's left of the day," I objected. "We'd better run for Cottonwood and make camp ahead of the rain."

"There's no point in stampeding," Bert retorted, thinking of the Highland Mary trout. But we had to move somewhere, particularly if a bulldozer was on the way. We cleared the loose rock off a piece of semiflat ground and began to maneuver the car around, inch by inch. While we were at it, our wives walked back down the hill.

We found them near the tumbled buildings. Mildred had started looking for discarded bottles, their glass stained a delicate purple by decades of mountain sunlight. They are prized collector's items; some people work prodigiously to dig them from overgrown dumps. Mildred was not so intent, however, and soon let herself be distracted by a dusky grouse hen and its covey of chicks, scurrying among the stalks of crimson fireweed.

Becky was sitting on a barkless gray log, looking over the landscape with a pair of binoculars. We gathered around her while we discussed alternatives —whether to learn the county's plans or go to Cottonwood Creek.

The women did not seem to grasp the seriousness of the situation. They swapped the binoculars back and forth, exclaiming over the old mine buildings perched in incredible places on the weather-ravaged slopes. After a while Bert and I took our turns with the glasses. Over and over we repeated their amazement. "Was there anywhere those old boys wouldn't go for mineral?"

At that point Becky made a real discovery. High on a cliffside was a pinpoint of white. "A tent!" she squealed.

We told her she was mad. No one would pitch a tent in such a spot. But after passing the glasses around, we decided that it really was a prospector's tent. "What these new boys won't do for mineral!" Bert murmured. Then a sliding cloud blotted it from sight.

I jumped to my feet. Beguiled by the lingering sunlight and by these mute hieroglyphics of adventure, we had let more than an hour slip by. "We can't sit here all day," I said.

Bert turned the binoculars on the road. No bulldozer was visible. "Okay," he said resignedly, "Cottonwood it is."

We drove on up the Animas to the point where the river forked. There we turned up the narrow road that slashes a diagonal across the hillside above the last straggling evergreens. A deluge enveloped us, and we saw little but the windshield wipers and the twin ruts ahead of us as we groaned and slithered across Cinnamon Pass, 12,500 feet high. The big peaks on the far side were dim shapes behind a gray veil. Then, as we inched down the hanging road that miners long ago had carved through the forest guarding the upper reaches of the Lake Fork, the clouds broke apart, showing wells of the deepest blue. "Ah!" we all said and opened the windows and unbuttoned our jackets.

Ahead we could see the tawny cliffs that marked the course of Cottonwood Gorge. As we crept eagerly on, the stream itself came into view. Bert and I groaned simultaneously. A mudslide had evidently oozed down those hills, too. The stream was the color and consistency of melted shoe polish.

"It's too late to go anywhere else tonight," I said gloomily. "We'll have to spend the night in Lake City. In a motel."

"Maybe we can go back to Highland Mary tomorrow," Bert said. He didn't sound very hopeful. After all, it had been raining there, too. Then he added, as if variety might somehow save part of this rain-scrambled trip, "We'll take a different road—up Hensen Creek and over Engineer Pass. We'll have lunch somewhere on top. It's slower that way, but the views are great."

*Learning to See*

The next morning we drove slowly up the Hensen Creek road. The clouds had returned, and there was just enough mist so that Bert had to use the windshield wipers every 100 yards or so. A sign by a big pool read, "Fly Fishing Only." The water was murky, and no one was out. No one bothered to make a remark.

The trees dripped. The thick grass looked scrubbed. Unexpected waterfalls leaped in side channels that normally were dry this time of year. We stopped once to watch two beaver puddling around a new dam, and several times to identify wild flowers.

As we crept down the far side of Engineer Pass to a rolling expanse of above-timberline ground called American Flats, patches of blue appeared overhead. Shafts of sunshine played like spotlights on the green tundra and dwarfed willow brush. One glowed on a large white rock close to the road.

"Lunch!" we cried simultaneously.

We went over with the picnic basket that our wives had filled at Lake City—cheese, dark pumpernickel bread, little cherry tomatoes, smoked turkey, and a tall, thin bottle of icy white wine. The wine was like the day, cold sunshine on our tongues.

A blatting came from the hillside. We watched lines of sheep moving along it like grains of rice. The herder stood on a hummock down below. He swung his arm in wide gestures. Obedient to the orders, his shaggy dog raced back and forth, driving the flock to new pastures. It was fascinating—1,500 animals managed with consummate skill by one man and one dog. I had seen many sheep before, had even worked with them as a boy, but this was the first time I had ever sat down long enough to watch them as a part of the mountain pageant.

A sight-seeing Jeep sloshed into sight, its occupants bundled to their chins. The driver stopped to ask about the road to Lake City. "Bad," we said cheerfully. Then we pointed out the sheep. The tourists glanced impatiently and indicated that they would rather drive on.

"You can't blame them," Bert said, tipping his paper cup to catch the last drop of wine. "They paid to see the views and all they're getting from the ridgetops is fog."

"Besides," I said, "they probably don't have much time and want to make the most of it."

It was our admission of surrender. No more hang-ups over the weather, at least on this trip.

For the rest of our four days we just rambled through alternate periods of sunshine and rain squalls. We prowled through old mine buildings, marveling at the mingled rich browns and delicate tans to which some of the planks had weathered. I had seen hundreds of abandoned mine buildings before, but this was the first time I had noticed in detail the magic that slow years of sun and snow can work on a spruce board. Unhappily others have started noticing, too. Pilferers are beginning to rip off the boards and take them to Denver and Colorado Springs to be used as paneling in dens and family rooms. Thus the loss of those relics of the mining boom accelerates throughout the state.

A gaudier experience was wading, soaking wet, through acres of blue-and-white columbine, spiked lupine, dark larkspur, flamboyant paintbrush. Each petal shone with its private drop of water. We smelled the rain-washed aspen and listened to the bicker of chickadees, the plaintive cry of tanagers.

Because our rented car belonged in Silverton, we slowly drifted back that way. We turned again up Cunningham Gulch with a vague idea of making another effort to reach Highland Mary Lake. A signpost, "Stony Pass," changed our minds and we swung to the left up a narrow canyon, intent on seeing what had once been the main route in and out of this section of the San Juan Mountains.

The road, very steep and tight with hairpin curves, climbs 2,300 feet in less than 2 miles. As we drove out of the dripping Engelmann spruce into the misted swales above timberline, we recalled the locally famous story of the miner's wife who, in 1875, had given birth to a baby here at the edge of the timber, lying on a bed of evergreen boughs under a sheet of wagon canvas. Reputedly it was the first child born in the San Juan Mountains.

On the other side of Stony Pass we came to the long swales where the Rio Grande begins its run to the Gulf of Mexico. As we moved along the edges of the meadows, looking for a place to camp, we saw an ingenious lean-to built of sheets of plastic as transparent as glass. The ground underneath was dry. Yet the onetime occupants had departed, discouraged perhaps by the wretched fishing in the rain-muddied stream.

On impulse we appropriated the transparent shelter and lined up our sleeping bags side by side. During the night another squall awoke us. The spruce roared with the wind. Bursts of rain rattled on the plastic like thrown gravel. Overhead the clouds broke and raced. A full moon turned the shredded sky into a boiling radiance. If we had been in tents, we probably would have shut ourselves away from the tumult by curling into our sleeping bags like groundhogs in a lair. But we watched this elemental uproar until it faded away, and in it each of us found a new definition for the word "awe."

By accident we even caught fish. We had decided to spend our last day looking over Mineral Creek, a little north of Silverton. Again a directional sign, this one reading "Clear Lake," twisted us aside. Up we went, under sodden evergreens. We chopped a fallen tree out of the way, rolled some rocks aside. We emerged at timberline just as the clouds were breaking into long streamers of mist. For a spellbound hour we watched the great peaks take shape out of that shifting blankness. A second creation. When we went on past the treeline to the lake, it was almost as if we were heeding an afterthought.

Rainbow trout were greeting the sunshine by jumping everywhere. We soon had our limits and were on the point of holding a fish fry then and there, using charcoal bricks we had brought along. But the clouds closed in again, and the lake hissed under a flurry of hail.

We retreated to a restaurant in town, where the chef agreed to cook the trout for us. A neighboring diner watched us attack the platter, and then came over to our table.

"Do you mind telling me *where* and *how* you got those fish?" he demanded truculently. "I came here from Texas on a week's vacation and I've worked every stream and lake I can reach, and I haven't had a nibble."

"That's the trouble," Mildred explained. "You've been trying too hard."

He stared at her. Even after she elaborated, he did not have the faintest idea of what she meant.

I wouldn't have, either, four days earlier.

1. Unremitting winds have shaped this fir into what is called, for obvious reasons, a banner tree.

2. "White-out." A raging blizzard batters defiant little evergreens near timberline on Niwot Ridge, a spur of the Continental Divide.

*3. The tops of these fence posts, rising just above a massive snowdrift on the lee of a small hill, enhance the otherwise stark line between snow and sky.*

*4. Starkly eroded clay hills near Montrose are highlighted by lingering scuffs of snow on their northern slopes.*

**OVERLEAF:**
*5. Shrinking snowdrifts streak the colored slopes of Willow Basin in the Snowmass-Maroon Bells Wilderness Area.*

6. *Winter intensifies the ruggedness of the San Juan country.*

7. *Crags.*

8. *Side gullies slash strong parallels down toward the Animas Canyon.*

# 4
# FULL COLOR

*The Summons*

Late in September Becky Tucker, once a newspaperwoman herself, called from Paonia to say that she had a journalist from Milan, Italy, in tow. During his search for material about the new American West he had visited the principal cities and had seen the obligatory natural wonders—Yosemite, the Grand Canyon, Great Salt Lake, Pikes Peak, Rocky Mountain National Park. His eye had been caught by the incredible massing of motorized campers in the National Parks, by artfully preserved mining towns, towering condominiums at the ski resorts, and the insect-legged steel pylons of power lines leaning into space from the edges of cliffs. Now Becky planned to show him something unique. She would not say what it was, but wondered whether Mildred and I would like to come along.

Almost on the instant we were in the car, headed up the north fork of the South Platte River. It was one of those gleaming days that promise everything you want from the mountains. On north-facing slopes a few clusters of aspens were already drawing patterns of gold against the dark background of evergreens. The shrunken stream was a ribbon of dancing light. The shadows at midday were noticeably longer than they had been a month ago. Where they stretched across a picnic table at which we paused for lunch, the air was cold. We moved to a sunny rock. In that briskness we wanted to run, even laden with picnic basket and paper bags.

We dropped down the far side of Kenosha Pass onto the broad flats of South Park. The close-cropped hay meadows were already showing a russet tinge. Men and machines were working in the distance. The result of their labors were hundreds of bales of hay scattered throughout the fields. Other tightly bound, rectangular bales were being piled into big, flat-topped stacks. What Becky's visitor from Milan would not see, I thought with nostalgia, were fields dotted with picturesque wooden derricks standing beside stacks of loose hay shaped into stacks that looked like loaves of fresh bread. What price efficiency?—a maudlin question the men in the field would have answered with loud snorts.

Instead of continuing directly across South Park, we turned southeast along Tarryall Creek. (Early prospectors, striking pay dirt in the stream's gravel, had reputedly cried, "Let's all tarry here!") Our intent was to visit briefly with old friends, writer Marshall Sprague and his wife Ejay, for Edna Jane. Their cabin—no one says cottage in those parts—stands on the back side of the Tarryall Range. It is a rugged area of steep slopes, scattered ponderosa pine, and islands of aspen trees, some of them already turning to an unlikely orange color. High above were heavily fractured cliffs and crags of pink, flaky Pikes Peak granite.

Awareness of autumn was even stronger here than it had been along the north fork of the Platte. For one thing we had time to notice the birds clustered on the hillside near the cabin, where the Spragues scatter food. The usual noisy residents were about—long-tailed black-and-white magpies, black-capped chickadees, and Steller's jays, hopping raucously from branch to branch, their crests jaunty, their heads black, their sturdy bodies a dark, handsome blue. Mingling with these familiars were other species fleeing from the rigors of timberline—rosy finches, nuthatches hanging upside down on the tree trunks, and flocks of juncos, their white tail feathers flashing as they burst out of the grass in short, erratic flights.

Another harbinger of cold weather was Marshall's eagerness to gather firewood. I recognized the symptoms. In the old days the cowboys on the ranch where I grew up would file the teeth of a two-man crosscut saw, hitch a pair of white mules to a wagon, beckon me aboard, and rattle off to the pine forest below the camp. Marshall beckoned, too, but he uses a Jeep and a chain saw, modernizations which I regard without nostalgia. Besides, the rituals haven't changed. You sniff the air and announce the obvious: the job cannot be postponed any longer. With studied deliberation, as though to lend weight to the importance of what you are about to do, you pull on heavy, gauntleted gloves and shrug into the sheepskin coat that has been hanging all summer at the cluttered back end of the closet.

Off you go, headed for an area that you know was burned over years before. Your eyes search for fallen limbs or sections of tumbled trunks that have been charred on the outside but remain solid inside. Somehow the charring seems to have sealed in and concentrated the pitch in the dead wood, so that it burns fragrantly for a long time with a hot flame. Because it also gives off a thick black smoke, it is not as suitable for stoves—clean, quick-burning aspen is better for them—as it is for rock fireplaces.

*First Snow*

As we worked, clouds covered the sinking sun. Wind stirred a deep humming from the pine boughs, and we guessed what was coming. Later, when we walked out through the starless dark to make sure the pasture gate was closed, we knew we'd been right: the year's first flakes of snow stung our cheeks.

"Perfect!" I exclaimed, thinking of Becky Tucker's journalist. For autumn is never so glorious as when it is ushered in by an early snowstorm.

Mountain dwellers often call these September disturbances equinoctial storms. Whether or not they are really related to the equinox, except by coincidence, I do not know. At any rate, a storm generally occurs during the last two weeks of September. (There is generally one during the last two weeks of August, too.) At elevations above 8,000 feet or so the September precipitation comes as snow. At rare intervals the fall will reach as low as Colorado Springs or even Denver. If the drop of wet flakes in the cities reaches a depth of a foot or more, it does painful damage to the elm and maple trees, for they are still in full, green leaf. Branches break off with a distressing sound of splitting wood and create a twisted maze in the residential areas that completely confounds traffic.

Although this first dazzling fall of snow and the accompanying plunge in temperatures seem like a fitting announcement that autumn has arrived, the chill actually has little direct bearing on the coloring of the leaves. The sudden change is apparently the result of a shut-off mechanism in the plants that is triggered by the reduced length and intensity of the daylight hours. Water no longer reaches the leaves. Unable to continue manufacturing chlorophyll, they lose their greenness. The red and yellow pigments in the fibers show through and the leaves prepare to drop. A hard frost then is destructive to tree beauty, for the extreme cold instantly reduces the red leaves of the oak brush and the blazing yellow of the aspens to drab brown ruins.

When we awoke in the morning we found that about 4 inches of wet, cold fluff had fallen during the night. It capped every fence post, bent the grass into fuzzy humps, lay like cotton on the tops of the evergreen branches. Some of the aspens looked bent and pained. In most cases, though, the flexible leaves had let the snow slide harmlessly off. Even though the morning was dull, the trees glowed like fire against the whiteness.

Because the unimproved road serving the cabin was slippery, Marshall escorted us with his Jeep as far as the gravel highway beside Tarryall Creek. We followed it a short distance, then cut through a fairyland of whitened spruce to Highway 24, which strikes from Colorado Springs west across South Park. At the top of Wilkerson Pass, on the low eastern rim of the Park, we stopped dead, stunned by a mountain phenomenon that is rare only in the sense that to see it you have to be lucky enough to be in the right place at the right time.

As most widespread storms do, this one was moving east toward the plains. Overhead the sky was a flat, thin gray. In front of us the drab sagebrush on South Park's wide flats was stippled with white. The western horizon was a row of glimmering, snow-shrouded peaks. Above the peaks on the horizon was a thin streak created by the imperceptible drift of the storm to the east. This knife-edged shearing-off of the trailing end of a storm is relatively common and always beautiful. Today, however, the play of light on the pristine whiteness below made it breath-catching. Car after car pulled up onto the Pass, slowed abruptly, and swung into the parking lot so that the occupants could watch.

There was no color in the opening above the peaks. It was a slash of pure radiance, almost unbearably bright. Light flowing toward us from the glow struck an infinitude of sparkles from the tops of the frosted hummocks of sage. Then, almost before you could breathe, "Look at that!" the intensity waned and the front border of the sparkles retreated swiftly to the horizon. The slash above the peaks widened and filled with baby blue. The edges of the clouds grew ragged, and it was just one more beautiful morning. The parking space filled with the grinding sound of starting motors.

"I wish the Italian could have seen that," I said, and then I wondered again, "What on earth do you suppose Becky is planning to show him?"

*The Italian Cowboy*

The visitor's name turned out to be Guglielmo Mairani. We promptly called him Bill. He was middle-aged, tall, and lean with a long nose, thinning black hair, and a wide, winning smile. His English was exact but heavily accented. Wherever he went, he carried two cameras hung around his neck. Learning that our expedition would consist of a four-day horseback ride into the back country, he bought, in lieu of riding boots, a pair of greenish rubber overshoes to cover his oxfords. He wore stiff new, ill-fitting jeans, a sweater, and no hat. He called himself, in amusement, "the Italian cowboy," the most unlikely cowboy, surely, that the mountains ever saw. He had never before been on a horse. He rode awkwardly and did it for several hours at a stretch with only a sleeping bag on the ground to soothe him betweentimes. He must have been sorely chafed and strained, but he never complained or lost his good nature.

Our guides were a couple named Grant and Mamie Ferrier. They must have been close to seventy years old. They had run cattle for years in the West Elk Mountains east of Paonia, Colorado. Now, during summers, they and their sons operate a dude ranch near the hamlet of Crawford and lead trail rides through the West Elk Wilderness Area. In the fall they take deer and elk hunters into the hills. The hunting season was due to open shortly after our arrival in Paonia, and they planned a routine check on some of their camps. Becky had arranged for us to go with them on part of the survey. But she still wouldn't say what she hoped to see.

I let my dubiousness show. "Sure, it's great country, especially with the color coming on. But the peaks aren't much. There are half a dozen more spectacular ranges—"

"A man who climbs and skis in the Alps every year isn't looking for mountains."

"But—"

"We'll spoil it if we keep talking about it. It will have to happen naturally —if it does happen."

We began the trip by truck, driving up the north fork of the Gunnison River to a tributary named Coal Creek. A wretched road, slippery from the storm, took us up Coal Creek's narrow canyon past stands of Colorado blue spruce—the tips of their evergreen branches truly are a deep cerulean—to a sidestream known as Robinson Creek. The hill to our left culminated in a magnificent rampart of brown pinnacles called locally The Rooster's Comb, the boundary for a short distance of the West Elk Wilderness Area.

Similar rock walls—pillars, domes, crenellations—are characteristic of the massive roll of land between the two forks of the Gunnison River. Some of the best examples are inside the wilderness area, notably a 12,000-foot crest known as The Castles. "Toothsome rock" is the way Robert Ormes, playing on words, describes them in his climber's *Guide to the Colorado Mountains*. If you are unable to hike in to see the wilderness ramparts at close range, look north from Highway 50 across Blue Mesa Reservoir into the canyons there. The buttes and cliffs you glimpse will give you the general idea.

Saddle horses and five pack mules, the latter intended primarily for carrying supplies to the hunting camps, were waiting in the corrals at the end of the road. We loaded up and started along Little Robinson Creek, its narrow, earth-walled stream bed filled with a succession of beaver ponds. The water was murky, for the beaver, too, knew that winter was near and in their diligence to make ready were stirring up quantities of mud.

Soon we were engulfed by forests of aspen threaded here and there with spruce. It was a glorious experience of gold and white. Not a breath of air stirred the leaves. The hooves of our animals made little sound in the moist earth. Though the snow had vanished from the open meadows, it still lay in rumples on the forest floor. Out of its whiteness rose a maze of white trunks bare of branches as far as the golden canopy overhead. The scattered brush of the understory was golden, too. Even the air was golden, filled with the refulgence of sunlight striking through the yellow leaves.

The Ferriers' camp stood near two big beaver ponds in a broad swale known as Elk Basin. Oddly the trees there—the elevation is a little over 9,000 feet—were just beginning to turn. Streamers of green still laced the prevailing yellow, muting the hues until the hillside looked like a soft blanket that you could pull up around your chin when you went to bed.

The ponds caught the glow of sunset and of yellow aspen leaves. We watched a family of beaver swim back and forth through shimmers of crimson and gold until the light faded and we retreated to the dining tent to listen to Grant tell tales of hunting. It was cold when we turned in. The Milky Way laid a bridge of radiance across the infinite depth of the night. The bells on the horses clanged; at intervals coyotes chorused back and forth. When we got up the next morning, the grass was white with hoarfrost, and lenses of ice glistened along the edges of the ponds.

*New Looks at Old Vistas*

That day and the next we took long rides out from the base camp. On the first day we crossed a high ridge crested with red-barked Engelmann spruce and dropped down to Soap Creek, which, like The Rooster's Comb farther north, forms part of the western boundary of the West Elk Wilderness Area. Eventually we reached Sheep Lake, set in dense spruce under a curving gray cliff crosshatched with snow. A wooden fence whose single opening was too narrow for livestock prevented range cattle and horses from reaching the shore. So many backpackers have camped at Sheep Lake, however, that they have stripped the immediate area of firewood, and we had to bring in kindling for our lunch from outside the fence.

The concept of wilderness puzzled Bill even after we had explained the legalistics involved. No firewood at a camp inside the wilderness, yet plenty outside? Odd. But he did like the idea of protecting sections of the mountains from commercial exploitation and motorized travel. "A motorcycle or—how do you call it?—a Jeep? (he said "jep") is not what Europeans picture on these paths. Don't let go of your wild places. Our children need them to think about, just as you need our cathedrals to think of when your hearts are sore."

The next day we made a circuit of an 11,000-foot dome called Haystack Mountain. It rises between Elk Basin, where our camp was, and Coal Basin, where the creek of the same name heads. Around the upper edge of each basin curl rows of gentle peaks. On that day they still glistened with the remnants of the equinoctial snow. Thin cirrus clouds, shaped like turkey feathers, stood out against the vivid sky. One often hears of the lazy haze of Indian summer, but such days are rare in the high mountains. Most, like this day, are polished as clear as diamonds by the wind. Distant ridges are limned as sharply as if shaped by a steel razor. We could even make out the forms of individual trees on hilltops miles away.

We rode slowly across open meadows toward the western snout of the haystack. Underneath the thin mantle of snow was a myriad of tunnels left by pocket gophers. The horses sank up to their fetlocks in the soft earth, so that the animals lurched rather than walked. But the softness did not appear to bother three antlered bucks, as red of coat as any Robin Hood ever shot, that bounded away from our approach downhill into the trees.

At the prow of the ridge we halted. The huge basins on either hand rolled away beside the diminishing ridge, joined, and flowed through a gap in the mountains to the blueness of the low country. The grays and whites of the peaks slid down to ragged collars of black spruce. The spruce in turn merged unevenly with the vast cover of aspen and oak brush—green, yellow, orange, red, brown, and threads of white, a Persian fantasy.

After a long silence, Bill asked Grant, "Can you point to where there is a house people live in?"

"No," Grant said. "Not down there."

"A summer place perhaps?"

"No. There's a sort of a cow camp at the edge of those meadows, but it isn't used much any more."

"I don't see a road," Bill said.

"The closest one ends where we packed up."

Bill persisted. "We have ridden three days and have not met one person."

"That's partly because it's the quiet time of year," Grant told him.

"Will we see anyone tomorrow?"

"Probably not."

"Four days—no one! Is this wilderness?"

"What we're looking at? No."

Bill gave his head a wag of bafflement. Then his arm flung wide. "Ah, but it is space! In Italy . . ." He broke off, to say reflectively, "One would not want to be lonesome forever. But sometimes . . ." Again he did not finish, but asked instead, "Are there many places like this?"

I thought of all the high basins dropping between long plateaus into wide valleys where little farm towns nestle. I thought of the eastern plains. I remembered the light flooding across South Park, engulfing with its radiance all sign of the ranches that are there. We live in an ambiance of vistas so overwhelming that we grow impervious, until someone like Guglielmo Mairani comes along.

"Yes," I told him, "there are places like this all over the West."

He nodded, very pleased, as though a faith had been reaffirmed. For many Europeans, America still means space and all that space can suggest to a hungry imagination.

I saw Becky smiling. "Okay," I grumbled. "You win."

For several minutes after that we sat silent on our tired horses, looking across those tousled miles of color as though we had never seen anything quite like them before.

PART TWO

# *The Way the Land Lies*

# 5
# THE PLAINS

Because Colorado's mean elevation is 6,800 feet above sea level, first-time visitors approaching from the east often expect—indeed, yearn—to see mountains almost as soon as they cross the state border. Their hours have been monotonous. The ascent of the highway or railroad tracks, a steady 7 or 8 feet per mile, is not enough to relieve the impression of interminable flatness. The slow change in vegetation is equally indiscernible. If one has been following the South Platte or the Arkansas River, there is just more of that winding green ribbon of cottonwood trees and irrigated farms. Or if the route has been spearing across the drier country between the streams, the only things visible are low shrubs and dun grass, an occasional mirage, and here and there pale strips of corn and wheat planted by men who are betting that this may be the year when dry farming will pay off.

Sooner or later such travelers pick up and repeat with relish a folk saying that is indigenous to every section of the West whose main feature is uninterrupted breadth: "You can look farther around here and see less than anyplace else I've ever been."

Countering that, though not made with the saying in mind, is the remark of an acquaintance of mine who lives on the plains in the southeastern part of the state. "Sure, I like to go to the mountains on short trips. But after a week I feel penned in. I can hardly wait to get back where I can see something."

Though the mountains are not immediately visible to new arrivals, they nevertheless are the determining factor of plains ecology. The soil itself derives from them. Its base is thick layers of sandstone laid down in ancient seas by sediment washing out of ancient mountains. During the geologic past, seas ebbed and returned; mountains rose and were eroded to peneplains (a peneplain translates as "almost a plain"). Then, perhaps 70 millions years ago, a vast upheaval known as the Laramide revolution lifted up the predecessor of the long chain of mountains we call the Rockies. Again the seas retreated. Debris tumbled onto the lowlands. Clouds of ash streamed out from exploding volcanoes. Less spectacularly, ice and water and wind carried on their relentless scourings. The products of this erosion—gravel, sand, and silt—were carried far out from the base of the mountains and deposited in merging alluvial fans whose constituent parts disintegrated still more under the impact of alternate sun and frost. This massive decay left the first mountains almost as flat as the plains. Then another cataclysm occurred, pushing up more mountains. Now they too are eroding, sending new washes of sand and gravel onto the plains. The result is a profoundly deep soil rich in minerals and aching (from man's standpoint) for enough water to make things grow the way man would like to see them grow.

The hope is frustrated by the same mountains that provided the soil. Their peaks suck unto themselves most of the moisture carried in the storms that roll east each winter with the breaking of the Pacific high. At least five times as much snow mantles the Rockies as drops on the plains. Fortunately for the lowlands, summers are moister. Warm air currents curving north out of the Gulf of Mexico clash with colder air pushing down from Canada. The result, at times, is a fierce display of lightning and brief, torrential rains and hailstorms. Almost three quarters of the annual precipitation received by the plains comes from such storms, spaced at wide intervals from the beginning of April through September.

Since the annual average is only 10 to 13 inches, depending on locality, three quarters of the total is not very much. The average, moreover, is made up of figures that fluctuate erratically. Some years the total barely reaches 6 inches. And whether years be wet or dry, the forces of desiccation are continuous. After the rare clouds retreat, the sun hangs as naked as an arc light in a vault of brilliant blue. The wind *s-shushes* interminably. Evaporation is so rapid that you can feel it puckering your skin. Within hours after those short, slashing rains the land again looks as dry as a bone.

In spite of all that, the plains cannot be classified as desert. Although trees will not grow except beside the widely spaced streams or where they are nurtured by hand, certain grasses and shrubs thrive. Chief among the former are curly buffalo grass and blue grama, their seedpods shaped like the plumes that Greek warriors once wore on their helmets.

They cling close to the ground, their deep roots forming a tight sod that helps form cool vaults for storing traces of underground moisture. Rice grass is taller, its tops lacy; Indians once harvested its hard, tiny seeds. Salt grass grows where the soil is alkaline; pale, fluffy New Mexico feather grass on shaly limestone. Western wheat grass, whose spiked head looks like an emaciated version of the head of domesticated wheat, is widespread.

Except when snow falls or during a brief period in springtime, the land at first sight looks uniformly brown. But when your eyes start dividing it into sections, you see that the tones, though muted, range from dusky to pale tan —almost white in certain slants of sunshine. Here and there are the whitish beds of intermittent streams. From these shallow creases the land climbs slowly, then falls gently away into unexpected swales. It is prickled at intervals by silvery buffalo brush, spindly sage, and the bayonet leaves of yucca. In places, generally on land that was once plowed and then abandoned, dense strands of sunflowers push up chest-high, dry out, turn dark and rattly and ugly—but play a useful part in catching and holding wind-blown snow.


*The Nimble Creatures of the Plains*

Wet springs bring forth bursts of color—pale green on the undulations of the open range, vivid green where winter wheat has been planted. Dwarf yellow flowers blanket the unplowed ground as far as the eye can see. Gray-leafed mallows (their juice was once used for making marshmallows) send up spikes of bloom covered with what look like miniature hollyhock flowers. Prairie asters and primroses riot. Flat-leafed prickly-pear cactus put out pale yellow, satiny flowers; barrel cactus has red blossoms. Queen of all are the waxy white pendants of yucca, tightly clustered on swiftly growing spikes.

Birds sings constantly then. Most loved is the western meadowlark, a solid, chunky bird with a striped gray back, white tail feathers, and a bright yellow front set off by a black bib. He carols so lustily from fence posts or in flight that you can catch snatches of the song even when racing by on the interstate freeways. Another spectacular songster is the lark bunting. At mating time the male is jet black, with vivid white patches on his wings. He entertains his drabber mate by soaring perpendicularly toward the sky, then fluttering back while warbling joyously, just as any bird bearing the name lark ought to do. The lark bunting is Colorado's state bird, a showy but not altogether fitting choice since the birds occupy only the eastern two fifths of the state for only part of the year, migrating south for the winter.

Lark buntings, which feed in flocks, are shy. The smallest disturbance sends them whirring for the closest shelter in wildly zigzagging courses. Their nervousness comes from their conspicuousness in a land where the sharp-winged falcons of the prairie strike hard and fast.

Contrary to the buntings' reasonable suspicions, however, most hawks prefer small mammals. Unhappily, because of human hunters and the encroachment of farmland and suburbs on nesting grounds, the population of the larger species is slowly diminishing. Still, it is a rare day when a traveler does not note a redtail hawk riding high on the air currents while now and then uttering his penetrating shriek, or a powerful, ferruginous rough-legged hawk—he's even bigger and more powerful than his name—beating along a fence line in search of the rodents that live where weeds have escaped the blade of plow or mowing machine. Smaller but no less dramatic are hook-billed, strongly marked gray, white, and black shrikes. Though no bigger than robins, they are so ferocious that they have been named "butcher birds." They will strike down horned larks and lark buntings if they can, but mostly they prey on grasshoppers and other insects, which they store for future reference by impaling them on thorns or on the barbs of barbed-wire fences.

Animals are less conspicuously marked than are these highly noticeable birds. Prairie dogs and ground squirrels look like the earth into which they burrow for protection. The buff-and-gray fur of coyotes and of long-eared, black-tailed jackrabbits blend into the muted tones of the brush. The only exception to this camouflaging is the fleetest of the prairie animals, the lovely pronghorn antelope, whose white rump shines like a flag.

The antelope's undoing is it insatiable curiosity. One famous plainsman of the last century, Marcellin St. Vrain, used to lure the animals within rifle range by standing on his head and waving his legs tantalizingly in the air. You can amuse yourself nowadays by exploiting the same trait. The best time

9. Alpenglow, Courthouse Mountain beside the Uncompahgre River near Ridgway.

10. Nature's reservoir. The scores of square miles visible in this picture all lie well above 11,000 feet in elevation, a vast catchment plain for snow. Towering in the middle is the great north face of Uncompahgre Peak, northeast of Ouray.

*11. Boaters thrive on spring run-off. This raft is tackling a rapids in the Dolores Canyon. In a few more weeks the river will shrink to a trickle.*

*12 and 13. Cliffs hemming in the Yampa River.*

*14. Spring evening: Although the Yampa River, northwestern Colorado, has broken free of its ice, no leaves have yet softened the bare branches of this lone cottonwood as it reaches toward a rising moon.*

15. Hay once was put up for winter in stacks shaped like loaves of bread. Now it is baled by machine before being hauled to the barns where it is stored until needed. South Park.

16. The delicate seedhead of the pasqueflower is almost as beautiful as the blossom.

*17. A scuff of snow and yellowing aspens herald the approach of fall in the West Elk Wilderness Area.*

is the fall, when the animals are gathering into flocks. A good area is the rolling country south of the Arkansas River towns of La Junta and Las Animas. Drive down some remote back road until you have spotted a group. Leave your car, walk a short distance onto the prairie, and sit down. What's that strange hump?—the animals will edge nervously closer to investigate. A sudden panic will wheel them about, and they will race out of sight over a hill. Sit tight. For they will reappear at full speed. When they reach the spot where they veered before, they will stop abruptly, stamping and snorting and staring. Then away they'll go again, white rumps bobbing, to return a third or even a fourth time if the game has not grown tiresome first or if they have not been distracted by something else.

*Bringing Moisture to Dryness*

This vast biome of grass—it occupies the eastern two fifths of Colorado's 104,247 square miles—is threaded by two major strips of green, the valleys of the South Platte and Arkansas rivers. The first named breaks out of the mountains a few miles south of Denver and flows north near the base of the foothills, picking up tributaries as it goes. In the vicinity of Greeley it bends east and then northeast, entering Nebraska almost at Colorado's northeast corner.

The Arkansas breaks out of the mountains through the awesome Royal Gorge west of Pueblo. From there it flows a bit south of east until it reaches Kansas. At one point in the high country, where the Mosquito Range divides the upper Arkansas Valley from South Park, the heads of some of the two rivers' tributaries are only feet apart, yet where they leave the state they are separated by 200 miles—only to mingle at last in the Mississippi.

Both are "braided" rivers. That is, their shallow waters split into channels that twine sluggishly among almost innumerable low, brush-choked islands. Both are subject to rampaging spring floods that spread sheets of water across the valley floors and pile clutters of debris into the lower limbs of the cottonwood trees on their banks. Together they constitute the mountains' greatest gift to the plains.

Their impact on the development of Colorado can hardly be exaggerated. They were the highways of the first traders pressing west to make contact with the Indians of the high plains and with the Spanish outposts in New Mexico. Wagon trains followed their winding courses to the gold camps of the southern Rockies. Railroads and interstate highways utilize their easy gradients.

More importantly, they transport water. Settlers at the cooperative colony of Greeley learned a century ago that if the barren-looking benches above the river bottom were irrigated with ditch water from the South Platte and its chief tributary, the Cache la Poudre, the soil would produce bounteous harvests of wheat, vegetables, melons, sugar beets, and alfalfa. The abundance attracted odorous sugar factories and feedlots for fattening sheep and cattle. When the natural flow of the streams proved unable to meet the increasing demands, huge transmontane diversion projects were devised for bringing in more water from the far side of the Continental Divide, a billion-dollar effort that has extended to the Arkansas as well as to the Platte.

Beneath the visible rivers percolate broader underground streams that are now being tapped by ever-deepening wells. Attached to some of these wells are horizontal pipes an eighth of a mile long mounted on what look like overgrown bicycle wheels. The force of the water turns these monsters in a slow circle while rainbird nozzles spout glistening fountains onto the planted land beneath. From the air the pattern is extraordinary. Western farms, traditionally rectangular, are in places becoming circular.

Irrigation has meant the building of storage reservoirs at intervals along the main streams. Runoff water has created marshes. Artificial ponds dot the drainage courses of the uplands. Cottonwoods and willows, no longer chopped down for firewood by emigrants in wagon trains and no longer browsed on by buffalo, grow densely in the river bottoms.

This altered ecology has attracted hitherto unfamiliar forms of wildlife—muskrats, innumerable song sparrows, geese, eighteen species of wild ducks, herons, egrets, and dainty-legged avocets with their long, uptilted bills. Brilliant yellow-headed and red-winged blackbirds teeter on the cattails. Solitary bitterns escape detection by pointing their long bills straight upward so that they look like sticks, while the stripes of their bodies blend deceptively with the shadows of the reeds. The male bittern's springtime mating call, a booming *ump-ump* produced by a kind of bellows in his throat, has earned him the nickname "thunder pumper."

Beyond these small oases are a few sections where precipitation is slightly higher than average. Here farmer-gamblers plant winter wheat in the hope that moisture stored in the rich loam underneath the plowed sod will germinate the seed and that enough rain will fall to bring the sprouts to maturity. Because many of these men do not live in the areas they farm but simply move in with their machinery to handle the crops, they are called "suitcase farmers." In good years they make a killing, but not all years are good.

Beyond and around the dry farms lie thousands of square miles of livestock range, dotted with tens of thousands of cattle and, less frequently, with sheep. Although the low, curly grama grass on which they feed is nutritious, it is also sparse. In places 60 acres are needed to support a single cow. Many of those cows have to walk miles to reach muddy ponds, where they drink by wading out up to their bellies, or they seek out galvanized tanks filled by thin trickles pumped from the ground by lonesome windmills. Winter blizzards sometimes create havoc. Herefords in particular will drift with the wind until they jam up in some fence corner and freeze to death. In order to reduce fatalities, many ranchers build shelters in the southeast corners of their big pastures—southeast because most winter storms howl out of the northwest.

It has been a hard-used land. Entire species of game—buffalo, wolves, grizzly bears—have been exterminated. In the east-central part of the state is the weather-grayed hamlet of Wild Horse, named for the huge herds that used to water nearby in Big Sandy Creek. They are gone now. Even the grass they grazed has been threatened by overstocking. Of the high plains Indians who, with their neighboring tribes, developed one of the world's distinctive cultures nothing remains in Colorado except the names attached to three of the counties through which they once roamed—Kiowa, Cheyenne, Arapaho.

During and after the First World War, the high price of grain and the blandishments of land speculators lured farmers into all sections of the plains in the hope that they could flourish by dry-farming wheat. They tore up the sod for miles, exposing it in long furrows to the wind. For a little while nature was kind. The moisture that had once accumulated under the sod and the rains that came in the nick of time produced bumper crops. Inevitably this encouraged more reckless plowing. The end came when the Depression of the 1930s coincided with a heart-wrenching sequence of rainless windstorms. Towering clouds of dust sweeping up from the sodless fields blotted out the sun, buried fences and sheds, seeped into every corner of the houses, and drifted east as far as the Atlantic.

The hardest-hit sections of Colorado lay north of the South Platte and south of the Arkansas. The topsoil in both areas is thin. Erosion has exposed the bones of the land in the shape of scrawny outcroppings of rock, low bluffs, and, most spectacularly in the north, in the twin, slab-sided Pawnee Buttes, rising in grand isolation hundreds of feet above the flatlands.

*The National Grasslands*

During the duststorm years many destitute families abandoned their wind-scoured farms to the mortgage holders and tax collectors, and vanished. Others lived hand to mouth on relief, hoping that next year would be better. The land in its way needed help as much as the people did. To relieve both, the federal government in 1934 purchased thousands of farms throughout the Western states, assisted the displaced families in finding new homes, and then began the difficult work of restoring the ravaged countryside.

In 1960, after various vicissitudes under diverse agencies, nearly 4 million acres of drylands were consolidated as National Grasslands and placed under the administration of the National Forest Service. Of the West's nineteen Grasslands two are in Colorado. Fittingly each has an Indian name. The Pawnee National Grassland, divided into two sections, lies north of the Platte, near the buttes of the same name. The Comanche National Grassland, also split into two parts, lies below the Arkansas. Intermingled with the government lands are many private holdings.

In a sense Grassland is a misnomer, a hope rather than an actuality. Erosion gullies still scar both areas. Dust still swirls. Yucca and sagebrush have affixed themselves to flats that were once heavily overgrazed. But the slow process of rehabilitation—slow because these semiarid lands cannot be hurried—is at last showing signs of progress.

Some reseeding is being done, but mostly the native vegetation is given a chance to reestablish itself through limitations placed on the amount of grazing permitted on a given section. (Ranchers and the Forest Service seldom agree about what the proper amount is.) Wells and ponds help both wildlife and livestock. "Guzzlers"—ground-level tanks covered with low corrugated metal roofs that catch and channel rainfall, provide shade and water for small animals and birds.

Outside the marginal grasslands some dry farming continues, but not in the thoughtless ways of half a century ago. The ground is not pulverized as ruthlessly as was once the case. Plow furrows run crosswise to the direction of the prevailing wind, whose sweep is further mitigated by leaving strips of grass between the bands of cultivated earth. Near the little town of Akron the federal government maintains an experimental station devoted to investigating dry-farming procedures.

### *Ecological Ranching*

Private individuals are also seeking for ways to improve their land. The most controversial among them is Tom Lasater, who came north from Texas shortly after the Second World War. After long search he settled on 25,000 run-down acres near Matheson, midway between the two rivers. Wanting an animal that would return the greatest amount of meat per pound of grass consumed, Lasater mixed together Shorthorn, Hereford, and Brahma strains to produce what he called the Beefmaster, recognized in 1954 by the Department of Agriculture as a distinct new breed.

The ponderous Beefmasters require no more land for their support than do the smaller Herefords—about 50 acres per animal in the Matheson area. Lasater does not keep them continuously in the same pasture, however, but rotates them from plot to plot as the condition of the grass suggests. Nature rotated the buffalo, too, he believes. The huge herds would devour everything in a given area to the roots, meanwhile fertilizing it copiously. Then the herd would move on, not to return until the range had had a chance to restore itself. Pushing the land to capacity without rest is what hurts, Lasater says, for as the supply of grass dwindles the hungry animals of necessity injure the sod, browse down the cottonwood trees that provide them with winter shelter, and eventually devour the locoweed that kills them—things they will not do if ample grass is available.

Because Lasater believes that nature is keyed to maintaining healthy balances, he has posted his land as a wildlife refuge. Within his fences all creatures great and small live as nearly in their primitive ways as is possible—except that he does provide artificial ponds for his cattle and, as a corollary, for non-domestic animals and birds. He rarely loses a calf to a coyote, he says, because coyotes would rather feed on their accustomed insects and rodents than face an angry cow. It is only when their natural food has been eliminated by thoughtless poisoning programs that coyotes trouble livestock—a theory, it should be added, that is vigorously rebutted by many sheepmen.

In spite of these bold attempts at restoration, public and private, a sadness still lies on much of the land. Children seep away toward the cities from the farms and the elm-shaded villages. Once six hundred families lived in the southern part of Otero County, where part of the Comanche National Grassland is located. Now there are twenty-three. Ghost towns and ghost farms are commonplace. Spindly clusters of trees reveal their locations even when no buildings remain—trees planted in defiance of nature and coaxed into growth by barrelfuls of water hauled by wagon for indeterminate distances. Those green banners of confidence vanish last, their leaves dying gradually until only snags are left.

Unquestionably the farms and ranches that remain are better managed than were their predecessors. That knowledge is heartening. But then you read of the serious overdrafts being made on the water tables by the huge, circular irrigating machines—and by wells sunk deep to supply masses of suburban homes east and southeast of Denver—and you wonder. Later, perhaps, you stop in the sagging hamlet of Firstview on Highway 40, named so because it was there that earlier travelers first glimpsed Pikes Peak, and you see nothing through the distant lens of smog thrown up by the cities ranged along the foothills. The opaque barrier is symbolic. Linkages between those invisible mountains and these plains are as fundamental now as they ever were. Yet in some ways we are as unable as the dry-land farmers of the thirties to see far enough through the veil of our local concerns to realize that our lives are all of a piece. It is the lesson of the Yampa repeated under different circumstances on the opposite side of the state: we cannot damage a basic resource in one area without eventually bringing injury to the whole.

# 6
# TRANSITIONS

For a visually dramatic approach to the Rockies from the east, leave Interstate 70 a few miles outside the town of Limon and strike west along State Highway 86. It is the quickest way to reach trees—in this case widely spaced ponderosa pines—and the sight of their olive-green boughs builds anticipation. After endless miles of flat brownness you have gained enough altitude, here on the wide, rolling divide between the South Platte and Arkansas rivers, so that a new life zone is beginning. There are different forms of vegetation to see and (if you can spot them from the car) different kinds of birds and mammals.

But your main concern, built of impatience, is for the mountains. The blue wall of them shows clearly through openings in the thin forest. Even so you are not prepared for the panorama that lies ahead. Of a sudden the land drops into valleys carved by little streams winding north to meet the South Platte where it breaks out of the ramparts to the west. Elevated thus, you look across space with no foreground to belittle the impression of height. Even more striking is the tremendous north-south rush of that gouged and ragged barrier.

Each person who contemplates the view will distill from it his or her own dominant impression. Majesty will certainly be one, yet overshadowing that for me are the twin sensations of contrast and tension. Vertical lines break upward out of horizontal. Grasslands give way to forests. As the forests climb the slopes, their color changes from green to black. The black in turn is cut off at timberline by the gray of rock or, in winter and spring, by the sheen of snow. Although the main thrust of the mountains is north and south, the canyons that cleave their sides drop as a general rule from west to east. Within these canyons, you can well imagine, is the clash of water and stone.

*The Urban Strip*

There is even a contrast between emptiness and congestion. Behind you is the loneliness of the plains. To your right, to the northwest, you can make out the smoky sprawl of Denver's suburbs. The traffic moving southward from there toward Colorado Springs reminds you that approximately 70 per cent of Colorado's 2,250,000 residents live in a narrow band, scarcely 20 miles wide, where the plains bump against the mountains.

Why this particular band? Because three of its principal cities—Denver, Boulder, and Colorado City, precursor of Colorado Springs—began life as jumping-off points for the mines, there is a tendency to overemphasize the role of the gold rush in determining population centers. The theory leaves out too much. Pueblo, for example, began life as an Indian trading post; Fort Collins, as a cluster of homes around a military installation; Greeley, as an agricultural colony. In all cases except Greeley's, the original *raison d'être* faded, but the towns endured.

They endured largely because they could draw on the best of two environments, the storm-created waters of the mountains and the sunny days and long growing season of the plains. While gaining these advantages, moreover, they were able to avoid most of the disadvantages. The winds that wrack the plains seldom trouble the urban shoestring along the foothills. The violent storms that Denver residents can see hammering the 14,264-foot summit of Mount Evans to the west of the city rarely extend to the base of the hills. Rapid fluctuations in weather do occur, but as a rule summer nights are cool, summer days no more than pleasantly warm. Although December and January temperatures occasionally drop below zero, the lack of humidity keeps the cold from penetrating unbearably. All this is psychologically important: most people are stimulated by the dryness of the air, the floods of sunshine, and the mile-high elevations.

Added to the allure of the climate is the appeal of the mountains. People like the recreational opportunities, both in summer and winter. Imaginations are stirred by the tensions visible in their battered height. It is hard to believe, for instance, that the seventeen tightly aligned spires of the amazing glass-and-metal chapel of the United States Air Force Academy were not inspired in part by the pinnacles on nearby Devil's Head. Chapel and devil—that implicit conflict awakes memories of two dry canyons, named Christian and Devil, that come together near the old wheel ruts on the Santa Fe Trail beside Timpas Creek, southwest of La Junta. What the story behind the naming is I cannot learn, but surely it says something about living in that contradictory land.

Hoping to use the foothills environment for attracting and holding high-caliber employees, industries began moving west during World War II. The armed forces added several huge complexes, particularly in the Colorado Springs area, and the new rush to the Rockies was on. With it came the world-wide paradox of people perverting their own desires through overcrowding and ill-judged boosterism. That tension is also integral to Colorado, as it is to every other beautiful region threatened with too much loving at the hands of a highly industrialized people.


*The Warped Earth*

The contrasts that are part of the land's appeal result primarily from two massive physiographic conditions—the convulsions produced by the upheavings of the mountains and the variations in ecology that result from the rapidly changing elevations.

Everywhere along the base of the foothills are topographic welts that give evidence, we are told, of the earth's past warpings. West of Denver twelve bands of protruding sedimentary rock—sandstone, limestone, shale—have been analyzed and named. Once they lay horizontally, in beds whose aggregate thickness amounted to almost 2.5 miles. When the mountains rose, these bands were bent upward. In places they became almost vertical, but mostly they sloped steeply, at angles of 45° or so. Once they probably formed a broad, rounded arch over the entire mass of the Rockies—an arch perforated here and there by volcanoes and perhaps by pink granite pushing up through the fault lines. Then, as aeons passed, the bulk of the covering eroded away, so that only the lower sections now remain, hanging on the chests of the mountains something like a battered necklace on a decaying dowager.

Generally we are asked to accept statements such as these on faith, though it involves believing that layers of stone more than 2 miles thick can be warped as readily as putty. Still, an instinctive doubt must linger, for why else are we jolted so when we are confronted with direct evidence of nature's titanic strength? For instance: a hogback west of Denver contains the huge, unmistakable, three-toed footprints of what must have been a monstrous dinosaur. When the creature made the prints, it almost certainly was walking across a flat marsh. Mud settled into the depressions and hardened into a mold. Then sand washed in, was compacted, and preserved for millions of years the record of that prehistoric passage.

During that time the rock tilted upward. It had to. You stare at those tracks on a smooth piece of sandstone rising at an angle to which no dinosaur could possibly have clung, and you are forced to admit that the upending took place after the print making. So the sight does open a door a little ways onto comprehension, and afterward it is never possible to be wholly casual about the mountains behind the hogback—mountains whose rising rumpled a large part of the earth's smooth, round surface from Alaska to Chile.

### The Impact of Altitude

Closer to the mountains and hence older by several million years than the grayish Dakota sandstone bearing the dinosaur tracks are the red beds. They appear irregularly along many miles of the foothills. By coincidence the most spectacular protrusions occur near three of the state's principal cities—Boulder, Denver, and Colorado Springs. Fortunately each municipality has been able to acquire for public use the main parts of each uplift.

The slabby protrusions near Boulder are called the Flatirons. They make a fine backdrop for the newer, russet-hued, tile-roofed buildings of the University of Colorado and, especially, for what is perhaps the finest example of modern architecture in Colorado, the blocky pink buildings, reminiscent of Indian pueblos, that house the National Center for Atmospheric Research. For rock climbers the Flatirons have a more strenuous appeal. Over the years adventurous young men and women have worked out scores of hair-raising routes, some of great technical difficulty, up every face of those leaning towers.

Denver's 600 acres of red rocks are part of the city's superlative system of twenty-seven mountain parks. The chief feature of the Park of the Red Rocks, aside from the whale-backed, nose-raised sandstone grotesqueries, is an open-air auditorium of ten thousand seats, cupped in an acoustically perfect amphitheater of deep red cliffs.

More widely heralded is the Garden of the Gods near Colorado Springs. The monoliths, both white and red, are slimmer there and warped into stranger shapes than those in the other uptilts. "Kissing Camels" is one. (It gave its name to, I regret to say, the Kissing Camels Golf Club on a nearby mesa.) For a time there was even a "Seal Making Love to a Nun." The monstrosity has fortunately weathered away, though not as fast as did the publicist who was fired for perpetrating the title. Such folderol may have lain behind writer Julian Street's dismissing the area as "a pale pink joke." Happily for Colorado Springs boosters, Helen Hunt Jackson, author of *Ramona*, was more ecstatic. Here, cried she, was a wonderland of "red rocks of every conceivable and inconceivable size and shape . . . all motionless and silent, with a strange look of having been stopped and held back in the very climax of some supernatural catastrophe." Yet whatever else may be said of the rocks, some of them do frame magnificent views of America's most famous mountain, Pikes Peak.

As one approaches these spiny guardians of the foothills, one realizes that soil and vegetation are changing almost as rapidly as is the slope of the land. Beyond the last ridge of sandstone is a huge mold of intrusive pink-gray granite. Though it is often given the limiting name of Pikes Peak granite, it spreads across most of the lower parts of the Front Range. Much of it sparkles with feldspar. It disintegrates readily. The gravelly soil that it produces drains rapidly after precipitation and hence places stern demands on the vegetation that grows in it.

Curiously latitudinal variations occur in the plants that occupy the lower reaches of the foothills. The scrub oak that forms tight clusters on the buttes south of Denver does not extend north of the city. The gnarled piñon pines that blacken the mesas around Walsenburg and Trinidad in the south are likewise missing in the north—with one notable exception. Tucked into the foothills almost at the Wyoming border is a grove of twisted patriarchs with trunks 4 feet in diameter, by far the largest piñon trees in the world. According to the guidebook *Colorado,* their age approaches that of the most ancient of California's redwoods.

Even more striking changes occur with altitude. As you contemplate the slopes, another textbook generality turns into reality: there is direct correlation between traveling north and traveling up. Botanists have a rule-of-thumb formula for expressing the relationship. Rising 1,000 feet in elevation, they say, is the ecological equivalent of journeying 300 miles toward the North Pole. Thus driving along the highway that spirals upward 9,000 feet from Denver to the summit of Mount Evans presents travelers with as much variety in vegetation as they would see during a journey to the Arctic Circle.

A gentler trip that allows a leisurely study of the transitions is the one from Loveland west up Highway 34 to the high point (12,183 feet above sea level) on the Trail Ridge Road in Rocky Mountain National Park. The route begins amid lovely cherry orchards backed by typical foothill protrusions—huge hogbacks and weathered sandstone pinnacles. After leaving these it plunges into the narrow, pink granite jaws of Big Thompson Canyon. Willows and cottonwoods crowd close beside the stream. Clinging conspicuously to the gravelly hillsides are majestic ponderosa pines, their lines echoing the uprights of crags and granite spires. They are called ponderosa because the trunks of mature trees rise 150 feet or more with relatively little taper, a characteristic that makes them beloved by lumbermen.

Ponderosa crave sunlight. Their long, light green needles glow in it. Their huge branches, the outer ends heavily tufted, reach far to obtain it. Even the bark of the older trees is a sunny, deeply furrowed orange-yellow.

A ponderosa's root system spreads wide in a search for water. Partly because of that competition but mostly because the ground that ponderosa like is inhospitable to other growth, the forests are quite open. Juniper will cling to rocky nooks that pines avoid. There is a scattering of sumac and of kinnikinnick, a ground-hugging shrub whose leathery green leaves and clusters of bright red berries are often used in the mountains for Christmas decorations. But the main ground cover of a ponderosa forest is a carpet of warm brown needles, humps of granite, and tufts of grass through which grasshoppers whirl noisily.

You begin to notice, too, that there is a difference between growth on slopes facing south and those facing north. Southern slopes receive more sunlight, especially in winter. At lower elevations plants typical of the plains, notably yucca and flat-leafed cactus, invade the parched soil. By contrast north-facing slopes are shaded and cool. Mixed with the ponderosa on those slopes are stands of short-needled, thick-barked Douglas fir. Colorado blue spruce, the young trees delightfully symmetrical, appear among the willows on shaded stream banks. Watching this, you realize that vegetation changes are a result of local temperature variations as well as of altitude and that demarcations between life zones are not clearly defined.

The names of the life zones are revealing. The one that embraces the plains and some of the desert mesas of southwestern Colorado is called Upper Sonoran. Sonora, of course, is a province in Mexico. In Colorado the Upper Sonoran Zone reaches roughly from 3,500 feet to 5,500 feet above sea level. Above this "Mexican" zone—on above the Transition Zone—is another zone named in some botanical texts for a neighboring nation, the Canadian Zone. To that contrast add this: the Sonoran Zones are termed Austral, which means southern. The Canadian and the zones above it are called Boreal, northern. As the words suggest, a kind of climatic war is waged along the foothills, aridity pushing sun-loving plants from the south up the slopes, moistness counterattacking with downward thrusts of cool northern growths. Quite naturally this belt of conflict is often known as the Transition Zone—it lies between 5,500 and 8,000 feet—and it lends the lower slopes of the mountains much of their variety.

*The Topmost Life Zones*

Beyond the tourist-jammed streets and cluttered souvenir shops of Estes Park village, the highway to Trail Ridge enters Rocky Mountain National Park. After passing through the last glades in the ponderosa forests, it leaves the Transition Zone for the montane or Canadian life zone.* Deciduous aspens appear—the only deciduous trees existing in quantity in the southern Rockies. Like ponderosa pines, they crave sunlight. When a breeze sets their lightly notched, egg-shaped, pointed leaves to dancing, the lighter undersides

---

\* Botanists are not in agreement about zone names or the lines of demarcation between them. One list speaks of the Transition Zone (5,500–8,000 feet); the Canadian (8,000–11,000 feet); the Hudsonian, for Hudson Bay (11,000–11,500 feet); and the Arctic-Alpine (above 11,500 feet). Another speaks of the montane zone (6,000–9,000 feet), subalpine (9,000 feet to timberline, whose elevation is variable); and alpine (above timberline). To point up the difference further, some lists begin zone names with capitals, some with small letters. In the main this account will follow the montane-subalpine-alpine division.

reflect the day's radiance like dusty mirrors. As the trees grow, the lower branches, deprived of sun, die and break off, leaving round or oval black scars on the green-white or dun-white trunks. Other black scars are caused by fungus, by scratches made when elk rub their horns against the trunks, when stretching bears claw parallel gouges into the soft wood, or when small-time human boasters carve their initials.

The thin canopy in mature aspen groves is high overhead. The trembling leaves create a dappled shadow full of shimmers. Enough light comes through so that tall grass, wild geraniums, blue-and-white columbine, butterflies, and hummingbirds flourish.

Because aspens propagate from root extensions more readily than from seed, they are often the first trees to establish themselves on burned-over ground. If they do this near stands of spruce or fir, they in effect commit suicide, for they furnish shade needed by young conifers. Under favorable conditions the vigorous evergreen seedlings will eventually crowd their nurses to death.

Another seed that establishes itself quickly on burned ground is the lodgepole pine, so called because Indians once used the slender-trunked trees as supports for their portable buffalo-hide tipis. The cone of a lodgepole pine, each of its scales fortified by a sickle-shaped thorn, opens only during periods of unusually hot sunlight or after a fire. Because fire-stricken areas are stripped of competing vegetation, the young lodgepoles grow profusely in what foresters call "dog-hair" stands. Drought and self-crowding will thin these tight ranks somewhat, and the remaining trees then grow tall, in such uniform masses that to the human eye they appear monotonous. Mountain lupines like them, however, and send up multitudes of rich blue spikes along the edges of lodgepole groves or in small openings within the forests.

Curving easily, the road swings into the subalpine life zone on the flanks of Trail Ridge, a long hump that runs east from the Continental Divide. (The name Trail Ridge comes from trails used by Ute Indians when crossing the Divide to hunt buffalo on the plains.) Sidestreams scallop the edges of the ridge. For a brief time each summer the sunny meadows that spot the small valleys are exquisite with wildflowers. Almost universal in the subalpine meadows are crisp white flowers of brookcress, glowing against shiny dark green leaves. Equally lush is mertensia, sometimes called chiming bell from its drooping clusters of tiny, intense blue flowers. Where the grass is thinner, paintbrush gleams, its colors ranging from deep cerise to lemony white. Still more dazzling are clumps of shooting stars. The big blossoms ride proudly atop leafless stalks a foot or so tall. Their black stamens hang down in sharp points. Behind the base of the stamen is a band of yellow-white and then five narrow petals streaming backward so that when air stirs them the flowers indeed look like colored meteors flashing toward the grass.

In the twilight of morning and evening, elk and mule deer, the latter named for their huge, questioning ears, sometimes frequent the meadows. Beaver dam the streams, leaving on the adjoining hillsides a prickle of gnawed, cone-shaped stumps as testimony of their industry. Such meadows lead doomed lives. Sedge, grass, and willows take root along the marshy edges of the ponds. They catch drifting leaves and particles of earth. Dying, they add their own humus to the new earth across which their progeny will inch toward the heart of the glade. Spruce trees follow. In time the meadow will turn into a forest, and the little stream will clatter between banks bare of everything except low brush, spruce duff, and chunks of fallen, moss-covered timber.

Almost imperceptibly your car enters a dark green belt of intermingled Engelmann spruce and alpine fir, the highest forest biome of the Rockies. In rare cases where these trees grow in isolation, they resemble Colorado blue spruce. Their branches brush the ground; their outer needles are coated with a cold-resistant, waxy substance that gives the trees a bluish cast. Botanists can distinguish between the spruces by noting small differences in the needles and cones. Laymen can do it by remembering that Colorado blue spruce generally grow at lower elevations and seldom in thick stands.

In dense forests, the intermingled Engelmann spruce and alpine fir both grow tall and spindly and as alike, you first think, as the slats in a picket fence. But several clues exist for distinguishing one from the other. An unusually thin, spire-like top probably belongs to a fir. The small cones of the fir, which generally grow near the top, are as erect as Christmas candles; those of the Engelmann spruce, which also grow on the upper boughs, hang down. The bark of a mature fir is grayish; that of an elderly spruce is a strong, russet red. As you walk by a questionable tree, take hold of a branch tip. If the short needles prickle your palm, the tree is a spruce. If they feel soft and feathery, it is probably a fir.

The heaviest stands of Engelmann spruce and alpine fir occur, with variations, at elevations ranging between 10,000 and 11,500 feet. Except where man-made trails exist, travel in the groves is difficult. Snow lingers long in the thick shade. Where the ground isn't steep, it is generally boggy. Down timber abounds, limbs tangled and trunks crisscrossed, much of it felled by the high winds that blast through the shallow-rooted forests late in winter. When rain comes, the clouds sit right on the treetops. One of the gloomiest experiences I know is to ride horseback or hike under the dripping bows during a cold downpour, winding slowly past a monotony of soggy, moss-grown logs and in and out of the sucking black mud of the marshes. Yet the value of such forests during storms is inestimable. The humus in the soil holds moisture tenaciously, filters it clean, and, until the earth becomes saturated, lets it percolate into the creeks without flooding.

*Timberline Struggles*

As the road nears timberline, the size of the trees diminishes sharply. Where islands of them protect each other, they still stand straight. In more exposed places, the wind torments them cruelly. It deforms the trunks, twists the branches, scours away the bark with abrasive pellets of sand and icy snow. Limber pines and bristlecone pines, which at high elevations sometimes mingle with the spruce and fir, are particularly susceptible to wind sculpturing. They lean; their limbs stream and writhe; dead stubs protrude starkly from scattered tufts of tightly bunched needles.

Of all life, the bristlecone pine is the most enduring. Trees have been found in the White Mountains of California whose age surpasses that of the redwoods. Resistance continues long after death. After the bark falls away, the coarse-grained wood decays slowly, taking on with infinite patience rich, subdued hues ranging from deep tan through maroon to odd patterns of black.

Just above treeline you sometimes find strange clumps of evergreens called Krummholz, or "wind timber." These clumps begin to form when a misplaced fir or spruce seed somehow manages to lodge on the naked slope behind the shelter of a boulder or small roll of earth. Unable to grow upright, the seedling sends out prostrate shoots that in time form a thick, protective mat. Some of the shoots in this mat take root, sending up new trees. Each

18. *A sudden rush of flowers brightens the West Maroon Creek drainage in the Maroon Bells-Snowmass Wilderness Area near Aspen.*

19. Mountain water nurtures fields near Greeley. Spray from long pipes mounted on overgrown bicycle wheels has eased the burdens of irrigating but draws heavily on limited water supplies.

20. One use for junked cars: checking erosion caused by spring torrents slashing through the sandy plains.

21. *A lonesome road stretches endlessly across the Comanche National Grassland south of La Junta.*

22 and 23. Spring rain brings a profusion of dandelions to overgrazed sections of the Pawnee National Grassland on the high plains of northern Colorado.

24. When the soil dries, duststorms blow.

25. Water from the mountains fills dozens of turquoise reservoirs. This one is on the plains near Denver.

26. Irrigation brings life to desolation. The uprights are power poles that carry current to the pumps that lift the water from underground aquifers.

27. Wheat grown by "dry-farming" the high plains is stored in this grain elevator. If rain fails, the dry-farming gamble does not pay off.

28. Rancher Tom Lasater of Matheson has attracted wide attention by adapting his cattle operations to the plains environment rather than by forcing the environment to fit his preconceptions. The huge animals, called Beefmasters, are a new breed that he developed on his ranch.

29. Lasater shows a group of 4-H youngsters how easily his huge bulls can be handled.

30. A Denver residential district at sunrise, the Front Range in the background. A smear of smog is already gathering over the city.

grows an inch or two higher than the original parent. Eventually the impenetrable clump will extend 10 feet or so beyond the sheltering boulder. Its top is shaped like a gently sloping roof over which the wind slides with a minimum of resistance. There is a harsh limit to height, however—the average depth of the winter snow blanket. Any twig that protrudes above this for long is burned brown by reflected sunlight or sheared off by the wind.

Timberline, where the subalpine life zone gives way to the alpine, is the most abrupt of the division points between the mountain biomes. It is not a level line, however, as you quickly note from the windows of your car. In Colorado it varies from an elevation of a little over 11,000 feet to 12,000 feet in protected areas. It sags where cliffs or rockslides eliminate footing or where deep snow, lingering in the valley bottoms, prevents seeding. A vivid example is Hidden Valley on the Trail Ridge Road. There is not a tree in the bottom of the deep notch that marks the valley's upper end. By contrast, tongues of black forest climb far up the valley's sides. And even here there is a difference. The reach goes higher on the south-facing slope than on the north.

Beyond timberline, all growth is Lilliputian. Although rydbergia, or alpine sunflowers, sport bright yellow disks up to 4 inches in diameter, all facing east, they grow on woolly stems hardly as tall as the blossom is wide. Adaptations are extraordinary. Mats of white, yellow-centered marsh marigolds grow right beside the receding snowbanks or in the middle of tiny streams coiling among the sedges. Side by side with them, making islands out of their own roots, are blood-red Parry primroses and purply king's-crown. Meanwhile, only feet away from the wet places are dry, sun-smitten gravels where white phlox, pink moss campion, and sky-blue alpine forget-me-nots exist by forming domed masses only 2 or 3 inches tall that shed the wind the way the clumps of Krummholz do. Where boulders, gay with orange, chartreuse, brown, and gray lichen, reflect the sun's heat, yellow saxifrage blooms, as do Jacob's ladder and sky pilot, whose funnel-shaped blue flowers are possessed of a dismaying juice that smells, when the plant is crushed, like the emissions of an outraged skunk. All told, Colorado's tundra fields hold roughly three hundred species of flowers, far more than are found in any other mountain state.

More animate forms of life are also surprisingly common. Deer and elk graze the deep basins. Now and then mountain sheep appear on exposed ridges, although for some unknown reason their numbers in Rocky Mountain National Park are diminishing. Gophers, meadow voles, waddling marmots, lean weasels, and whistling little rabbit-like pikas dart among the boulders. Except for marmots, which hibernate, these animals stay busy throughout the winter, scampering through tunnels under the rocks or in burrows they dig beneath the snow. During summer the pika is as industrious a storer of food as is the beaver, piling flowers, grass, and sedge indiscriminately beside his sunny tunnel entrances so that the hay can cure before he drags it inside.

Rosy finches and pipits walk the surface of the snow fields in search of chilled, wind-blown insects. Horned larks—the same sweet singers that nest on the plains—find the grass of the tundra congenial enough that some of them migrate there to raise their young. Winter drives these birds to lower elevations. Not so the ptarmigan, a small grouse that depends for protection on changes in the color of its plumage. During summer its feathers are a mottled brown, gray, and white that make it look like one of the stones among which it wanders in search of willow buds, tender leaves, seeds, and insects. In winter it becomes pure white and grows feathers on its feet and legs for easier, more comfortable maneuvering in the snow. Color, however, does not protect ptarmigan nests from being trampled by herds of sheep, and so, except in the National Park, where sheep are not allowed, their population, too, is shrinking.

In spite of singing birds and glowing flowers, no one would call this a kindly land. Except where snowbanks melt or springs ooze under cushions of dwarfed willows, its surface is desiccated by constant wind. The blazing sunlight is unsoftened by the cushioning effect of the denser atmosphere at lower elevations. Because of lack of binding roots, the land is constantly in motion. In the spring the briefly wet hillsides creep downward to form what are called solifluction terraces, a constant slippage that over the ages has rounded off the steep ridges and has brought a wavelike look to the meadows.

Ice, which always lurks a few inches below the surface, heaves up hummocks of earth and sometimes masses of boulders called fell-fields. Snow melt trickling into cracks on the cliff faces freezes at night and gradually chisels loose a piece of ancient stone. Sometimes, seated on the lee side of a sun-warmed upthrust, you will hear the dislodged fragment rattle down onto the talus slope beneath the precipice, and you will look up startled, wondering what is walking over there—only to see loneliness.

Perhaps you would see another such land if instead of stopping here on Trail Ridge you drove all the way to the Arctic Circle. I don't know, never having been to the Arctic. But I think the differences must be profound. Unlike a camera, the human eye, or at least the mind behind the eye, carries memories with it. Even if you hunker down where you cannot see the waves of peaks that surround your spot of tundra; even if you turn your back on the view of the distant plains and the chasms that your road has crossed, you remember. Your senses are suffused with an awareness of height. You'd not take that feeling with you, I think, to the Arctic, most of which is flat. You'd know, moreover, that the Arctic wasn't the end, that beyond it lies one more zone, the land of perpetual snow. Here, however, is a culmination. You are on the ridgetop of the continent and there is nothing beyond except the sky.

# 7
# THE MAIN RANGES

Many skeletons of heroic endeavors attest to the influences that the Southern Rockies, like all mountain ranges, have exerted on the lives of the people who dwell among them. One thrilling example is the old railroad bed by which the narrow-gauge trains of the Denver, South Park & Pacific Railway once surmounted the central part of the Continental Divide. It can be readily examined today because the grade on the western slope of the divide has been turned into a narrow dirt road that can be negotiated with ease by four-wheel-drive cars and, with care, by standard automobiles.

The route rises out of Quartz Creek on a long diagonal slashed across a heavily timbered hillside. After leaving the hill it bends around gulches and for brief stretches levels out on flower-spangled terraces. At one point it curves tightly back on itself in order to get a manageable run at a series of cliffs whose sheer faces it crosses by means of hanging shelves of hand-hewn masonry. The journey ends at an altitude of 11,600 feet at the collapsed western portal of the old Alpine Tunnel.

*Relics of the Mining Rush*

Along the way the Forest Service has erected explanatory signs. One declares, perhaps with hyperbole, that the grade is a visible memento of the greatest feat of railroad building ever undertaken in North America. Other signs point to the sites of mining camps, most of which have vanished with scarcely a trace. One, Woodstock, was obliterated in March 1884 by a snow avalanche that killed thirteen people. Across the valley is an unconscious touch of irony—a round-shouldered peak still known as Paywell Mountain.

Those vanished towns, like hundred of others throughout Colorado, were there because of random deposits of valuable minerals precipitated from molten rock during the upheavals that created the mountains. Located at strategic spots among these ganglia of high-altitude camps were trade centers, some of which boasted mines of their own. At those centers miners could buy supplies and have their ores milled or smelted as circumstances demanded.

Quantities of coal, lumber, and machinery and a constant flow of people were involved in the processes. When volume became sufficient to attract a railroad, its construction engineers began the arduous work of conquering the inhospitable terrain. Often they acted in fierce competition with the builders of other railroads for rights-of-way through narrow canyons or across low places in the high mountains. In laying out the Alpine roadbed, the Denver & South Park was racing the Denver & Rio Grande for the trade of the Gunnison country, which included bonanzas of coal, a fact that reminds us of the sedimentary beds that once overlay the rising cores of mineralized basement rocks.*

Although a few gargantuan mines still tear at the mountains—for molybdenum at Climax, lead and zinc in the Eagle Canyon, and mixtures of lead, zinc, gold, and silver at Ouray and Telluride—the emphasis now is on other treasures. Chief among them are the well-filled pockets of vacationists in search of summer and winter recreation, and rivers that can be captured in reservoirs and then made to flow in ways contrary to nature's original pattern. Success in these pursuits, no less than success in the older pursuits of gold hunting and railroading, depends on understanding the high country. Thus learning the shape of the mountains and the reasons why those shapes came into being retains much of the importance that attached to it a century ago when the first geologic surveys were crisscrossing the state in search of both utilitarian and abstract knowledge.

---

* The Denver & Rio Grande won the race by crossing the Divide at Marshall Pass, a score or so miles south of Alpine Tunnel. Because Marshall was about 800 feet lower, a protective snowshed could be used in place of an expensive tunnel. The Rio Grande, indeed, won enough races that it still exists. The Denver & South Park does not.

*The Tortured Mountains*

To repeat what was stated in an earlier chapter, the precursor of the Rockies arose some 70 million years ago during what was known as the Laramide revolution. In a sense the connotations created for laymen by that statement are unfortunate. Because nothing is said to the contrary, the words suggest that the end product of the convulsion was a single, massive north-south barrier thousands of miles in length. There is a further impression that though the barrier may once have been much higher than it is today, it has always looked pretty much as we see it now.

These notions do not accord with the actual sequence of events. There are, first of all, two main ranges in Colorado, not one. Although they make contact, here and there, they are separated for the most part by a necklace of wide depressions known as North Park, Middle Park, South Park, and the San Luis Valley. Furthermore, though the foundations of the two chains remain as they were created 70 million years ago, the upper stories have been totally altered.

Under the impact of sun, snow, rain, wind, and localized earth shifts, the first product of the revolution eroded down to an undulating plateau called a peneplain. Rising out of that plain were occasional lumps that had escaped the general leveling process either because they were far enough from main drainage systems to avoid the water's full abrasiveness or else were composed of unusually resistant material. Longs Peak, Mount Evans, and Pikes Peak are the descendants of such monadnocks.

The peneplain did not stay level. Once again granite and metamorphic rock welled up from the earth's hot interior. This second upheaval is not considered a revolution. It followed paths already established. It did no major new violence to the already upturned bands of sedimentary rock.

The second uplift may also have eroded to a peneplain and then have been followed by a third arising. At least N. M. Fenneman's *Physiography of Western United States* names two apparently distinct peneplains that have been identified by means of stream-washed gravels lingering on the shoulders of mountains where streams no longer flow. Be that as it may, the summits at which we look today are not originals but are reprises of what went on 70 million years ago. It may even be that our current mountains are still in the process of rising. If such activity is indeed taking place, we do not notice because the rate is slow and our senses are more attuned to the showier processes of local erosion.

Cataclysmic stresses accompanied the successive uprisings. Fault lines tore apart, with the result that each of the main ranges has in places been offset by a few miles from its original axis. Volcanic eruptions, particularly in the San Juan Mountains of southwestern Colorado, have covered the basic structures under thousands of feet of lava and cemented ash.

Because of those torturings, the state's two main granite belts do not present enough uniformity in appearance to be accorded uniform names throughout their whole extents. This is true even of the easternmost belt, the one that three quarters of the state's population see every day rising out of the plains as far north and as far south as they can look. They call the expanse loosely the Front Range and then proceed to divide it, in words, into several segments.


*The Varied Faces of the Front Range*

The verbal fragmentation preserves some fine local names. Stretching across the Wyoming border to the northwest section of Rocky Mountain National Park is an extension of Wyoming's Medicine Bow Range. Coloradoans sometimes call their part of the Medicine Bows the Rawah Range, Rawah being an Indian word for "wild country." (The long, narrow Rawah Wilderness Area occupies the most rugged part of the range.) Just south of the Rahwahs is the Never Summer Range, a short but beautiful line of mountains that marks an aberrant northward turning of the Continental Divide.

In the northwest part of the Rocky Mountain National Park, we at last pick up a section universally called the Front Range. It, too, is a part of the Continental Divide. It runs south through the park and along the Indian Peaks to the drainage system of the north fork of the South Platte River. At that point more fragmentation occurs. The Continental Divide wanders off to rejoin the western belt of granite while the eastern belt sags down to about 9,000 feet elevation and continues south under the name Rampart Range, a heavily forested stretch enlivened by spires of pink granite.

The Ramparts end at a fault line whose ancient subsiding created one of the principal gateways into the interior, Ute Pass. Immediately south of Ute Pass towers the vast dome of Pikes Peak, 14,110 feet above sea level.

Although thirty other summits in Colorado are higher, Pikes Peak remains in the minds of millions of people *the* mountain of the Southern Rockies. It sits farther to the east than does any other major peak. No other mountain of comparable height is near enough to compete with it for interest. Fur traders pushing up the Arkansas River and gold seekers following the Smoky Hill route through the central reaches of the high plains saw its dim blue helmet before they could detect any other mountain. Though none of the early gold camps were located on its huge flanks, "Pikes Peak or Bust!" became the slogan of the mineral stampede of 1859.

Soon the peak became so powerful a magnet for tourists that promoters risked fortunes devising means of lifting them at their ease to the summit. A carriage road was completed in 1889, followed almost immediately by a cog railroad. An automobile highway was opened in 1915. (Impatient motorists had reached the summit several years earlier by following the old carriage road.) Not everyone takes advantage of the easy ways, however. Marathon foot racers hold annual meets along the automobile highway's 20-mile course, and, every December 31, adventurers struggle up the cog road's snowy bed in order to greet the New Year with bursts of fireworks. All told, well over 6 million visitors have set foot upon Pike's capacious summit, a record not approximated, so far as I know, by any other mountain of comparable height in the world.

Southwest of Pikes Peak the front belt tumbles down to the great gorge of the Arkansas River. At the Arkansas, the uplift makes a V-like bend southeast. The displacement has created two ranges. The main one is the narrow, splendidly crenelated Sangre de Cristo. (Sangre de Cristo means "blood of Christ," a reference to the alpenglow that impressed Spanish settlers who lived within sight of the range's southern extension into New Mexico.) Hiding most of this lively uplift from the plains is a subsidiary range, the Wet or Greenhorn Mountains. Between the two ranges is one of the handsomest and, from a tourist standpoint, least exploited troughs in Colorado, Wet Mountain Valley. Neither the valley nor the mountains to the east of it are particularly wet. The clouds hovering over the green hills just made them look that way to early travelers weary of the arid plains.

*Intramountain Flatlands*

West of the unevenly elevated and sometimes erratically wandering eastern belt of granite is a series of extraordinary parks. In this usage a park is not a place of public resort but an expanse of relatively flat ground on which few trees grow. Some mountain parks are small grassy meadows ringed with spruce or aspen. Others are huge and girt by mountain ranges. Colorado's four principal parks—as noted earlier they are named North, Middle, and South parks, plus the San Luis Valley—together occupy about 13,000 square miles. This amounts to 8.3 million acres, or about 12.5 per cent of the state's total area. These wide openings between the granite walls do almost as much as the plains to give Colorado its liberating sense of spaciousness.

In spite of elevations ranging from 8,000 to 10,000 feet, North, Middle, and South parks are famed as cattle and sheep ranges. Their fertile soils produce during their short growing seasons remarkable tonnages of hay for winter feed. The southernmost and lowest of the parks, San Luis Valley, whose average elevation is about 7,600 feet, also produces livestock and hay, plus copious fields of potatoes.

All the parks are frequented during winter by game animals. In the 1830s South Park, then known as Bayou Salade, was beloved by the mountain men because of the fat buffalo that gathered there. One massif on the western rim is still known as the Buffalo Peaks, the home today of a small band of mountain sheep. The streams of all three of the northern parks offer delectable trout fishing for those who make arrangements with the ranchers that control long stretches of the banks.

*The Winding Divide*

West of the parks is the second of the state's great granite belts. It is even less unified than the eastern core. The broken plateau country still farther west provides no sweeping view of major portions of it. Great spurs and offset lobes hang onto its western sides. The best-known of these tangential ranges are the precipitous Elk Mountains in the central part of the state and the sprawling San Juans in the southwest.

It would be convenient for writers of descriptions if the Continental Divide steadily followed either the eastern or western granite belts. That belt could then be designated beyond dispute as the state's main range. The Divide does not act so obligingly, however. In the northern part of the state it wanders away from the western belt to join the eastern range. After several miles of this it returns to the west.

Sometimes the Divide is very high. Sometimes it sags low, as it does in the Rabbit Ear Mountains that separate North Park from Middle Park. Its only consistency is the way in which it separates the waters that flow into the Gulf of Mexico from those that flow into the Gulf of California. And even this uniformity has been violated by man, whose canals and gigantic tunnels move water underneath the ranges into drainage systems never intended by nature.

Farms along the Platte and Arkansas rivers as far as the borders of Nebraska and Kansas, together with hundreds of thousands of householders in Denver, Colorado Springs, and Pueblo, exist in large part on water that used to find its way to the Pacific. Because other states in the Southwest also have claims on that Pacific-bound water, Colorado's borrowings have to be repaid by means of intricate systems of storage reservoirs. These safe-deposit vaults dole out the banked water into the Colorado River late in the summer when the need is great and in that way compensate the lower states for what has been taken from them. A side benefit has been providing the state of Colorado, which has few natural lakes, with broad blue bodies of liquid that foster a variety of water sports.

There is a penalty, however. At low stages reservoirs are ringed with stark water marks and ugly mud flats. Eventually all of them will fill with silt. Pondering these demerits and mourning lost meadows and drowned canyons, some ecological Cassandras are beginning to wonder aloud whether the time has come to call a halt to further monumental tamperings with the normal shape of things.

*River Patterns*

Meanwhile the water that is not diverted by man continues through canyons whose awesome walls are as vivid a proof of the mountains' rising as are the dinosaur tracks on the tilted sandstone west of Denver. Consider the strangeness of their patterns. One would expect rivers to go around mountains that appear in their way. But, contrary to logic, every major stream in Colorado—the Arkansas, the North Platte and the South Platte, the Rio Grande, the Colorado and its principal tributary, the Gunnison—attacks a mighty barrier head on and chews its way through with implacable force.

The most likely explanation for the phenomenon is this. The course of the streams was established during the aeons involved in weathering down the mountains formed during the Laramide revolution. By the time a peneplain had resulted, the rivers meandered sluggishly along set routes. Then, very slowly, the next mountain uplift took place. As hillsides tilted upward, the streams quickened. Meeting new barriers, the water dug in and began to grind. Generally the brawling streams were able to scour out their beds as rapidly as the mountains arose. Occasionally, however, a swelling took place at a brisker rate than the river could match. In such cases a huge lake resulted. The Rio Grande, which flows out of the eastern side of the San Juan Mountains into the San Luis Valley, apparently lay frustrated in such a lake until finally the mountains ceased their rising. It broke loose then along the lines of its old channel and gouged out a wild gorge through northern New Mexico.

Some of the mountain-breaching canyons have made history as well as scenery. The most famous example is the Royal Gorge of the Arkansas River. After rising in the central part of the state, the Arkansas foams southward along a deep fault line floored with glacial gravels. To the east are the domed peaks of the Mosquito Range. To the west is the Sawatch Range, loftiest part of the Continental Divide. Fifteen of the Sawatch's peaks exceed 14,000 feet in elevation. One, Mount Elbert (14,433 feet), is Colorado's highest.

After passing today's Salida the river swings southeast and then east, a shift that brings it up against shaggy hills fingering southwest from Pikes Peak. The result of several million years of conflict between water and pink granite has been a spectacular canyon whose visual charms are now being thoroughly exploited. Tourists are lured to the area by a suspension bridge that crosses the chasm merely for thrills—its road doesn't continue to any destination—and by an inclined railway that slides down the walls into the bottom at a hair-raising 45-degree angle.

The abyss through which the Arkansas River passes is barely wide enough in places to allow the laying of a single set of railroad tracks. The limitation became critical a century ago when the town of Leadville, located near the headwaters of the Arkansas, boomed into prominence as one of the richest mining camps in the West. Two railroads, the Atchison, Topeka and Santa Fe and the Denver & Rio Grande, promptly locked horns in a bitter struggle to gain control of the gateway.

After mutual threats of violence, acidulous lawsuits, and manipulations by Jay Gould in the East, the Denver & Rio Grande won the right-of-way. In return it surrendered its claims to the Raton Pass crossing into New Mexico. For the Rio Grande this meant giving up its dream of growing into a north-south trunk line connecting middle America to Mexico and becoming instead the famed Little Giant of the Colorado mountains. Meanwhile the loser of the Royal Gorge, the Santa Fe, swung south over Raton Pass and, as the years passed, grew to be a major transcontinental. Thus do mountains change destinies.

*Ice Carvings*

Like the canyons, the sheer cliffs, notched arêtes (high, thin ridges), and cirques of the high peaks are also the result of water action—water compacted long ago into ice. When the Rockies first arose, their tops were rounded like long loaves of bread. The winter storms that buffeted them came mostly from the west, although in places local conditions varied the direction. (The storms that swept the San Juans, for example, often came from the south or southwest.) Much of the wind-borne snow settled in deep piles on the lee slopes of those bread loaves of rock. There it lingered.

Although the successive ice sheets that covered a large part of North America during the ice ages did not reach what is now Colorado, their chill was in the air. Winters were severe, snowfall heavy. The accumulations on the lee slopes thickened. Under pressure they turned into glacial ice whose own weight set it to creeping down the steep slopes. With it the ice carried boulders that acted like scouring pads. Foot by foot, year after year, ice and rock dug into the flanks of the mountains. It created cirques whose walls curved out like the sides of a wing chair. Occasional anomalies resulted—knobs on the outer wingtips of some cirques are higher than the main range. Thus Colorado's two highest peaks, Elbert and Massive (together with several other of the high peaks of the Sawatch Range), are not on the crest of the Continental Divide, but are on short spurs protruding eastward from it.

The ice grinding down the sides of the cirques gathered at the bottom into "streams" that crowded into high valleys carved by earlier water erosion. Relentlessly these glaciers widened narrow canyons into U-shaped troughs. An example readily apparent to tourists traveling from Loveland to Rocky Mountain National Park is the bed of the Big Thompson River. Its lower canyon, into which the glaciers did not reach, is a sharp V. Its upper section in the National Park is a broad U filled with spruce.

The masses of rock that rode the glaciers downhill were deposited as moraines—lateral moraines if they paralleled the sides of the protruding tongues of ice, terminal moraines if they marked the glaciers' farthest downward extent. The lateral moraines we see today are generally low ridges disguised by thin accumulations of soil that support dense growths of shrubs and scrubby trees. Terminal moraines often function as dams, creating exquisite lakes near timberline.

Other tarns lie at the foot of tall cliffs in depressions scooped by glacial action out of the floors of the high basins. Their surfaces are free of ice only for two or three months of late summer. Steely cold and as clear as the mountain air, they draw the eye downward past sequences of sharp-edged rocks into tantalizing blue-amber depths. Their capricious surfaces mirror every mood of the mountain weather, shimmering with each puff of wind and changing color under the fluid sky from black to purest sapphire. When two, three, or four such lakes are strung like beads down some gray gorge, they are called "paternoster lakes."

Most of the high-altitude lakes that contain enough food to support fish have been stocked with rainbow trout. Such tarns are well worth long hikes to reach, for even if the fish prove temperamental about striking at lures, as high-altitude rainbow generally do, the lake itself is reward enough.

Of the multitude of high-altitude tarns in the Western United States, probably the best-known is Bear Lake in Rocky Mountain National Park. So many cars wind up the 9-mile road leading to it that the Park Service is contemplating banning automobile traffic in favor of a system of shuttle buses. Buses probably will not affect normal reactions, however. The majority of first-time visitors will content themselves then, as they do now, with walking a few hundred yards along a paved path to the nearest, spruce-fringed shore of the lake. They will look dreamily across it at the striking cliffs of Hallett Peak, feed the striped ground squirrels (which visitors are not supposed to do), and return to their transportation. But then, according to one of the rangers to whom we talked, a subtle dynamism takes hold of some of them. On their next trip they are likely to hike entirely around the lake. From there to more difficult trails and eventually to the peaks is an inevitable progression for an enthusiastic handful. The lure of the high country has caught them.

### *High-Country Driving*

It is possible, of course, to enjoy the mountaintops without using your feet. Automobile highways twist upward to the summits of Pikes Peak and Mount Evans. As indicated earlier, the Trail Ridge Road in Rocky Mountain National Park affords views of some of the finest tundra country in the state. From these places and from the tops of several high passes short hikes are in order. Be warned, however. The drama of the wind-tossed sky, the sharp clarity of the enormous vistas, the coolness, the decreased amounts of oxygen and atmospheric pressure, and an increased intensity of ultraviolet light are stimulating and may tempt unacclimated people to overexertion. The results can be an onslaught of short breath, pounding hearts, dizziness, headaches, and sometimes nausea. At that point, in the words of a stale mountain joke, tyros join the Daniel Boone Club: they go out and shoot their lunch.

People wanting more adventurous mechanized tours turn to four-wheel-drive vehicles capable of climbing 25-degree slopes and negotiating more abrupt curves than standard automobiles can manage. These sturdy work horses capitalize on the same geologic patterns that the earlier miners used. Foremost is the fact that with only a few exceptions Colorado's main peaks are glaciated on one side only, if at all. The remaining slopes, especially to the south and west, roll gently. Their drainage basins are not cliff-walled cirques but friendly cups whose floors are bright green with scrub willow and atinkle with the sound of small streams. The ridges between the basins are not knife-edged arêtes, but are broad and gain altitude at easy stages. They lead to wide expanses of mingled fell-field and flower-bright tundra. In such places primitive road building obviously does not present insuperable difficulties.

During the mineral booms of the past century miners wove a network of rudimentary wagon roads up those kindly slopes to weather-exposed veins of silver ore at timberline or higher in the Georgetown district of the Front Range, in the Mosquitos west of South Park, and in parts of the San Juans—to name only three of the most prominent areas. Much of this road building was the result of unfounded optimism. The majority of the mines did not justify the roads and were abandoned. Other properties closed down during the sharp decline in silver prices that accompanied the depression of the 1890s.

The storm-battered buildings and the old roads were quickly discovered by the purchasers of army surplus four-wheel-drive jeeps thrown onto the market after the close of World War II. Sensing the popularity of the new recreational activity, other manufacturers began turning out competitive vehicles. Owners banded into clubs devoted to furthering the sport. Entrepreneurs in small mountain towns began running sight-seeing trips for tourists. County road supervisors were badgered into clearing out snowbanks as early as possible in the summer and removing boulders and tumbled trees. Still other roads were opened by timber cutters and by construction crews working on remote dams.

It has all been a great deal of fun for a great many people, but unfortunately it has been accompanied by serious abuses. Tundra is very fragile; clumps of plants that easily fit under a jeep driver's hat may represent more than a hundred years of growth. Unaware of or indifferent to this tenderness, motorists who are swept away by the challenge of reaching a difficult spot will sometimes leave the regular roads and zigzag recklessly across meadows that appear to open a way to their goal. Others, irked at being blocked by snow or mud, swing wide around the obstructions and tempt others to follow their tracks. The ruts that such wanderings gouge into the friable soil will remain visible and sterile for decades.

Aware that objections to such antics can result, and have resulted, in road closures, the operators of sight-seeing tours and the responsible members of four-wheel-drive clubs are urging restraint. The nation's heightened ecological awareness lends force to the arguments and is producing results. Still, one cannot roam very far in the mountains without concluding that machinery in self-interested hands, whether miners, dam builders, tree cutters, highway engineers, or jeep drivers, has always been the high country's greatest threat.

*Climbing the Fourteeners*

All peaktops offer attractions to hikers and climbers, but the most compelling ones in Colorado are the "Fourteeners"—peaks that exceed 14,000 feet in elevation. There used to be forty-eight. Later there were fifty-four. Today the number has slipped back to fifty-three. These variations have resulted not from mountain rising or erosion, but from increasingly accurate surveys and from settling debates over what constitutes a mountain.

Suppose, for example, that you are confronted by a ridge with a knob at either end. How much distance should lie between them and how low should the connecting ridge drop before the two summits can be classified as separate peaks? By carefully calculating such matters many years ago, my brother was able to prevail on both the Colorado Mountain Club and the United States Geological Survey to accept El Diente, 14,159 feet high in the San Miguel Mountains, as a separate summit from Mount Wilson, 14,246 feet, to which it is bound by a pinnacle-bristling arête. By contrast Mount Cameron in the Mosquito Range has been humbled into anonymity as a mere appendage of Mount Lincoln, which is only 52 feet higher.

Because at least one side of most ranges escaped heavy glaciation, an ascent of all but a handful of Colorado's peaks can be turned into outings that require little more than time, stout lungs, and stout shoe leather for success. Often, however, the other side is different. You can all but stroll up the south flank of Uncompahgre Peak, rising 14,309 feet in the northern part of the San Juan Mountains. People have even spent several nights on Uncompahgre's summit. When I was there many years ago, we ate lunch on a wooden tent platform laid down by scientists experimenting with heliography—flashing code messages with huge mirrors reflecting the light of the sun. But one glance over the brink of Uncompahgre's north wall suffices to dispel any feelings of superiority that you may have developed during the ascent. That astounding cliff, 3,000 feet of loose, treacherous rock, has never been climbed and is one of the last great mountaineering challenges in the United States.

Someone will succeed, for such is the story of "impossible" climbs. The prime example is the east face of Longs Peak. That 1,700-foot cliff, the back side of an overwhelming cirque, is well worth hiking or riding horseback up the trail from the Longs Peak Ranger Station to see. The trail itself stops at a

31. *Part of a steel mill at Pueblo.*

32. Factories in the field: agribusiness in the shadow of the Continental Divide near Loveland.

34. Foothills daisies of genus Erigeron. Other members of the group, including fleabane, extend as far up the slopes as the subalpine regions.

*33. A ranch near one of the hogbacks that signal the shift from plains to foothills.*

OVERLEAF:
*37. Bare aspens and white cloud streaks draw a cold frame around Mt. Sneffels.*

*35. Ball cactus, a foothills echo of the arid plains.*

*36. Wild roses spread from the foothills to elevations of about 10,000 feet.*

38. *Cottonwoods stand dormant beside a frozen stream.*

39. *The lines of winter.*

40. *Spring green: The first tender freshness of aspen leaves is one of the most welcome sights in the high country.*

41. *The blaze of autumn.*

small stone shelter cabin. From there you scramble across a moraine to Chasm Lake, a bright jewel all but encased by soaring, ice-polished granite. The main cliff above the lake is Longs' stupendous east face. The sheer central part of the East Face is called the Diamond. We used to avoid it by swinging to the left up tight chimneys and along a narrow ledge mockingly named Broadway. No one, I remember thinking, would ever scale the Diamond itself. But in 1960 it succumbed to a 52-hour assault by two climbers who spent the dark hours of night lashed to the rock with ropes. Since then the feat has been duplicated several times.

In spite of that implacable east face, Longs Peak is the most frequently climbed peak in Colorado, even though several other Fourteeners are easier to reach and gentler of slope. Indians once climbed Longs to trap eagles. Since then some 75,000 other people, using a variety of routes on the north, south, and west sides, have made about 100,000 ascents. Several people, some of them professional guides, have climbed Longs more than a hundred times each. An eighty-five-year-old man and a seventy-year-old woman have reached the top. So have at least two children aged five, and two others on crutches. One couple were married on the summit.

For a time those who climbed the north face were able to pull themselves over the hardest 150-foot stretch by means of two lengths of iron cable installed in 1925 by the Park Service. On some holidays the crowds at the foot of the cable were so thick that would-be climbers had to wait for up to two hours for a turn. That is ended now. In June 1973 the Park Service removed the worn cables for safety's sake and then, for aesthetic reasons, decided not to replace them. Climbers were warned either to use ropes on the north pitch or seek an easier route through what is called the Keyhole.

Protest about the removal was expected, but little came. No one is quite sure why, but it is heartening to think that one reason is honesty: most people who are willing to expend the energy required to come to grips with one of America's great peaks prefer that the contact be direct, with no artificial aids intervening between them and the fullness of the mountain experience.

# 8
# BREAKAWAY COUNTRY: THE PLATEAUS

Anyone who is unfamiliar with the Rockies and draws an imaginary cross section of them will probably fall into the error of making both slopes look much alike. Nothing could be wider of the mark. In descending the mountains to the west one passes through the same sequence of life zones—alpine, subalpine, montane, Transition, and Upper Sonoran—that prevails on the eastern side, but that is the only similarity.

### Colorado's Rugged Western Slope

The fall of the land toward the Pacific is so distinctive that it has received its own name. When speaking of the Mississippi side of the mountains, one uses the term "eastern slope" as a matter of geographic convenience. Western Slope by contrast is spelled with capital letters. It is a human as well as a physiographic entity. It is also a mystique. The people of the Western Slope feel superior to lesser mortals. They like to think that while shaping the land, they have been shaped by it: by its long vistas, its angularity, even its stubbornness. It has yielded its resources grudgingly. When a person has at last wrested from it his portion of good things, he hangs on hard and is proud—this despite his turning, after the fashion of other people, to the state and federal governments for subsidies whenever the problems of mastering the land grow too much for him.

In theory the Western Slope is easily delineated. It is that part of Colorado

—about three tenths of the state's area—whose waters drain into the Pacific Ocean. In actuality, the boundaries are erratic and confusing. In the north the arbiter of waters, the Continental Divide, bulges far eastward to encompass the headwaters of the Colorado River in Middle Park. In the south the Divide loops far westward in order to contain the sources of the Rio Grande. The result is a north-south line that on paper looks vaguely like an abused crankshaft.

Another cause of topographic confusion is the lack of any clear line of demarcation between the westernmost granite belt and its adjacent physiographic province, the plateaus. In the east the mountains rise abruptly from the plains in an almost straight line. In the west the mountains drift off into a jumble of uplifts—coxcomb peaks, long ridges, and lava-topped mesas rimmed with cliffs. Outstanding in this mélange are two westward-thrusting ranges as spectacular as any part of the main belts. One is the jagged Elk Mountain spine whose human focus is the famed resort town of Aspen. The other is the much larger San Juan area, a hodgepodge of high peaks and profound canyons, much of it veneered with the remnants of ancient volcanic eruptions.

On the eastern slope sedimentary rocks are noticeable only where they have been upturned against the base of the foothills. On the Western Slope gigantic horizontal beds of limestone, shale, and sandstone are evident everywhere. Generally speaking, these layer cakes of rock were eased upward by the heaving earth without much folding. Where they have weathered, they present viewers with rising tiers of cliffs, sometimes on the sides of 14,000-foot peaks like the Maroon Bells southwest of Aspen, and sometimes in deep, terraced canyons, like that of the San Miguel River, which drains northwest from the San Juans.

### *Exclamation Marks in Granite*

Reaching like knobby fists toward the Utah border are a series of plateaus. Near their upper ends are isolated peaks that serve as the concluding exclamation marks of the high country. Because of their lonesome positions their summits show forth splendidly. One is the pyramid of Mount Sopris, lording it over the triangle formed by the junction of the Roaring Fork and

Crystal rivers. Totally different in shape but no less effective is the wall of thumbs and buttresses that line the crest of the plateau bordering the Uncompahgre Valley below the town of Ridgway on Highway 550. But none of those last-stand summits is as lovely, in my mind, as the Lone Cone, an offshoot of the San Miguel Mountains west of Telluride.

The peak's name is its description. Though it is not particularly high (12,631 feet), it is visible across enormous distances. I admit to prejudice in writing of it. As a boy and young man I spent more than a dozen summers on its flanks. In the soft twilights of Indian summer I'd wander with the rest of the family through its sagebrush skirts looking for low-growing, prickly-leafed Oregon grapes or along the narrow draws in search of black chokecherries, from both of which we made delectable jelly—even, when crops were plentiful, sweet wine. Sage grouse startled us by bursting out of the cover with a wild whir of wings, and it was a rare evening when we did not see at least a doe bounding off through the scattered yellow pines in high, four-footed leaps. I discovered, too, how hard it is to run down a wild steer in the dense mats of oak brush that cover the lower hillsides, and how delicious is the sound of a small stream in a dappled aspen forest. It was on the Cone's summit approaches that I first felt the slippery roughness of gray, mottled granite slide rock under my feet and hands, and grew aware, very suddenly, that an electric feeling in the air can be more than just a metaphor.

All peaks draw salvos of lightning from passing thunderheads. The Lone Cone attracts more than most because of its exposed position. When the air up there—or on any high ridge—is charged with power, you feel a fluttering in your hair as if trapped moths were struggling to get untangled. Sometimes there is a sizzling on the rocks. If you hold up your hand, little crackles of sound pop off the tips of your fingers. It is well then to drop below the skyline, where you are the tallest object around, or at least to lie flat. Avoid small stream channels while doing it. Part of the millions of volts that will be discharged at the flash will race along moist strips of earth for considerable distances before expending themselves.

If the flash is close, you see none of the forked daggers customarily associated with lightning. Rather there is a sourceless, all-encompassing brightness that eliminates, during a fraction of a second, every other visible object. The noise that follows is a crackling *spl-l-i-it*. A coppery smell of ozone fills the air, and the crash of thunder, after rolling between the cliffs, fades off with sullen slowness among the clouds.

Cowboys I know can tell you exactly what it is like. Three of them once climbed the Cone on impulse—in high-heeled boots, though they did remove their spurs. Because a storm threatened, one carried over his shoulder a rolled yellow saddle slicker. A light rain caught them on the top. All three sat huddled under the slicker while writing their names on the summit register. They heard the warning sizzles, but after you have reached the top of a peak, you want to record your triumph: Kilroy was here. While they were indulging in that harmless boast, lightning struck the yellow target. One died. By some wild quirk of luck—records of lightning strikes are full of tales of caprice—the other two suffered nothing worse than painful burns and a moment of indescribable terror.

*The Marvelous Plateaus*

Whether or not the Western Slope's plateaus support peaks, they are delightful places, yet seldom visited by tourists. Of the few automobile roads that climb to their crests, most are unpaved. Such roads are worth exploring, nevertheless. Three among several that never disappoint include one that winds southwest out of Delta to the top of Uncompahgre Plateau and another that goes northwest from near Ridgway in the same valley over Owl Creek Pass into the palisaded Cimarron country. Best of all, perhaps, is the one that thrusts north from Rifle over the White River Plateau to Buford.

Except on the Owl Creek road tall peaks are not a distraction. You become totally absorbed in sequences of tree-girt glades spotted with pink and white wild geraniums and tall penstemon, its deep, tubular, purplish-blue flowers clinging to one side of the stalk only, like the branches of a banner tree. Even more conspicuous is scarlet gilia, another tall plant whose trumpet-like blossoms also tend to grow on a single side of the stalk. Masses of gilia will set a whole hillside aglow. And always, in drier spots, is paintbrush, cerise in higher elevations, more brick-colored lower down. The plant is not as independent as its flamboyance suggests, however, for it finds part of its sustenance by sending out underground tendrils to tap the hard-working roots of neighboring shrubs.

The high points of the plateaus are tufted with Engelmann spruce. Lower down, especially on northern slopes, Douglas fir grows in thicker stands than it does on the eastern slope. When a rider approaches, dusky grouse burst up from the understory to sit on dead tree limbs, craning their necks with so little effort at concealment that they have been nicknamed fool hens. An even tamer bird is the ubiquitous gray-and-white Canada jay, called camp robber from his brazenness in invading a tent or picnic area and snatching up, under the occupants' noses, any loose object it can carry. Chickadees and nuthatches pry insects from the scaly bark; red Fremont's squirrels (chickarees) send down showers of cones from the treetops, meanwhile chirring in exasperation at any sign of intrusion.

Below the conifers are some of the most magnificent stands of aspen on the continent. In places the slender, off-white trunks soar nearly 50 feet before the branches begin. Air moves freely under the lofty ceiling of trembling green. Grass and flowers reach high for light. Two of the loveliest—purple monkshood and deep blue larkspur—kill cattle if the animals overindulge in the tasty roots, leaves, and stalks when juices grow toxic just before the flowers appear. Another effective flower when it grows in masses is cow parsnip, its umbrella-like clusters of small white flowers riding high above big, notched leaves. But the queen of the groves is the columbine, Colorado's state flower. Though its zone lies from the foothills to boulder fields above timberline, it flourishes best where it can throne itself close to the white aspen trunks. The stems grow taller there; the long-spurred sepals are creamier, the halo of petals a bigger, richer blue.

As the plateaus reach farther west, rainfall and, as a rule, elevation decrease. Scrub oak, juniper, and flats of sagebrush become common. Scatterings of scarlet gilia, Indian paintbrush, and penstemon grow here, too, along with bright locoweed, dwarf lupine, and yellow late-blooming rabbit brush. As in the aspen groves this zone also has its queen, called sego lily by the Ute Indians and mariposa by the Spanish. What sego signifies I do not know. Mariposa means butterfly, a name that rests appropriately on the chalice-shaped blossom swaying on the slenderest of stems. Mostly the lily's three petals are ivory white, though sometimes you'll see one that is pinkish, lavender, or lemon yellow. Inside, at the bottom of the chalice are crescents of purple and an exquisite cluster of golden hairs and stamen. At the bottom of their deep, stubborn roots are small bulbs that are edible. Though hard to dig up, the bulbs on occasion saved both Indians and the Mormon pioneers of Utah from starvation. Partly for that reason the sego lily, as it is commonly known among the Mormons, is Utah's state flower.

## The Long Valleys

Any opening in the plateau forests provides distant views of the adjoining river valleys. Each rises in the granite of the main ranges and eats its way down into sedimentary rock. Otherwise there is little similarity between them. Even their directions appear illogical. Only the White and Yampa in northwestern Colorado flow as due west as our nation's east-west orientation suggests they should, until the Green absorbs them in Utah and whips them south. Below them on the map the muddy Colorado shoulders an impetuous way southwest. An irresistible magnet, it bends its principal tributaries, the Roaring Fork and the Gunnison, abruptly northwest to meet it. Meanwhile, the Uncompahgre, a small stream in a gargantuan valley, flows almost due north in order to meet the turbulent Gunnison at the agricultural town of Delta.

Most erratic of all is the Dolores. After plunging out of deep glacial basins among the Wilson Peaks near Telluride, it flows southwest almost to Mesa Verde. There, wheeling about, it enters a heavily forested, seldom visited canyon that takes it north among increasingly barren, red-walled uplifts to the Uncompahgre Plateau. Bouncing off the plateau's terraced flanks, it swings northwest to join the all-absorptive Colorado.

The Western Slope's other south-flowing streams, all of them draining the southern part of the rumpled San Juans—the Animas, the Vallecito, the Pine, the Piedra, and, farthest east, the San Juan—are more orderly. They keep to their courses as predictably as the teeth of a comb until the San Juan all at once remembers the distant Pacific, veers west, and sweeps the lot of them away through northern New Mexico.

The passageways these streams carve are as inconsistent in appearance as in direction. Remember the South Platte and the Arkansas, coursing the plains like identical green ribbons? Not these waterways. The Dolores is deeply canyoned throughout its length, as is the San Miguel, which meets the Dolores in the bottom of a great red well little known to anyone save uranium miners. The Uncompahgre bursts out of the northern San Juan Mountains through the narrowest rock slits in Colorado, but then settles down to a placid journey in the widest of the Western Slope's broad troughs. By contrast the Yampa and the Gunnison begin in open parks and curl lazily past smiling ranch lands and prosperous towns before diving into tremendous gorges.

A special quality of the upper Gunnison country is the sky that arches over tributaries flowing gently toward the main river from north, east, and south. Much of that huge area is treeless. Summer twilight is the most poignant time to see it. As you drive or ride horseback along the rippling, sage-covered hills that slide downward into the valley, the thunderstorms of late afternoon end their belligerent grumblings. Dusk flows softly through the rain-washed air. The flat-topped buttes, the distant peaks, the far-off ridges crested with a fuzz of trees—all are muted beneath cumulus clouds piling upward to the limits of the atmosphere. Slanting sunlight strikes a silver dazzle from their mushroom tops. The lower convolutions are opalescent, dim pastel hues defying definition. In the distance one last gray ravel of rain reaches toward the shadowed land. The glint fades from the water in the irrigation ditches beside the darkening hayfields, and only the vast tumble of the sky is left to promise tomorrow.


*Colorado River Country*

As the key river of the Western Slope, the Colorado embodies the characteristics of them all. Its first waters gather in Grand Lake at the southwestern edge of Rocky Mountain National Park. From there it flows easily, a clear and sparkling trout stream, through the hay meadows of Middle Park. But when it reaches the first layers of sedimentary rock, it grows boisterous and starts gouging out canyons, burdening itself with fine, almost colloidal red sand. The canyons it creates, broken along the way by a broad sage basin where the Eagle joins the flow, are splendid: bands of vertically furrowed cliffs alternating with steep slopes of red soil where pines and scrub oak cling precariously.

Below the town of Glenwood Springs the river confronts a high uplift protruding eastward from Utah. Geologists, but almost no one else, call the whole of the plateau by the Ute word Tavaputs. Local people use more descriptive names for its different segments, only the easternmost of which concern us here.

The Colorado River has created those segments by slicing a broad-bottomed, steep-walled valley through Tavaputs' southeastern shoulder. The barricade on the west side of the river consists of dull-toned but otherwise impressive gray cliffs. In 1853 explorer John Gunnison named them the Book Cliffs because he thought they resembled a ragged line of upright, open volumes, the V's between the pages being caused by the shallow gullies that creased their faces.

The southern extremity of the Book Cliffs overlooks the principal city of the Western Slope, Grand Junction. (The Colorado used to be called the Grand; "Junction" derives from the city's location at the confluence of the "Grand" with the Gunnison.) Below Grand Junction the combined river valleys spread out to almost a plain, or, more accurately, if you look away from the central quilt of irrigated farmlands, to a stark desert. Bordering the desert on the north and disappearing dimly off into Utah is that same barricade of cliffs, now called the Roan Cliffs because of tinges of pink in the rock.

A curious narrow-gauge railroad once struggled up through a dry break in the Roan Cliffs to the wild country north of the rim. Curves were so sharp and grades so steep that special locomotives had to be designed for the run. The line's principal freight was a cousin of petroleum called gilsonite, useful in making paint, varnish, and certain rubber substitutes. Gilsonite is so explosive that early-day miners (who lacked electricity) dared not use open carbide lamps around the rock that contained it and so dug the stone out by groping around in the dark.*

It may be that more dark gropings loom ahead for the northern part of Tavaputs Plateau and the encompassing Uinta Basin. This is oil-shale country. Impregnating the crumbly soil behind the Book Cliffs, in an area that reaches from a little north of Grand Junction to the White River and then back into Utah, are billions of barrels of black energy whose recovery is beginning to look commercially feasible. What will happen to the land during the process is a murky question still being hotly debated.

Opposite the southern part of the Book Cliffs and riven from the rest of Tavaputs by the Colorado River rises the imposing bulk of Grand Mesa. The

* Gilsonite is now transported out of the area in a pipeline as slurry.

topmost point of the mesa, which has been protected from severe erosion by a cap of lava, approaches 11,000 feet in elevation. The views of the valleys—the Gunnison, the Uncompahgre, the Colorado, and their satellites—are extraordinary. Even more staggering are the contrasts created by elevation. The southern snout of the mesa leaps more than a mile upward from the valley floor. The spruce and aspen forests back of the rims are thick and shady. The small streams that crease the mesa's surface feed scores of bright little lakes. Near the brink of the tabletop, ski and toboggan runs curve insouciantly a long stone's drop above dry, treeless sand that, startlingly enough, is seldom whitened by more than a scuff of snow.

*The First Residents*

The meaning that these abrupt variations in climate can bring to the economics and pleasures of life was discovered first by the Ute Indians. The Utes tend to be a round-faced, stocky race, darker of skin than are many Indians. They probably appeared in what is now western Colorado and eastern Utah about the fourteenth century A. D. Before they learned from Navajos and Apaches how to make bows, and before they obtained horses from Spanish settlers in northern New Mexico, they lived dismayingly close to the bottom margin of subsistence—scanty clothing of plant fiber and rabbit fur, shelters built of heaped-up brush, meals of piñon nuts, serviceberries, rose hips, seeds, snakes, insects, and such small rodents as they could catch from time to time.

Their new acquisitions, the bow and the horse, lifted them from misery into affluence. They developed a brisk trade with the Spaniards, bartering buckskin and child slaves, most of the latter seized from neighboring tribes, for knives, cloth, beads, and still more horses. They crossed the mountains to the plains to hunt buffalo and fight the Cheyenne and Arapaho. (Ute Pass behind Colorado Springs and Trail Ridge Road in Rocky Mountain National Park follow two of their paths.) From the Indians of the plains they borrowed a fondness for decorative feathers and learned to make hide tipis in which to live. But no other tribe ever learned from them how to tan soft deerskins as beautifully as the Ute women did.

Like all Indians, they watched their horses with care. They developed, almost instinctively it seems, adaptations in herding them that fitted exactly the demands of their environment. Like the deer and the blue jays, they wintered in the valleys, where the weather was mild and the sun-cured grass was seldom covered more than a day or two at a time with snow. When spring came they drifted the animals upward, just as the deer and the jays drifted, until they reached the greening meadows of the aspen glades.

In doing this they did not follow the valleys to their headwaters. Rather, they moved laterally from the bottomlands up the sides of the plateaus. In autumn, after the red and yellow leaves had turned brown and had fallen, they urged the horses back down into the swales they knew. Thus, though they took long trips just for the fun of the rides, they were not true nomads, but periodic migrants within limits loosely defined by the flux of the seasons. It was a pattern that white ranchers would also develop years later for their sheep and cattle without the least idea that the heathen Utes had thought of it first.

The Utes were not a numerous people. It is unlikely that more than 3,500 of them lived in what is now Colorado. That handful was fragmented into small bands, each occupying its favorite valley on the Western Slope or the lower ones between the two granite belts—the San Luis Valley, for instance. Although they visited easily back and forth, they seldom acted in concert on major issues. Thus they had no chance whatsoever of working out a viable compromise when white miners and homesteaders began encroaching on their lands.

In 1879 the frustration of one of the bands exploded in the massacre of eleven people living at the government agency on the White River and in a subsequent battle with a column of soldiers marching to the agency's relief. That fruitless blowup ended Ute occupancy of Colorado, except for a few families in the south who were granted a narrow reservation beside the boundary with New Mexico. The rest were herded out of the state to a reservation in Utah.

Their imprint has stayed in the names attached to plants and places, including the state name, Utah. In addition to the sego (mariposa) lily there is another flowering plant with an edible root that the Utes and we call yampa, which is also the name of a river. As they did, we use the word Uncompahgre to denote both a valley and Colorado's longest plateau. The loftiest section of the Continental Divide retains its Ute designation, Sawatch. (The word used to be spelled Saguache, as a town name in the San Luis Valley still is, until baffled Anglos declared that the only way to pronounce such a spelling was to sneeze it.) The name of one of their tribes, Tabeguache, is now attached to both a 14,000-foot mountain peak in the Sawatch Range and to a huge terrace of oak brush and junipers on the San Miguel side of the Uncompahgre Plateau. Famous chiefs are remembered in peaks—Antero, Shavano, Ouray. Ouray is also the name of a town, deep-set in a mountain bowl where hot springs kept the adjoining grass green throughout the winter and where Chief Ouray's people once loved to camp and soak their aches away.

The settlers who followed the Utes into the valleys wanted farmland where they could raise produce to sell to the gold and silver mines at the headwaters of the streams. They found that they had chosen a resistant and contradictory area. Their progenitors on the Ohio side of the Appalachian Mountains had been forced to clear away forests to make room for corn. Here, where there was only gnarled sagebrush to grub away, they had to climb the sides of the mesas just to find enough wood for fence posts and barn timbers.

Their epic struggle, as in all the Far West, was for water. Except in favored places the main rivers were either too headlong or too deeply entrenched to be mastered by the dabs of horse-drawn equipment they could muster. Many of the first settlers accordingly retreated to benchlands from which cooperative groups could dig small ditches back to easily raided sidestreams. Some of their shallow canals—I am thinking especially of those on the sides of the Lone Cone—wound for miles along pleated hillsides, their scarred banks fragrant with wild roses, their shallow waters delightful places for a small boy's adventuring.

When bigger efforts were needed, the settlers formed united water districts, besought and sometimes received federal aid, built dams, erected giant trestles, blasted tunnels through intervening ridges, quarreled over the division of the spoils, united to repair catastrophic breaks, and then spent most of their summer days in rubber boots anxiously herding insufficient trickles across their yellowing fields. Once in a while they reaped enough harvest to pay off some of the mortgage.

After the mines played out, they turned to supplying cattle and sheep ranches with alfalfa, redtop, and timothy hay. Some of them managed to acquire a few animals of their own. Joining forces with their neighbors, they formed what they called "pools." After obtaining permits from the Forest Service for the communal herd, they hired a cowboy or two to move it to the summer grass atop the nearby plateaus. In the fall they brought the animals back, sold off the steers or young wethers, and ran the she-stuff on the open range in the juniper breaks, supplementing the scanty grass with hay from their fields.

Industrialism infringed only gradually. Although the sedimentary foundations of the plateaus contain extensive deposits of coal, the local markets were not extensive, especially after the mines and smelters closed, and hence the collieries never grew big. Another sedimentary product was carnotite, a soft yellowish ore that contains both uranium and vanadium. During the first quarter of this century carnotite was a primary source of radium. It was supplanted then by pitchblende from the Congo, but roared back with the development of atomic power. The deposits that produce the low-grade ore are scattered, however, and so are the dismal, dust-powdered, rust-scabbed industrial plants that were built to process it. After a hundred years of chasing after small rainbows of industrial promise, the economy of the Western Slope remains tied tight to what can be grown from the soil.

Outsiders keep edging in, nevertheless. Travel is easier now for people and freight—by air, along the asphalt ribbons of interstate highways, aboard the Rio Grande Railroad, which has worked out a relatively direct route across the state by means of prodigious tunnels through the eastern granite belt and curving tracks along the Colorado River. Literally millions of visitors are now discovering the recreational advantages of the Western Slope's high country in both summer and winter. Inevitably some are settling near the resorts. Others are drifting down the valleys.

Among them are resort developers and speculators (add now the hangers-on of the oil-shale boom) who are boosting land prices to unprecedented heights. The old-timers can understand such people. What puzzled them was the growing infiltration of young people whose clothes, hair, and ambitions were not cut to traditional patterns. These newcomers lived in outrageous ways. Some associated in communes. Others patched up decayed cabins that had been sitting delinquent and unwanted on county tax lists for decades. A few were even content with tipis. They spent their working hours turning collapsed whorehouses into fancy restaurants, published newspapers that made no sense whatsoever to readers nurtured on "Items of Local Interest," and produced for sale such unlikely articles as clay pots that met no utilitarian need, barbaric jewelry, beads, and macramé. Fruitgrowers who had spent endless hours with chemical fertilizers and insecticides developing trees whose boughs bend low under the weight of plump cherries, fat peaches, and crisp red apples could not fathom their requests for organic produce, however nubbly it was. Sheepmen, cattle ranchers, and some deer hunters resented fiercely the newcomers' support of environmental bans on the poisoning of predators, especially coyotes. Most of all, remembering their own years of scrabbling to make a living in regions remote from social amenities, they were bewildered by the outsiders' unyielding opposition to progress.

*A Hard Way to Make a Dollar*

Patiently the invaders explain that "progress" is what put them to flight from the other side of the mountains. Nor are they content just to talk. In places like Aspen and Telluride, young newcomers have gained partial control of the municipal governments and are seeking to impose their own visions of order on those revitalized mining towns. They just might succeed. Not long ago a middle-aged businessman in Telluride admitted to me,

"When this ski promotion began to catch hold after we'd been stagnating for years, I sang hallelujah. A ten-story Holiday Inn on the flat below town would have looked to me like the most beautiful sight in all Colorado. Now I'd fight it, because I've finally come to see that we can lose the things we love most just by promoting them too hard. The trouble is, a fast buck in a poor country is a hard argument to answer. If we manage, it will be at least partly thanks to these kids, crazy and impractical as I sometimes think they are. So give 'em their heads, I say."

Commitment to a different faith. Maybe it does breed a special kind of people. Anyway, that's what they think over on the Western Slope.

PART THREE

*The Thirsty Land*

42. *The slim, tall trunks of aspen lace a morning sky.*

43. Scarlet Parry's primrose and white bitter cress like the flashing small streams near timberline.

44. Moss campion and alpine clover (above) are among the more familiar of the matlike plants that bloom above timberline.

45. Krummholz, or "Twisted wood," domed and matted by wind and snow for perhaps three hundred years.

*46. Marsh marigolds often appear at the very edges of retreating snowbanks.*

*47. Sky pilot. Despite its loveliness it smells, when crushed, distressingly like an angered skunk.*

*48. Queens crown, or rosy crown, a member of the succulent family, can grow among fractured rock where soil seems almost non-existent.*

49. *Ever since the gold rush of 1859 Pikes Peak has been a beacon to travelers across the high plains.*

50 and 51. *The first greening of the cottonwoods starts a new cycle of activity on this horse ranch near Estes Park.*

52. *A hayfield dreams under the summer sun. Gore Range in the background.*

53. *Herefords put on weight as the season advances.*

54. *In September an equinoctial storm drops the first snow on range cattle fattening near Tarryall Creek.*

55. *A lone horse waits for the next greening of the cottonwoods.*

# 9
# THE ANCIENT ONES: VISTAS IN TIME AND SPACE

For the purposes of this foray into the baffling civilization of the Anasazi, the Ancient Ones, who once lived in what is now southwestern Colorado, the best approach is along Highway 160 from Monticello, Utah, southeast toward Cortez. The best time is late May, when the thrust of spring has finally turned back the blades of frost.

The first part of the road runs like a seam through a quilt of silver-gray sagebrush erratically patterned with thick stands of piñon pine and juniper. As you progress, farmlands become more frequent. Some fields are vividly green with winter wheat that has just sprouted and is growing with almost visible exuberance. Alternating with the green are stretches of red-brown earth being plowed and harrowed by lonesome yellow tractors whose color makes them visible almost as far as the eye can reach. Their purpose becomes clear when you pass through a false-fronted town 8 miles inside the Colorado line and decipher a weather-blurred sign, "Dove Creek, the Pinto Bean Capital of the World."

Beans, you reflect with mild surprise, were also a principal crop of the Anasazi, who dry-farmed the edges of this region centuries before Columbus first touched the continent. When you reach the hamlet of Pleasant View a few miles beyond Dove Creek and see another sign—this one is directional, "Lowry Ruins, 9 mi."—you swing that way, west through the bean fields, curious about the persistence of these rhythms sprung from the soft brown earth.

*The Culture of the Ancient Ones*

The graveled road leads gently upward toward the top of the long ridge that the main highway has been paralleling. As the car climbs, it comes close enough to one of the yellow tractors for you to notice that the operator is wearing big earphones so that he can hear, by means of the radio in his cab, the latest news and music from the broadcasting station in Cortez. You also notice when he veers his ponderous machine slightly in order to skirt a low mound of stones. It is an Anasazi ruin, all but lost under the earth. Soon, like uncounted others in the bean and wheat fields along the easy slope of the ridge, the hummock will be lost, for each year the tractors edge closer. No one worries. Ruins abound in this section. Besides, it is the way of new cultures to build atop the detritus of older ones.

How old?

So far as is now known, the Anasazi began spreading through the present Four Corners country (the regions fanning out from the common meeting point of Colorado, Utah, New Mexico, and Arizona) about the first century before Christ, as we date time. Anthropologists call those original settlers Basketmakers because they wove baskets so skillfully that the receptacles held water; by dropping hot stones into that water, cooks could boil food. They made sandals out of yucca fiber, collected roots and seeds and berries (they had not yet learned agriculture), and now and then killed a deer by using a throwing device, the atlatl, that enabled them to hurl short spears with devastating force but indifferent accuracy. They did not build houses, but sought shelter in the numerous shallow caves that pock the sandstone walls of the winding canyons.

Shortly after the opening of our Christian era, the Anasazi learned to dry-farm corn, an Aztec art that for some time had been seeping northward from Mexico, along with the necessary seed. Squash and beans arrived later. All three items kept well if stored in dry, cool places away from rodents. To that end the Basketmakers began digging shallow granaries in the floors of their canyonside caves. In time the granaries were strengthened by being lined and covered with thin slabs of sandstone.

As the centuries passed, the granaries grew to be pit houses, single-room dwellings dug 2 or 3 feet into the ground and walled, very crudely, 2 or 3 feet above it, the whole covered with a flat roof of brush plastered over with adobe. Because these new dwellings gave ample protection from weather, some of the settlers moved from the caves onto the mesa tops, presumably to be near favorable locations for their crops. (It was probably a pit house that the yellow tractor was nudging toward oblivion.) Meanwhile they domesticated turkeys, both for food and for feathers, which they wove into warm robes. They learned to use bows and arrows, which let them augment their larders, and to make pottery, which eased household work while solving storage problems.

They discovered how to work stone, whose surfaces they sometimes dimpled with pointed tools for effect (and then often covered with plaster, hiding their artistry). They solved the secret of mixing mortar strong enough to hold the stones in place even when piled to remarkable heights. Thanks to those innovations they were eventually able to abandon their pit houses for structures built wholly on the surface. Yet the subterranean chambers in which their ancestors had lived for centuries retained so strong a hold on their imaginations that they retained them, in a rigidly standardized form, for ceremonial purposes. These were the kivas, a word we have borrowed from the modern Hopi (as Anasazi is a borrowing from the Navajo). Although the more solemn of the rituals that were carried on in the kivas were performed by men only, it seems likely that women were admitted from time to time for purely social events.

As techniques improved and population grew, say around A.D. 1000, the mesatop villages began to pull together into urban complexes built around the heads of many of the almost innumerable canyons that crease the land. (Such was the one now called Lowry, after a white homesteader in the area.) Rooms were piled on top of each other; some pueblos were three and four stories tall. Although small kivas retained their family functions, the communities as a whole pooled labor to build what can be very loosely compared, from the standpoint of service, to churches—great subterranean kivas as much as 50 feet in diameter which must have housed community rituals.

As the pueblos, or towns, expanded, a flourishing trade grew up between them. Some anthropologists believe that extensive specialization followed, with some villages becoming known for their pottery, some for cloth, some for tools and jewelry. It may be that some ceased growing their own food and depended on agricultural pueblos to fill their needs, even as modern cities do—as witness southwestern Colorado's bean farmers, whose produce is now shipped throughout urban America.

### The Long View from Lowry

The cracked, weedy surface of the small parking lot at Lowry Ruins suggests that few people drive the 9 miles to visit the site. This is unfortunate, for just the physical experience is exhilarating. The wind-cleaned air is pungent with the resinous smells of juniper, piñon, and sage. Gray mourning doves flash up on knife-like wings, white tail feathers flickering. Thousands of them pass through the area each spring. Hundreds stay and nest. The cooing sound of their lovemaking floats in from every direction.

In that crystal atmosphere the view leaps at you with such impact that you want to absorb it even before studying the ruin. Eagerly you scramble onto the ancient stone walls. The venture is safe enough. Although the pueblo once reached three stories in height, only remnants of the walls still stand. They are from 4 to 8 feet tall, and their uneven tops have been converted into footpaths by cappings of cement.

Eight feet are enough to put you on top of this part of the world. Your eyes travel unimpeded around the converging sweep of four states, a vast bowl whose rim is prickled by an array of peaks blue in the distance: the dim spire of Ship Rock in New Mexico; the cliff-rimmed Lukachukai Mountains in Arizona; Comb Ridge, the Abajo, and La Sal Mountains in Utah. In Colorado you recognize the sentinel Lone Cone, the bundles of snow-streaked gray peaks that mark the main sectors of the San Juan Range, and, closer by, the pyramidal La Platas. Due south is the 2,000-foot-high escarpment of Mesa Verde, topped by salmon-colored cliffs, the great center of Anasazi culture, which we will visit later. To the right of Mesa Verde is the heavy-shouldered laccolith of Ute Mountain.

Ute Mountain merits a digression. It stands isolated in the Southern Ute Indian Reservation. Because it is highly visible from all directions, it has become the subject of a good deal of lore, some patently phony. At one point on the road from Durango to Cortez, its outlines suggest to fervid imaginations a reclining woman—a head with streaming hair, tall breasts, elongated body, and upturned feet created by a pinnacle at the southern extremity of the uplift. On postcards the laccolith is called Sleeping Ute Mountain, an adjective not employed by professional geographers. Local people say that if clouds settle on the sleeper's breasts at sunrise, rain will surely follow by evening.

Although jurisdiction over the peak itself is in the hands of the Bureau of Indian Affairs, its shadow is so persuasive that officials of the Bureau of Land Management call the adjacent territory that they administer the Sacred Mountain District. Whether or not the Utes or Anasazi ever considered the mountain sacred, I cannot say, but anyway the connotations spread a faint patina of solemnity across the area, including the ruins that the Bureau also supervises.


*Altering Nature's Rhythms*

The Bureau of Land Management, more commonly known as the BLM, is a Johnny-come-lately among the federal agencies—the Forest Service, the Park Service, and so on—that supervise all lands not held by private individuals or corporations. Much of the area it administers is winter range, where livestock driven by snow from the high country (and thousands of deer and some elk as well) find sustenance grazing on grama grass, the feathery tips of rabbit brush, and the silvery, parchment-like seedpods of saltbrush. The budget of the Sacred Mountain District is expended in large part on projects designed to improve the range's carrying capacity.

One program involves creating ponds where animals can drink. This is done by catching the sheet water that flows off slick rock after a storm, slick rock being platter-like surfaces from which the thin soil has been stripped by wind. The sheet water eventually converges in shallow draws where it is readily impounded behind low dams. Bureau engineers have discovered that many of the places they select for dams were utilized in the same way a thousand years ago by the Ancient Ones. In fact, BLM dams sometimes make use of the remnants of Anasazi dams. It is notable, though, that no ditches led out of Anasazi reservoirs. The water they collected had to be carried to the fields, just as Hopi Indians still carry water to their corn, by hand in jugs.

Another program of range improvement involves "chaining" sections of piñon and juniper forest. Overgrazing has eradicated such grass and browse as once existed under the shaggy trees, creating erosion problems in the adobe soil. After a site has been selected for rehabilitation, grass seed—generally crested wheat grass or western wheat grass—is sown on it by airplane. Then a monstrous chain about 100 yards long and weighing up to 90 pounds per link is spread out between two powerful tractors. As the big cats drag the chain ahead, the iron links uproot the trees in the way. The tumbling stirs the air-dropped seed into the ground, where, given a boost from favorable weather, it sprouts lustily.

The area does not turn into a meadow, however. Not every tree is torn completely loose from the soil, and new evergreen sprouts appear from intact roots. The down trees lie in ugly, twisted heaps, and because this is arid country, they do not decay readily into nurturing duff. Thus although the program's ability to foster forage and soil conservation is proved by now, casual passers-by invariably object vehemently at what seems wanton destruction.

The Anasazi, too, cleared away patches of forest. They had to. Wherever enough moisture fell to make dry farming possible, the gnarled piñons and shaggy-barked junipers grew thick. By what must have been the most laborious of processes, those all-but-forgotten farmers used fire, stone axes, and pry poles to clear out enough growth to let sunlight onto their gardens of corn, squash, and beans, using the wood they gleaned from their labors for fires and roof beams.

It is unlikely that they understood crop rotation, and so they may not have alternated their corn and beans as today's farmers alternate wheat and beans. Instead, when the soil of one patch was depleted, they probably cleared another. The abandoned plot then went to grass and brush, but even that was a gain. Like today's clearings, those old openings attracted deer and thus made hunting easier for the Anasazi—all of which brings us back to the Lowry complex, whose excavation was sponsored by the BLM through a contract with the Department of Anthropology at the University of Colorado.

*Persistent Patterns*

In terms of today's geography the Lowry ridge, which runs from northwest to southeast, functions as a dividing line between waters draining into the Dolores River of Colorado and those flowing into the stretch of the San

Juan River that slants northwest out of New Mexico into southern Utah. The two slopes are very different, as will become evident shortly. The point now, however, is elevation. The 7,500-foot crest of the ridge is the highest land for miles around. Consequently it draws moisture from whatever storms happen to blow across the area from the Southwest. The magnet pulled the Anasazi into the area just as it pulls today's dry farmers. The pattern of precipitation is so pronounced, indeed, that one of the agricultural clubs serving the area's bean farmers calls itself the Rainbelt Grange.

Current custom yields clues about ancient practices. Every tilled field on the ridge—100,000 acres of them—faces toward the big bend of the Dolores —that is, to the east, with a slight inclination southward. The fields are there because the slope, gentle and unseamed by deep canyons, is easily worked. The stone mounds that the tractors veer to miss show that the Anasazi bean farmers also sought the same slope, although they did not venture as far down its sides as do today's agriculturists.

(An irresistible aside: like the Ancient Ones, today's rainbelt farmers build no fences. The reasons, of course, are different. Having no conception that the earth could be privately owned, the Anasazi saw no need for apportioning it. Their successors, by contrast, are trying to increase individual profits. Because big tractors and big harvesting machinery cannot maneuver close to fences, their presence would create strips of unproductive earth whose weeds would harbor grasshoppers and other injurious pests. Neighbors accordingly divide by agreement, not by mechanics. The result is, I think, unique in America: a 30-mile scarf of uninterrupted, curling fields of intertwined colors—in May emerald green and red-brown—broken only occasionally by a shallow draw grown to gray sage or black juniper. To the Anasazi the apparent communality would not have seemed unique at all.)

Except for natural precipitation, there is no water on this east-facing slope of the ridge. The sandstone beds beneath its rich soil tip toward the San Juan, so that the underground waters drain that way. Hence the Dolores side of the ridge has neither living streams nor wells. The farmers, whose small homes are scattered at wide intervals along the scarf of fields, live on rainwater spilling from their rooftops into cisterns and barrels. They keep no horses or milk cows that require water, and as a consequence have no barns— just houses and machinery sheds. Since the average annual precipitation is about 18 inches, divided evenly between snow and rain, they manage to save enough liquid to grow a few shade trees. During favorable springs their wives plant tulips inside discarded tractor tires whose rubberized sides retain the moisture that is applied by watering cans. When cisterns run dry as generally happens once or twice a year, they load tanks onto their trucks and rattle off to Pleasant View or some other community to buy a few hundred gallons, just for housekeeping needs.

The Anasazi who lived near their fields in the summer collected drinking water by steering little drainage ditches toward natural rock cisterns among the trees. When the cisterns ran dry, as they undoubtedly did at times, the families either left the vicinity until the next rain fell—or else lugged containers of water across the ridge from the canyons on the western side.

Beyond the foot of the ridge's eastern-facing slope, beyond the magnificent canyon of the Dolores River, lie thick forests of ponderosa pine. Sawmills hum in the area, but it is too cold and rough for farming. Today's agriculturists have made no effort to expand in that direction. Neither did the Anasazi. This ridge and the northern escarpment of Mesa Verde mark their civilization's deepest penetration into what is now Colorado.

Yet there must have been individual mavericks. There are a few small red cliff dwellings high on the red walls of the Dolores Canyon, well removed from the region chosen by most of the Ancient Ones. More baffling are the obsidian knives, reed baskets, a bonnet of ermine and feathers, and storage pits for grain—artifacts contemporaneous with Basketmaker culture—that have been found in a sandstone cave high above the Yampa River, more than 200 miles north of the Lowry ridge. Were those people wandering Anasazi in search of a new frontier that did not develop? No one knows. All we can be sure of is that most of the Ancient Ones preferred to face south, not north.

*Prehistoric Urbanization*

The western side of the ridge on which the Lowry pueblo sits is very different from the eastern side. It is rough, strewn with rocks, and clotted with timber. Long canyons, impassable laterally except at rare breaks in the walls, drain southwest through yellow-gray mesas to the San Juan. The country looks desperately dry, and most of it is except during rare flash floods. The exceptions occur in the heads of the larger canyons, which have eroded back almost to the crest of the ridge. Generally they contain water throughout the year.

This water may help explain why the Ancient Ones abandoned their small villages of pit houses in favor of multi-story apartment houses. It was an extensive movement that must have had enormous social impact. Lowry's three stories, for instance, held forty rooms that sheltered between seventy-five and a hundred people. In the same vicinity are unexcavated mounds that probably conceal between seven and nine additional clusters of a size comparable to Lowry's, a stern burden on primitive agriculture and hunting. Another group of mounds near the head of Sand Canyon on the same ridge covers 9 acres. At the Farview section of Mesa Verde sixteen apartment houses took shape within a radius of less than half a mile.

The easiest explanation is fear of attack from outsiders. The people grouped for strength. Of necessity they settled near the region's most dependable source of water, the pools and thin streams of the upper canyons. They built on the rims because there was space there and they were near their fields. Evidently the strategy succeeded in deterring would-be aggressors. At least the skeletons found in the area give little evidence of death in battle.

Associated with the growth of towns was tower building. The best surviving examples occur in the widely separated ruins that for administrative purposes are lumped together as Hovenweep National Monument. To reach them from Lowry drop back a few miles on the road to Pleasant View and then swing right as the signs direct toward the distant San Juan River.

It is a trip into almost unbelievable lonesomeness. By the end of May the country is empty. The deer that during winter browsed across the flats have started back toward the cooler, greener high country. Cattle and sheep have gone in the same direction, either trucked or driven by their tenders. Of large mammals only an occasional mountain lion or coyote and one small band of seldom-glimpsed wild horses have remained behind. Not a house is visible anywhere.

It was not always so desolate. Along the way you pass the remains of many small, single-family Anasazi units. The Bureau of Land Management has located within its Sacred Mountain District roughly 1,600 sites that were inhabited at one period or another during pre-Columbian times. The count does not include a multitude of similar sites on private land, in the Southern Ute Indian Reservation, on Mesa Verde, and in Hovenweep. It is probable, too, that hundreds of other sites remain undiscovered. Not all were occupied simultaneously. Nevertheless, Lloyd Emmons, a BLM archaeologist, is of the opinion that 100,000 Anasazi may at one time have occupied close to 10,000 habitations in southwestern Colorado alone. Only one fifth that many people now dwell in the lonely land.

A clustering of even 50,000 people in the many pueblos near the canyon rims would help account for the increasing sophistication of Anasazi pottery —lovely black designs on gray and white backgrounds—of the looms that were created for weaving cloth from cotton grown in the moister canyon bottoms, and of the community architecture, particularly the grand kivas and the towers. Certainly the creation of the towers in the Hovenweep groups demanded great skill and some technology.

*The Great Towers*

The largest of the groups, Square Tower, lies just inside Utah. Four others, linked by dirt roads that are impassable after hard rains, are inside Colorado. A further deterrent to sight-seeing is the voracious black gnats that swarm in the area each spring. Even so, it is worthwhile slathering on insect repellent and visiting the sites just to see how long true things can endure.

Archaeologists have a saying that the only way to preserve a surface ruin is to let it stay buried. As soon as it is excavated, snow water starts softening the foundations. Lizards and rodents dig into the mortar; vandals carve initials, rip off souvenirs, and sometimes deliberately topple leaning walls. The cliff dwellings escaped some of this attrition because they were hard to reach and were protected from the weather on three sides by the cavern walls. But the Hovenweep ruins had no such help. Their towers have stood naked to the elements for eight hundred or nine hundred years. They have lost their roofs and upper walls. Otherwise they are intact, even though their masonry, which in some cases rises in a direct line from the faces of the cliffs they overlook, is unfortified by mortar.

What function did these sturdy uprights and dozens of others throughout the region serve? Again defense is the easy explanation, though probably they served as lookout points rather than as citadels of war. Some were connected by tunnels to the kivas. (Once the kivas had stood apart from the villages, but as concentration quickened, they were moved to safer positions inside the village compounds.) A watcher in the tower could have notified the men in the kiva, a most vulnerable spot to be caught in, of an approaching enemy or, for that matter, of traders coming from a neighboring village.

There are a few towers, however, whose situations elude such pat analysis. In Hovenweep's Holly group is a tower perched exactly on top of a mammoth boulder in the canyon bottom. Exactly. Each of its four walls is an upward extension of the boulder. Those tan rocks could not have been piled so precisely one on top of the other without the exercise of great care and ingenuity. Why such effort? The buildings that stand above it on the enclosing horseshoe rim would have served much better as lookouts, if that was a tower's primary function.

And what of completely isolated towers, such as the double-walled rock cylinder, much shorter today than it used to be, that Lloyd Emmons showed us on a terrace of McElmo Canyon, close to the massive shoulder of Ute Mountain? Apparently there was no town nearby. So who manned that round upright, and when? What could watchers there do other than flash some sort of signal to another observation point in the distance? No, the theory of defense does not answer every question.

Some of the towers are round. Some are rectilinear with curved corners. Some have square corners. A few are shaped like the letter D. Does form signify anything about purpose?

Over them arches a sky that was once limitless. Today the air is veiled, however lightly, by smog from far away and, if the wind is wrong, by the coal smoke that pours twenty-four hours a day out of the tall chimneys of a power plant near Shiprock, New Mexico. Eight hundred years ago when there was no smog, when no electric lights glowed anywhere on earth, and when dry winds swept every trace of mist from the brittle air, how that wide canopy must have blazed each moonless night! Did the Ancient Ones, who had no calendars, align some of their towers in ways that aided astral observations and hence provided dates for planting and for accompanying ceremonies?

*The Mysteries of Mesa Verde*

It is time now to turn back through Pleasant View and Cortez to the road that twines up along the edge of Mancos Canyon to the top of the Mesa Verde escarpment. Again the vistas of the Four Corners country are superb, but the one that concerns us most drops southward across the area embraced by the National Park.

The great tableland of Mesa Verde, named in 1776 by the Spanish explorer Sylvestre Escalante, is a cuesta. That is, it is an asymmetrical ridge with cliffs on one side, in this case the north, and on the other side a much gentler southern slope. Mesa Verde's southern tilt is cloaked with dark piñons and etched by parallel canyons that, like those on the Lowry ridge, have eaten back almost to the crest. The far end of the slope is the huge trench of the Mancos River, which borders the mesa first on the east and then, swinging right, on the south.

Again the air is redolent with juniper and piñon and, at the end of May, with the heavy fragrance of cliff roses, a spindly bush frosted with small, white, five-petaled flowers whose centers hold an explosion of golden anthers. Later there will be scarlet gilia, red penstemon, blue spikes of lupine, vivid cactus blossoms, and, loveliest of all, the ever-swaying white butterfly blossoms of mariposa lilies. Gray jays scold; russet-crowned, greenish towhees mew like cats in the brush and occasionally break out their quick, bright songs. White-crowned sparrows chorus back. Overhead, hawks ride the turbulent air. On many afternoons purple thunderheads discharge awesome lightning bolts but little rain. "Dry lightning," it is called, and sometimes it creates serious fire problems.

Once several surface pueblos dotted the mesas between the canyons. Then, about 1200 A.D., the residents, both in Mesa Verde and on the Lowry ridge (but apparently not at Hovenweep), began deserting their towns for new habitations in the shallow caves that a thousand years earlier had sheltered their untutored ancestors. Though building problems must have been more troublesome in the caves than on the surface, the migrants managed to produce even more striking architectural triumphs. In some cases they raised walls all the way to the cave's ceilings. They crowded storage bins in high cracks, and devoted what seems to us a disproportionately large amount of floor space to their kivas. Much craft work and undoubtedly a great deal of gossip went on on the rooftops, and one wonders how children were kept sound of limb in those precipitous quarters.

What force could possibly have made the Ancient Ones leave the mesas for such inconvenient homes? Climbing up to the fields and down to water each day must have been taxing. Crowding was surely irksome. The 122 rooms of Spruce Tree House, it has been estimated, held two hundred people. Other cliff dwellings were almost as densely populated. Surely only great pressures could have compelled so drastic a change in life-styles.

Again the favored explanation is a need, real or supposed, for better protection against aggressive nomads. But other suggestions have been advanced. One has to do with weather. The mildest of winters are cold on mesatops whose altitudes reach 7,500 feet. Snow is sometimes deep. Many of the bean farmers north of Cortez escape the weather by loading up their campers and fleeing for a few months to the kindlier climes of Southen California and lower Arizona.

Perhaps the Ancient Ones reacted in as nearly similar a fashion as their limited mobility allowed. Their trash heaps have revealed the bones of birds that normally winter at higher elevations. So it seems likely that the period was marked by a general drop in temperatures. If so, the shivering Anasazi may have looked longingly at the caves. Those with southern exposures (and none of the inhabited caves face north) would be sheltered from the wind and would catch the winter sun, yet would be sheltered from summer heat. Why not move? And so, after determining that construction challenges could be met—note the series of terraces that level off the floors of Cliff Palace—down they went.

They did not stay long, relatively speaking. About 1300 they were again abandoning homes built with great labor. This time they forsook the area entirely. Migrating far south, they became, according to one theory, the progenitors of the pueblo dwellers of modern Arizona and New Mexico.

Perhaps the radical move was brought about by continuing fears of enemy tribes. And yet no serious attacks seem to have occurred. Perhaps they were starved out by a drought that began about 1275 and continued for more than two decades. But their predecessors had survived long droughts before them.

Or perhaps, as has been suggested by Ronald Switzer, Superintendent of

Mesa Verde National Park, they became unable to cope with the problems created by their own congested urban living. They had exhausted the fertility of the soil and had cut down the forests within practicable reach of their cities. Overcrowding made them increasingly susceptible to alarms about enemies and the threat of crop failure caused by dryness. Their seers may have added ominous prophecies drawn from the stars. Suddenly the culture that once had promised so much fell apart and they drifted away, not without terrible wrenchings. Recent discoveries indicate that cannibalism was at times resorted to during those years, though whether it was ritualistic (to gain strength by absorbing the vitality of a brave enemy) or merely for sustenance is not yet known. People from places like Hovenweep, who for want of suitable caves had not erected cliff dwellings, followed the migrants southward, and the land stood empty, awaiting the arrival of the much less numerous, far more primitive early-day Utes.

Cars must leave Mesa Verde by the same road they used on entering it. And so as you skirt the high north rim you reencounter those now-familiar long vistas across space and time. Far in the north you make out the green-brown scarf of the wheat and bean fields. You remember the yellow tractors lumbering through patterns laid down more than a thousand years ago by a vanished race. And you can't help wondering: how much have we learned in a thousand years?

# 10
# DOG TOWN

A plume of dust a quarter of a mile long hung behind the green Forest Service pickup truck as it slanted across the Comanche National Grassland on the parched plains southeast of La Junta. Inside the hot cab we were growing bored and uncomfortable, and it may have been that as much as anything that led me to ask, "Are there any prairie dogs left around here?"

Jim Hollenback of the Forest Service, who was driving, nodded. "I can show you some we are keeping an eye on."

We turned off the road through a wire gate in a fence corner. For a mile or so we bounced along over hummocks of autumn-brown grass. We dodged beds of prickly-pear cactus and wove between spiked yucca plants, the open seedpods on their dry stalks shaped like delicate chalices. With no word of preparation from Jim we dipped over the brow of a short, gentle slope. In front of us a small pandemonium erupted—dozens of little golden-brown bodies rushing crisscross towards mounts of earth shaped like miniature volcanoes.

Jim cut the motor. Through the open window we heard a barrage of staccato yelps as the prairie dogs dived into their burrows and then turned about to reassess the situation. At that, memory made one of its magical leaps. The years fell away and I was a teen-age boy on the other side of the state, walking over the lip of another low hill, seeing the same sort of scurrying and feeling myself the focus of scores of intent black eyes.

*Random Death*

When I was fourteen, my stepfather, who moved in mysterious ways, gave me a Marlin .22 rifle whose steel side plates (I thought they were silver) were engraved with pictures of leaves, quail, and cottontail rabbits. After I had passed his rigorous course in gun handling, he topped his munificence by saying that whenever I hunted prairie dogs, he would provide the ammunition and, in addition, would give me ten cents for every prairie dog tail I brought back to him. Jackrabbits, crows, and sage grouse late in the summer (the last for eating) were permissible targets of opportunity. All other living creatures were forbidden. If I indulged in ordinary target practice—I wanted to be a trick shooter, breaking two bottles simultaneously by splitting a bullet on a butcher knife set in front of them and lighting kitchen matches by skimming their heads with a bullet at 15 feet—I had to buy my own ammunition out of my prairie dog earnings. At the outset it seemed to me the greatest bargain ever struck.

Like all adults giving presents to children, my stepfather undoubtedly wanted to please. His other motives I cannot now fathom. He could hardly have expected me seriously to deplete the ranch's prairie dog population, but he may have thought that the effort would strengthen my steadiness of purpose, ingenuity, responsibility, and sense of usefulness. I am afraid that in the long run those gains were negligible. What the experiment did accomplish, however, and without his conscious intent, I am sure, was to solidify in me a cultural conviction already half formed by the context in which I then lived, namely that certain forms of wildlife are ruthless competitors of man and therefore merit extinction.

Our summer camp, as we called it, stood at the base of a sharp slope dotted with yellow pine and clumps of oak brush. The fan-shaped view to the northwest, north, and northeast was across wide flats of sagebrush to a distant forest of pine. The sage flats marked, in our vicinity, the upper reach of the dry zone preferred by prairie dogs. Within half a mile of the ranch house stood five dog towns, each an acre or so in size. Farther away were larger ones, as we defined large. Later I learned that on the plains east of the Rockies, prairie dog towns were cities, measured in square miles. There was a metropolis in

56. Spectacular mountain canyons were formed when "superimposed rivers" sliced through masses of pre-Cambrian rock as it rose across their paths. This cliff of crystalline gneiss and schist, laced with pegmatite, towers 2,000 feet in the Black Canyon of the Gunnison National Monument.

57. *The Black Canyon of the Gunnison National Monument. The abyss at this point is more than half a mile deep.*

58. About fifty species of lupine grow in the Rocky Mountains. Some varieties thrive on open hillsides at low elevations; others, like the clump shown here, prefer sunny openings in thick forests of lodgepole pine.

59. Clusters of tiny chiming bells hang like blue stars above their own dense foliage.

60. The range of Colorado's showy state flower, blue columbine, extends from about 6,000 to 12,000 feet. Its stems are longer and its colors deeper in aspen forests. Above timberline shorter varieties seek warmth in crannies between rocks or among scrub willow bushes.

61. Mariposa lilies like sunny hillsides and sagebrush flats.

62. Paintbrush flaunts its brightly colored bracts from the edge of the foothills to treeline. Hues vary from orange-red to a deep rose to creamy yellow.

63. Bistort: cotton tufts on slender stems. In this rock garden are also columbine, sky pilot, and chiming bells.

OVERLEAF:
64. The weathering away of sandstone hillsides sometimes leaves isolated monoliths like this one in Colorado National Monument. Rabbitbrush, which blooms in the fall, brightens the foreground. The rich farmlands of the Colorado River Valley below Grand Junction are in the background.

65. *A scud of rain swirls along the western side of the Sawatch Range, a section of the Continental Divide in central Colorado.*

66. *Water courses that are dry much of the year have creased into surrealistic forms the gaunt hills of the Four Corners area, the only point in the nation common to four states—Colorado, Utah, New Mexico, Arizona.*

67. Ancient round towers built by the Anasazi for unknown purposes dot the piñon-clad slopes of Ute Mountain.

68. Some of the towers in Hovenweep National Monument were placed unbelievably atop huge boulders and on the rims of sheer cliffs.

Texas, so I have read, that was 250 miles long and 150 miles wide, containing millions of residents.

The grass within and around each mound was kept closely clipped by the inhabitants. To ranchers who evaluated land in terms of the number of acres required to nourish one sheep or one cow, the pattern could be reduced to a mathematical formula of poignant exactness. To cowboys whose running horses sometimes stepped into prairie dog holes and fell head over heels the evaluation came in terms of broken arms and bruises.

The possibility that the animals might perform an ecological function in renewing the soil by bringing fresh earth to the surface and by increasing the soil's absorption of moisture never entered our thinking. Like wild horses and jackrabbits (but unlike deer or elk, whose hunting by outsiders brought quick cash into the country), prairie dogs were rivals for a limited supply of grass that we were already overcrowding. Hence they were classed, like mice and rats that raided storage bins and mountain lions, coyotes, and eagles, which occasionally slew a calf or lamb, as varmints—that is, vermin. And everyone knows what you do with vermin.

I can't say that my hunting helped the situation very much. After a few days the prairie dogs grasped the nature of the new menace that was among them and grew wary. About the only shot I got were at the beady eye of some curious pup as it peered over the edge of the family mound. Even when I scored a hit, the dog was generally able to drop out of reach in its burrow before it died. As my harvest of tails grew slim, my aim wandered. When my stepfather caught me shooting a flicker out of a pine tree, I lost the gun for the rest of the summer. Indiscriminate killing was not permissible.

Not because of my failure but because he had been talking in town with a man from the government Biological Survey (now the Fish and Wildlife Service), my stepfather decided to mount his next attack on prairie dogs by means of poison. He brought home a quantity of wheat that had been soaked, as I recall, in strychnine. Until such time as the ranch's two cowboys were free to distribute it, it was stored in a shed beside the log barn.

We kept two marvelous white mules around the place to do off-road hauling. (This was in the 1920s before rubber tire tracks and four-wheel-drive vehicles went everywhere.) They were family pets, larger than ordinary mules and far more tractable. They had pink noses and pink rims around their eyes, and were forever nuzzling us for whatever tidbits we might have in our pockets. At times my brother and I would climb onto their backs, without bridle or saddle, and stretch out in the sun, half dreaming, secure with that warm strength beneath us.

One night the two mules somehow got into the shed. The next morning we found them dead in front of the barn.

Because we no longer had mules for off-road hauling, we were hard put to move the carcasses to a secluded place at a tolerable distance from the house. For my brother and me, and I think for my stepfather as well, the effort was traumatic. I don't know that it changed my mind, right then, about prairie dogs and other varmints, but it did give me another and this time passionate insight into indiscriminate death. Although my stepfather sought with cool logic to distinguish between my deliberate aiming of the .22 at the flicker and the accidental nature of the mules' dying, I was much too upset to follow, or want to follow, his reasoning.


*Warring on Predators*

During the Depression we lost the ranch to the bank, and I did not see the place again until I visited it some years after World War II. That afternoon I walked for miles, marveling at the changes. New technologies and payments from the soil conservation service had enabled the new owners to grub out the sagebrush and seed the fields to grass. The growth was too sparse to be called a meadow, but it shimmered in the wind, and unquestionably a cow needed fewer acres for her support than had been the case a quarter of a century before. I noticed, too, that I didn't see a single prairie dog mound. Not one black eye assessed me from anywhere.

That evening I told my host about our abortive efforts to eliminate prairie dogs.

He smiled, with what I thought was just a hint of condescension. "We've got a new poison now—1080." The numerals refer to deadly sodium fluoracetate. "It really gets them."

"Coyotes, too, I understand."

"Oh, absolutely. It's been a long time since anyone lost a lamb that way. We never hear them yapping any more."

"Jackrabbits?"

"No, they haven't come back because the coyotes are gone. The poison controls them, too. No trouble."

"Sage grouse?"

He quit smiling. "I know what you're thinking, and you're wrong. The grouse were done for before the poison programs started. It's the sheep trampling out their nests that got them."

A millennium—no more losses to varmints. Hungry men have been working toward the goal ever since the first irate farmer erected a scarecrow in his corn patch. Out on the plains dry farmers once tried to handle jackrabbits by means of concerted rabbit drives. Whole communities turned out. Scores of men armed with clubs formed into a wide circle and then advanced toward each other, shouting and banging on tin pans. The terrified rabbits fled between narrowing fence wings into a wire pen in the center of the shrinking circle. The men waded in with their clubs while the onlookers, women, children, and senior citizens, whooped and cheered.

Our wild-horse drives contained similar elements. Once every three or four years cowboys built a wing-gated corral in a region where the horses were known to run. Then the circling began. We called the animals broomtails, or broomies, from the way their long, unkempt tails dragged the brush. We supposed that they had escaped from neighboring farms and ranches over the years. The present-day controversy about whether or not the West's wild horses still carry the blood lines of old Spanish stock imported into New Mexico more than three centuries ago never troubled us. Mustang was a Texas word. Our horses were broomies, and all we wanted was to get them off the grass we used.

Although we seldom captured more than a portion of the terrified horses that we jumped, we enjoyed the outings—the wild riding, the meeting with men we saw only occasionally, the prank playing, the old jokes, the tried and true stories. If someone's fancy was taken by one of the captives, he roped it for breaking at home. The rest were starved into submissiveness. A few gentle animals were put among them, and the herd was driven off for sale to some horse dealer who probably shipped the animals to dog food factories. Once in a while cowboys with nothing to do would drive a band all the way to the Navajo Reservation and trade the horses to the Indians, mostly for blankets.

Predators that killed domestic animals were hunted even more mercilessly than were the competitors for grass. Eagles and hawks were shot and their limp bodies hung to fence wires, presumably as a warning for other marauders to leave the country. Bounty hunters used dogs for running down mountain lions, black bears, and coyotes—grizzlies and wolves had long since been extirpated from our part of the country. When those measures failed, a rancher could call for help on one of the trained trappers of the Biological Survey. Sportsmen, most of them from the cities, were vociferous in their support of the programs, arguing that the elimination of predators would make more deer and elk available for their rifles.

In spite of the concerted attacks, wild animals did a fair job of holding their own until modern technology overwhelmed them after World War II. Eagles were shot from helicopters. Wild horses were run down with speeding trucks or herded by low-flying airplanes. So far as I know, only two tiny bands remain in Colorado, one in the desolate lands north of McElmo Canyon in the Four Corners area, and the other beyond the Book Cliffs near the Utah border. But the truly massive killers were poisons like 1080. A few ounces of the stuff in a hundred pounds of grain or raw horsemeat will destroy anything that swallows even a morsel of the bait.


*The Problems of Poison*

Possession of such awesome power seemed to breed a lust to use it. Prairie dog villages became ghost towns. The chorusing of coyotes no longer was a familiar accompaniment of the rising moon. Stockmen rejoiced. So did game hunters, whose bags in Colorado alone rose to more than eighty thousand deer and fifteen thousand elk each year. Some of the hunters even grew self-congratulatory, seeing themselves as nature's new balancers. Without their quick and merciful thinning out of the herds, they proclaimed, scores of thousands of animals would be doomed to a lingering death by starvation.

What undid 1080 was the indiscriminate way in which it spread death.

Not only prairie dogs and coyotes fed on the bait in which it was concealed, but also eagles, hawks, owls, magpies, songbirds, foxes, bears, badgers, skunks, and squirrels. The deaths, moreover, were chainlike. Anything that fed on meat disgorged by a dying coyote also died. Presumably no one wanted to kill the sleek black-footed ferrets that preyed almost exclusively on prairie dogs, but the ferrets became almost extinct, nevertheless, with only a dozen or so still surviving in remote parts of South Dakota.

As news of the slaughter spread, the urban public, already shocked by Rachel Carson's protest in *Silent Spring* against the indiscriminate broadcasting of pesticides, raised such an outcry that in 1971 the use of poison on federal lands was forbidden. Most state governments, which determine policies of predator control on all other land, tightened down their poisoning programs and on the issuing of permits for the use of poisoned baits by private individuals.

The controversy stirred by the edicts still resounds in the Colorado back country, as it does in all the Western states. Hunters insist that the number of game animals is declining noticeably. A furious rancher in the combined store and post office that makes up most of the town of Slick Rock beside the muddy Dolores River told me that he personally knows three men who had to quit sheep raising because of damage done to their flocks by coyotes and cougars. The federal government, he said, leases public land to stockraisers and is duty-bound as a landlord to see to it that the pastures are clean and safe. If these damned city-bred protectionists had their money where their mouths are, they'd talk differently. Why don't they stay home and tend to what they know?

Even as notable a conservationist as Tom Lasater of Matheson, Colorado, whom we met in Chapter 5, considers state rules about poison to be an unwarranted encroachment on personal freedom. Years ago Lasater had eradicated the only prairie dog colony on his land and then, noticing that grass grew better on the site of abandoned dog towns than on adjoining land, probably because of minerals brought up by the digging rodents, he wished he hadn't. He tried replacing the lost animals with imports. His intent was to keep the new towns drifting in directions he desired by poisoning the back edges. Before his dog colonies became established, however, the new regulations went into effect, and he discovered that he could operate on his own land only as governmental agencies decreed. At that he pungently abandoned the experiment.

Opponents of poisoning have replies for all this. They say that if every rancher were allowed to establish his own standards, indiscriminate killings would again leap out of hand. They insist that no one yet knows what the trends in deer population are or what really is causing changes, if any. They scoff at pretensions about balancing nature. A hunter naturally aims for choice specimens, leaving the weak to perpetuate themselves, whereas predators strike down the unfit, to the ultimate improvement of the herd.

As for having money where mouths are, what of the fact that stockmen are being subsidized in that they pay less for federal leases than they would have to pay for comparable private property? Why, the conservationists continue, should the taxpayers also be expected to foot the bill for reckless predator control programs? Moreover, the management of public lands is everyone's business, not just the stockman's, because America's heritage of wildlife on the public domain is a national resource of inestimable value even to people who see nothing more of it than pictures.

*A Dog's Life, Prairie Style*

We talked about some of these matters as we slid out of Jim Hollenback's pickup truck and sat quietly in its shade, waiting for the dog town he had revealed to resume business. At first the main attraction was a scattering of burrowing owls, a delightful bird that for some reason never crossed the mountains to the Western Slope. They stood on prairie dog mounds like trim soldiers in barred brown uniforms, watching us with eyes as round and yellow as sunflowers. If you approach them, they crouch; their legs disappear and, except for their staring eyes, they look like little stumps. As you come nearer, young owls back slowly down the holes until all you see above the ground are those saucer eyes. Older birds fly off in short, bobbing courses to a nearby mound and resume their staring. Credulous city boys are told that if they keep walking around and around the watching owls, the birds will eventually twist their own heads off.

Once it was believed that burrowing owls shared dens with prairie dogs. Actually they nest only in abandoned burrows. In springtime they dine now and then on small pups, but they do not tackle adult dogs, which are as big as they are. Most of their hunting is for crickets and grasshoppers.

Other occupants of prairie dog burrows are rattlesnakes. They are numerous around the towns, for they too relish tender pups. Sometimes several snakes collect in a single burrow. Local snake hunters, Jim says, discover the congregations by thrusting a hose 10 or 12 feet into the tunnels. If a buzzing follows, they pour gasoline through the hose, and out come the snakes to be slaughtered by the sons of Eve.

Snakes and ferrets (before the days of 1080) were the most effective enemies of the prairie dog. Other predators have a hard time reaching them. Badgers can dig but are slow-moving. Coyotes are quick but can't dig well enough to catch them underground. The prairie dogs make stalking difficult by gnawing down any tall growth that might provide a raider with shelter. In an effort to swing the odds a little more on the side of the hunters, and thus quiet complaints about letting varmints get out of hand, the Forest Service has set up roosts for hawks and has built slatted fences, like snow fences, behind which coyotes and foxes can slink within pouncing range. So far a shortage of personnel has not allowed sufficient observation for conclusions about the effectiveness of the devices.

The site we were watching, like all other towns I recall, was nowhere near surface water. How, then, do prairie dogs drink? Occasionally the cowboys speculated about it over their whittling. Some opined that they dug deep community wells. Others thought that the little bits of juice in the brown grass they ate sufficed. The facts, from what I read, are even more amazing: their digestive tracts are capable of converting food starches into moisture, so that they never have to drink.

Like most wild animals, prairie dogs are very wary of a human afoot, but pay little attention to automobiles. Soon gray heads began poking cautiously above the rims of the mounds. Not distinguishing us as people in the shadows of the pickup, the colony resumed its routines.

It is easy to grow sentimental about the creatures. They are about a foot long, fat, saucy, and strident. They look nothing like dogs and used to be called barking squirrels. They live in clans, or coteries. A member of one coterie quarrels and nips on encountering a member of a family group from the other side of town. Every now and then some chunky clan patriarch rears up on his haunches and yips out his territorial claims for all to hear. Belligerence vanishes, however, within the coterie. Members greet with what humans would call a kiss, and often stand upright nuzzling affectionately as they groom each other's soft, lustrous hair. Their barks of warning are for everyone. When the tocsin sounds, there is a general scurrying and diving, followed by that cautious eye-above-the rim appraisal.

As the sheepmen say, we can live without prairie dogs, ferrets, coyotes, and lions, just as we have learned to live without passenger pigeons and auks. Unquestionably, too, stockraisers and grain farmers do need some protection when predators grow increasingly numerous and bold. But how long we can live with the kind of arrogance that prefers to meet competition, either industrial or animal, by ruthlessly eliminating it regardless of side effects may be something else.

Anyway, for myself I am glad that in spite of 1080 a few special places remain where it is possible to sit for a while on the warm earth, watching nothing more exciting than a few survivors of a grim war go about their timeless business.

# 11
# FAREWELL TO A RIVER

A while back word came from the Bureau of Reclamation that travel on Colorado's Gunnison River between the influx of the Cimarron and the east boundary of the Black Canyon of the Gunnison National Monument would shortly be forbidden.

Except to a handful of people who cherish the area, the announcement was hardly earth-shaking. The interdicted stretch of water is only 10 or 12 miles long. But it is wild, really wild, and the first reaction of some of us to the ban was a determination to go back one last time. There would be the excitement of running the rapids in small rubber rafts. There would be a never-again chance to try our flies on what is one of the finest reaches of trout water in the United States. But mostly it would be a salute—and a farewell.

The stretch is a sort of remnant, a snippet left over from bigger concerns. First the government, in 1938, encased the magnificent lower part of the Black Canyon within the bounds of a National Monument. It is a spectacular section. The dusky walls, rising almost perpendicularly in places, are nearly half a mile high. Some of the giant cliff slabs are laced with bands of pink pegmatite that zigzag downward like congealed lightning bolts. Breathless spires, inappropriately called rock islands, soar at the end of crumbling thin arêtes separating side channels. The river twists through the abyss like a rumpled string. At the bottom of the Narrows—old-timers called the place the jaws—the cliffs are only 40 feet apart.

Rock climbers eager for more challenge than is offered by most of the rounded peaks of the Rockies visit the sheer walls in increasing numbers.

Hardy fishermen clamber down the few negotiable side channels in search of 3- and 4-pound trout. Once in a great while a party of raftmen try to push through the great slit but find themselves frustrated by piles of mammoth boulders that in places completely cover the howling stream.

Of necessity, adventure in the canyon is supervised and to that extent ceases to be a true wilderness experience. You are supposed to check in with the rangers before entering the canyon, and while you are in you have an uneasy awareness of dozens, even hundreds of eyes peering down from the rims. To those who prefer solitude it is as disconcerting as a roll of dislodged stones.

*The Dam Syndrome*

The upper part of Gunnison's Black Canyon has been tamed by dams that are part of the multi-billion-dollar Colorado River Storage Project, designed to slake the thirst of communities as far away as Los Angeles. The first you meet as you travel downstream is the earth-and-rock Blue Mesa Dam, completed in 1965. The barrier creates a reservoir whose shoreline, when the lake is full, winds for 96 miles around once-desolate sagebrush plains, the largest body of water in Colorado. Blue Mesa drowned miles of superlative river fishing. Much of that water was privately held, however, and available only to those willing to meet the demands of the resort owners that lined both banks of the pinnacle-bordered stream. Now the lake, heavily stocked with both trout and kokanee salmon, is open to everyone, the most heavily used recreation area in the state. Blue Mesa, a blue jewel in a dry country, also produces numerous kilowatts of power. So perhaps it would be misplacing values to cavil too stridently.

Below Blue Mesa and just above the junction of the Cimarron and Gunnison rivers is the newer, taller Morrow Point Dam. The canyon above Morrow Point is—was—narrow and deep. As a result the water behind Morrow Point nowhere overflows the rock rims, as it does at Blue Mesa Reservoir. The impounded lake is long and stringy, its edges scalloped by an irregular sequence of dark cliffs. The evergreens between the cliffs are stately; the water on which the powerboats of the vacationists float is a deep greenish blue. It is very beautiful and very placid.

Below Morrow Point and above the boundaries of Black Canyon National Monument is that 10- or 12-mile stretch of wild river mentioned earlier. For a time it seemed forgotten. No one supervised it. The hand of man had never altered it, except insofar as controlling stream flow at the dams is an alteration. It was seldom visited. You cannot walk along the banks because of the way the gray-brown granite precipices rise straight up from cold river pools of great depth. Casual boatmen shun the rapids. They are numerous and fierce, for the Gunnison drops faster throughout the course of the Black Canyon than does any other river in the United States except the Yellowstone in its chromatic gorge. Because the stretch is short, commercial operators have not been tempted to overcome the obstacles. And so for a few years that little bit of wild stream stayed wild.

A wasted stream, the Bureau of Reclamation decided, and set about filling it with another reservoir, to be held in place by what would be called, very brightly, Crystal Dam. The justification is hard to discern. Whenever Blue Mesa and Morrow Point fill completely, Crystal will hold some of their overflow. Proportionately speaking, the amount will be meager. Crystal's generators will produce less than half as much electric power as Blue Mesa's, less than a quarter as much as Morrow Point's. In Washington, however, those fractions seem worth more than the lift a rare bit of untrammeled stream can give to human hearts. And so the announcement came. The river was to be closed to travel lest incautious boatmen venture within range of boulders dislodged from the canyon walls by the concussion of dynamite blasts. After the blasting, the construction. After the construction, the drowning.

*Preparations*

A salute and a farewell: the impulse originated with Duane Vandenbusche—Bush when he is in the canyons. Track coach, headlong skier, and tennis player, Vandenbusche is a professor of history at Western State College in the town of Gunnison. He is also one of the very few people who have coursed the full length of the Black Canyon with a rubber raft, boosting it across cliff faces and over water-smoothed boulders more often than he floated in it.

With Bush was one of his former students, Chuck Cliggitt, track star and champion cross-country skier, officially tapped in 1972 as one of America's outstanding athletes. With Chuck was his wife, Mary Jean, another award-winning skier, brown-eyed and lithe, her curly dark hair cut close. And Marianne Viiding, fresh from Norway, where she had found recreation training race horses. Predictably Marianne—she insists on the Norwegian pronunciation Mah-ri-ah′-na—was as blond as Mary Jones was dark and just as tall and supple and lovely.

My wife Mildred and I were—well, older. But our connections with the canyon were older, too. I had fished for trout in the Narrows—the jaws—before the Monument had been set aside. Another time, also before the establishment of the Monument, four other then-young men and I had supposed we could do what had never been done before—walk in February upstream over the ice through the Narrows to an egress point near where Crystal Dam is to be built. The misjudged stunt ended in an ordeal of rope traverses across icy cliff faces in order to avoid the ice-flecked black water beneath, of frustrating struggles with boulder falls polished as smooth as glass by stream scouring, of collapsing ice bridges, and, on the rim, once we'd regained the rim, of wallowing endlessly through crusted, knee-deep snow. No, we didn't get through. But it was a canyon contact, and so Bush invited Mildred and me to join the farewell—historic relics, as it were.

We hit the river just as the sun was gilding the tips of the spires downstream from Morrow Point. We had two blue-and-orange "five-man" rafts of artificial rubber; actually each could hold comfortably only three persons and their gear. Each contained only a single air compartment (the raft we had used earlier on the Yampa, as described in Chapter 2, had been divided into several compartments) and they were dangerously light for this kind of river. We chose them, nevertheless, because we would be able to carry nothing heavier when we left the canyon above the interdicted dam site and climbed up the walls to the automobiles waiting on top. We also had six paddles, some stout cord, and a life jacket apiece. In addition to our food we had two plastic 5-gallon jugs of drinking water. Although the stream escaping from the dam was a profoundly clear, deep indigo delight, towns and tens of thousands of recreationists lay upstream, and so we thought we'd better take along recycled tapwater. So much for true wilderness.

We did not carry cooking gear because we hoped to use pots, pans, and a grill left some time ago by Vandenbusche and his fishing companions on a grassy, timbered flat 8 or 9 miles downstream. We each had sweaters and a complete change of dry clothing, but no sleeping bags. For the sake of saving space and weight, we intended to sleep on the ground, fully clad and rolled up in ponchos. I put my bulky camera in a plastic bag to protect it from spray and hung it around my neck. A waterproof iron ammunition box of the sort carried on organized river trips would have been too heavy to lug when the time came to clamber out of the canyon.

Recent rains had turned the Cimarron khaki-hued, but the clear water of the Gunnison absorbed the stain with only a tinge of discoloration. The early morning air was cold, and we were atingle with anticipation as we shoved off, Bush, Marianne, and I in the first boat, Chuck, Mary Jean, and Mildred in the second.

### White Water

Not as much water was being passed through Morrow Point Dam as we had anticipated, and so the current lacked the awesome surge that had characterized the spring-flooded Yampa. The Yampa's rapids, however, are much more widely spaced than the Gunnison's. The Gunnison is one of the steepest big rivers on the continent; it drops an average of 43 feet per mile in the Black Canyon as compared to 7.5 feet per mile for the Colorado River in the Grand Canyon. Rapids, often twisting violently around protruding cliffs, follow each other with stunning speed. Except in back eddies, the water flows with deceptive speed through the short stretches of quiet water that punctuate the white froth.

From previous encounters Vandenbusche and Cliggitt knew which of the tumults ahead marked a major cataract. Whenever we neared one, they had us land and walk ahead to study the run. Often it was difficult to pick out the main channel. Instead of being constricted, the water raged in a perplexity of passageways between multitudes of white and red and black boulders. We'd debate, occasionally toss in a small log to see how it traveled, then point to what seemed best, return to the rafts, position them, and shove off again.

If the bowman sat in the bottom of the raft, he could not reach deep enough into the water with his paddle to be effective, yet he dared not sit on the rounded prow itself. So he compromised, either kneeling or crouching as he swung his blade and bawled out his directions at the top of his lungs. Most of the work of holding the raft to the direction chosen by the bowman fell on whoever was in the stern, and a shoulder-wrenching job it was. The middle person—generally Mildred or I—had it best, sitting atop the lashed-in duffel and paddling frantically on one side or the other as the exigencies of each mad instant seemed to demand.

It is an indescribable thrill to hurtle toward water cascading into a deep hole and then, just as destruction seems inevitable, to feel the paddles bite and the boat veer away to safety. Or to aim deliberately toward a dripping boulder with the knowledge that if all goes well, your apparent recklessness is proper, for just as your breath begins to catch, the backlash of the current hits the raft a giant slap and thrusts it back where it needs to be. By the time we shot, drenched with spray, out into the feathered tail of each rapid, we were all whooping joyously, again and again.

Earlier we had talked of lining the rafts through the worst rapids—that is, disembarking and working the craft down close to shore by means of cords tied to the bow and stern of each. After some miles we came to a place where the caution seemed necessary.

There the main current was constricted. Almost the entire river roared through a channel between mammoth boulders to split itself on a prow of rock hundreds of feet high. The left part of the sundered water dashed into a maelstrom from which there was no escape. Trapped in there, one could not jump ashore, for "shore" consisted of a cove of glass-smooth cliffs, and of course there was no way back through the roaring current. So to run the rapid a boat would have to avoid both the eddy and the knife-edged cliff, trying to skim the right side of the slab with enough clearance so that the raft would not be dangerously scoured by the rough granite. It is not easy. Half a dozen years ago four Air Force men on leave had died while trying, and now the place is called Dead Men's Point.

With some difficulty we lined the first raft past the obstruction. Chuck and Bush went back to start lining the second raft—or so we thought. Mary Jean suspected first. She stood up suddenly, and the next instant we all saw that temptation had won. The two men were running the point.

Frantic with alarm, Mary Jean yelled epithets that her husband of course could not hear. The rest of us froze. It wasn't long. They missed both the eddy and the blade edge, but they hit the slabby side of the cliff a shuddering blow. One of them lost a paddle. Then spray obscured them. When we could see them again they had, by desperate reaching and great good luck, retrieved the whirling paddle and were driving hard for quiet water. When we scrambled down to meet them they were grinning broadly, and Mary Jean grew still more vocal. That risk just to say goodbye?

When trouble came, it was anticlimactic. Bush, Marianne, and I had taken the first boat—not the one that had run Dead Men's Point—through another rapid and were exulting in the froth at its foot when we felt as sickening a sensation as I, at least, have ever experienced. A valve had somehow sprung loose and the bright little blue-and-orange raft was deflating.

We paddled frenziedly toward shore. No use; the current was too swift. Bush pitched out first. He tried to hang onto the bow cord, but lost it. Marianne, though, managed to seize hold of the stern cord as she went out. When I came up, camera dangling around my throat, I saw a paddle bobbing out front. All I could think was that if we still had a raft, we might need paddles. I recovered it and kicked ashore. Praise be for life jackets.

Marianne had caught hold of the snout of a rusty-colored boulder protruding from the narrow bank. The limp raft had swung downstream like a yo-yo at the end of its cord and was threatening to pull her loose. Bush, thrashing up a froth in his life jacket, caught the craft and wrestled it ashore, relieving the tug. I floundered to the dry side of the boulder and held out the paddle handle. She caught it and pulled herself ashore. Thanks to the firm lashings that held our gear we lost only a single 5-gallon jug of drinking water. Plus one camera, quietly expiring in a sackful of river water

The valve proved impossible for us to repair. What now? Because of the cliffs that ever so often dropped into deep, fast water, we could not move ahead or back on foot. Nor could we, at that point, climb the canyon walls. Of necessity we piled our salvaged gear and the capsized boat into the one remaining, fragile craft, already hard used at Dead Men's Point. Then all six of us wedged aboard and off we went, looking like a cartoon of the survivors of a stricken ocean liner. All we needed was a flag fluttering at the end of a broken oar and the captain's wife carrying a parrot in a cage.

If an approaching rapid looked troublesome, some of us would disembark and skirt it afoot while the others took the raft through. This was slow work, however, and so whenever we dared we ran the white water, heavily overloaded, shipping curling waves into our laps, and yelling full throat to hide what in my case was considerable apprehension. We were glad to reach camp shortly after noon, spread our soaked clothing on sun-warmed white rocks to dry, and eat a soggy lunch. It was a pretty nook: evergreens, box elders, a cottonwood, and straggles of grass and rushes. Out front the white-fretted river roared endlessly.

A hard rain fell late in the afternoon. We sat it out, close-packed under a shelter patched together out of our ponchos and a piece of black plastic that had been used to cover the little table and the cooking utensils left by earlier visitors. The stream grew roily and we mourned the fishing.

About an hour before sunset the rain stopped. By twilight the water was clearing and we jointed our rods. Marvelous!—rainbow trout hunted no more than two or three times a year, if that often. We kept only as many as we could eat—Chuck had one 18 inches long—and at dark gathered around the fire. A delicious meal topped with roasted marshmallows, some sleepy banter, and we went to bed right there on the ground in clothes still faintly damp in spite of our care. The clearing skies brought a cold drift of air down the canyon. We huddled close for warmth, trying not to twitch when pebbles dug into hip or shoulder. It was a long night.

*Climbing Out*

We broke camp early, traveled a short distance downstream, and ferried ourselves across the river to the mouth of a narrow side canyon. This was Crystal Creek, source of the name of the dam-to-be, and our exit. We deflated the raft, folded it and its collapsed companion into tight bundles, and lashed each onto a backpack frame, one for Cliggitt, one for Vandenbusche. How much each pack weighed, I do not know; it was plenty. The rest of us divided up the remaining gear in our day packs and assumed responsibility for the paddles. Then up, toward the cars that the girls had taken to the head of Crystal Canyon the day before our departure.

There was no sign of a trail. The tiny stream wove intricate plaits and danced in miniature cascades amid a narrow, ascending line of boulders. The

69. Plateau country: Loghill Mesa beside the Uncompahgre River. Note the parallel lines on the mesa top, left center. Huge tractors with a chain stretched between them have uprooted windrows of trees in an effort to restore grass to the range.

70. The Sun Temple, Mesa Verde National Park.

71. Part of Long House, Wetherill Mesa, the most recently opened section of Mesa Verde.

72. The climax of Anasazi culture was the famed Cliff Palace in Mesa Verde. Why it was abandoned, no one really knows. One sobering theory suggests that the Ancient Ones abused the land to the point that it could no longer support them.

73. Isolated buttes girt with rimrock, like this one near Mesa Verde National Park, are a striking feature of the mesa and plateau country.

74. Sunset flushes the tawny north rim of Mesa Verde.

75. Some farmer built this rock house in McElmo Canyon near the Four Corners area, planted Lombardy poplars to soften the harsh lines of the land—and then, for forgotten reasons, walked away.

76. Sun without warmth: winter in the Gunnison country.

77. *A dazzle of light engulfs the Wilson Massif in the San Miguel Mountains of southwestern Colorado.*

78. The volcanic tuff that borders the headwaters of Cimarron Creek has been carved into grotesque patterns by trickles of melting snow.

79. Granite pinnacles along the edge of the Black Canyon show that wind, ice, and water really have been stronger than rock.

steep banks on either side were dense with brush and brambles. Above were gray cliffs a thousand feet high, glinting with mica and topped with tremendous spires. The only possible avenue was to teeter from stone to stone. We did it carefully. All of us were wearing lightweight tennis shoes, fine gear for rafting, but not, because of their slippery soles, the best choice for wet rocks. I fear the relics in the party held the others back considerably.

Noon was near before sunshine cleared the clifftops, and we began to feel its weight on our burdened backs. Sweating copiously, we halted in a grassy opening for lunch—a candy bar each. As we relaxed, adjusting to the strange sensation of lightness that comes from slipping off heavy packs, Mary Jean said into the silence, "A trip like this makes you glad to be alive. That *phtt* raft, your camera—they don't count. Only being alive."

Supposing that she meant it was better to be gasping in this chasm than to be tumbling along the bottom of the river with a camera wound round my throat and a salvaged paddle clutched in my lifeless hand, I agreed. But her perceptions were broader than that, as I slowly came to realize during the rest of the ascent.

It was a hard climb. The canyon narrowed steadily. The jumble of boulders that filled the bottom grew in size until some were bigger than houses. We boosted each other up the cracks in the giant piles when we could, bulled around them through clutching brush when we had to, and now and then crawled underneath through cold, gravelly caverns chiseled out by the little stream. Eventually we topped out—we would have used a rope on the last cliff if we'd had a rope—and then, as I looked back down the giant slit, I think I at last grasped something of what Mary Jean had meant.

She meant aliveness, not just being alive. She meant the preternatural alertness that comes to your senses when you find yourself nose to nose with challenges like this. Intense concentration and then the sweetness of rest. The satisfaction of looking back and knowing how little you really needed in order to get where you wanted to go. Camera, one leaky raft, sleeping bags, climbing boots, rope—she was right, none of it had mattered in the pinch. What had counted, outside of ourselves, had been helping hands unstintingly offered when needed and unabashedly taken. That had made the difference.

We walked wearily along a cattle trail to the cars, reached the paved Black Mesa road, and turned toward Gunnison. It is a beautiful drive, particularly if you are going upcountry. You are on the outside then. Here and there, where the aspen forests open briefly at the head of side canyons, you can catch fine views of the giant buttresses on the far wall of the main abyss. We stared hard. Where had the raft sunk? Which of those monstrous ribs ended in Dead Men's Point?

Then we came abreast of Morrow Point Dam. Its aquamarine waters were lovely and quiet and dead. We leaned back against the seats, not looking any longer. The run was over.

Forever.

# 12
# THE SALTS OF PARADOX: SERENDIPITY IN REVERSE

It seems that Paradox Valley in western Colorado has been troubling 10 million water users in Arizona, Southern California, and northern Mexico. For a secluded valley 24 miles long and from 3 to 5 miles wide, this is an unusual accomplishment—so unusual that the United States Bureau of Reclamation has been called on to meet the challenge.

The problem is a mass of salt nearly 3 miles thick buried originally under beds of sedimentary rock laid down by ancient seas. The uplifting of mountains on either side of this area created intense lateral pressures that rumpled the section into long pleats called anticlines. During the rumpling, the sandstone that roofed the dome-shaped anticlines was heavily fractured and thus made susceptible to erosion. The result in time was a series of long valleys chiseled out of the tops of the parallel, ridgelike anticlines. Paradox is the largest of these valleys.

Before Paradox was completely eroded another geologic cataclysm shook the area, just west of the present Colorado-Utah border. Molten igneous rock flowed in between the beds of salt and sandstone and buckled them upward still higher. On solidifying, this igneous intrusion became what is known as a laccolith, or "bubble" mountain. The central part of the oval mass rests in the northwestern part of the Paradox anticline. Eventually weather stripped the sandstone cap from the laccolith and produced a handsome, triple-peaked mountain visible from scores of miles away.

Because the highest peak of the laccolith reaches an elevation of 13,000 feet, it catches considerable precipitation. Water coursing down the flanks of the mountain into the fractured anticline quickened the chiseling of its dome into a spectacular, cliff-walled valley, whose floor lies nearly 8,000 feet below the peaktops.

These upheavals occurred after the Dolores River had already established a course that in this area trends northward toward the Colorado River. Declining to change its ancestral ways because of the anticline gradually rising across its path, the river chewed a way through. The result is some strange and spectacular scenery.

One striking feature is the anomaly of a river that goes directly across Paradox Valley instead of flowing along it. Such creeks as do follow the valley, generally underground, are rivulets of brine. This brine is created by storm waters dissolving the underlying beds of salt.

The underground flows ooze into the Dolores River from both ends of the valley. According to careful measurements by the Bureau of Reclamation the river picks up during an average year approximately 200,000 *tons* of salt, or almost 550 tons each and every day. The Dolores carries these trainloads of dissolved salt to the Colorado River in Utah, and the Colorado in turn wafts them on to the irrigated farms of the Southwest.

Some of the area's peculiarities were first noted officially by Ferdinand V. Hayden, who led a government surveying party through the then-uninhabited region in 1874. He called the hollowed anticline Paradox Valley because of the nonchalant way in which the Dolores struck across it rather than flowing along it. His party found salt flats and salt springs here and there throughout the trough and high on the sides of the laccolith that overlooks it in so striking a manner. Accordingly Hayden gave the name La Sal (The Salt) Mountains to the triple-peaked uplift.

It is an amazing country. An effective way to approach it is from the west, down La Sal Canyon, a deep, shaggily beautiful, cliff-bordered, perfectly normal watercourse that flows roughly parallel to the abnormal trough of Paradox. After climbing high onto the north side of the canyon, the paved road veers sharply left through khaki-colored rock and with breathtaking suddenness emerges onto the rim of the valley.

Seen from this vantage point, Paradox is a magnificent, wide, flat-bottomed gouge running from northwest to southeast between bright red precipices. From the road the peaks of the La Sals are not visible—just the deeply seamed, black-forested, red-soiled hills that close off the northwestern end of the trough. Settlers in what is known as West Paradox have captured the water that flows down that steep slope in Buckhorn Reservoir and use it for irrigating about 3,600 acres of alfalfa that during the winter is fed to cattle and sheep. The emerald fields contrast vividly with the red soil and red cliffs. Protected yet open, colorful and fertile, the secluded spot looks like a desert Shangri-La—if you don't mind almost total isolation.

The loose patchwork of hayfields reaches as far as the Dolores River, meandering across the valley near its midpoint. Beyond the river in East Paradox there is no fresh water and the land, its gypsum-streaked soil grown to scraggly greasewood and runty sage, looks shunned and forsaken, as it is.

Near the point where the river emerges from the southern cliffs is a combination store and post office and two or three shacks named Bedrock. The canyon into which Bedrock looks is sometimes called Slick Rock Canyon because it begins some 50 river miles upstream near another store-post office combination known as Slick Rock. Few places in the land are more lonesome than that canyon—roadless, uninhabited, seldom visited even by cattlemen. The river twists through enormous clover-leaf curves. Pools are long and quiet, fretted only occasionally by boulder-studded rapids. The walls, mostly of deep red sandstone blotched by black stains of desert varnish, are weirdly eroded and in places freckled with the mud nests of busy swallows. Here and there the current has undercut the bases of the cliffs to form arches that lean ponderously out across the streambed. Whenever enough water flows through Slick Rock Canyon to support rafts (generally in May), the trip is well worthwhile.

The river's history fits its looks. For instance: a short distance up La Sal Creek from its junction with the Dolores are the remnants of the Cashin Mine, for several years a rich producer of copper and in 1921 the scene of a bizarre murder. The killing sprang from the ambitions of several would-be outlaws who, enamored of Paradox Valley's isolated location, decided to make it their base of operations. Local inhabitants were to be terrorized into cooperation. One step in the program of fear was an announcement that the gang's work could be recognized by the decapitation of its victims.

The first to fall into the toils of the thugs was the watchman at the Cashin Mine, Lem Hecox, who habitually carried $3,000 to $4,000 in a money belt strapped about his waist. The outlaws slew him one November day. After robbing him, they cut off his head, hid his body in a pile of oats, and rode away with the severed member wrapped in a yellow slicker tied behind one of their saddles. An unconfirmed tale that I firmly believed in my youth insists that they halted at Bedrock, where a dance was in progress, tied their horses to the hitching rack outside, and sparked some of the local girls before continuing to the point where they disposed of the head.

Hecox's body was found, by smell, a few days later. Taken to the Paradox cemetery it was buried, as were all other deceased members of the community, in a coffin hastily extemporized from rare sawn lumber by a rancher doubling as carpenter and undertaker. Still later, detectives hired by the owners of the mine captured key members of the gang and persuaded them to reveal the location of the head. Some of Paradox's more sensitive members, feeling that the head should join its body in eternal rest, exhumed the coffin, only to find that it had been measured to an exact fit of the headless corpse. Since no one was willing to donate enough boards for a new coffin, the head was tucked into one of the corpse's folded arms, and the deceased was recommitted to the salty earth in the original box.

Most of the valley's other problems are more prosaic and predictable. One is the cattle's annual springtime struggle with temptation. On emerging from Slick Rock Canyon at Bedrock, the river enters a series of meanders bordered by scattered cottonwood trees, willow clumps, and treacherous mud flats. The first grass of spring grows on the warming mud. Hungry cattle venture out to get it and are sucked down by the bog until their barrel-like bodies check further submersion. Exhausted by their struggles to escape, they flop over onto one side. Their heads begin to droop. Sometimes crows start pecking out their eyes even before their nostrils fill with water and they drown—unless rescued first by cowboys delegated to "ride bog." These knights-errant in dirty blue jeans shove driftwood logs out beside the trapped creatures, teeter along the supports, and grunting profanely affix ropes to the animals so that they can be pulled loose with horses. On reaching solid ground the salvaged cattle, frenzied with fear, often try to gore their saviors.

The canyon by which the river leaves Paradox Valley is also dark red and sinuous. Here a dirt road runs beside the stream to the deeply engorged junction of the Dolores and San Miguel rivers, the latter of which arrives from the east. Big catfish lurk in the eddies set into motion by the commingling of muddy waters.

On the side of the river opposite the road is an amazing, horizontal prickle of badly weathered timbers protruding half a dozen feet from the face of the cliffs. Braces angling upward from a lower line of sockets drilled into the cliff support the outer ends of the protruding timbers. Not much else remains—in fact, only some of the braced timbers are still in place, but enough to help you picture the big hanging flume that once ran for miles along the canyon wall, 150 feet or so above the water and, in places, as much as 300 feet below the rim of the cliffs.

The purpose of the flume, which tapped the San Miguel River a couple of miles above its junction with the Dolores, was to provide water for placer gold mines on a high bench another 6 miles or so down the canyon. The work of building it lasted from 1889 through 1891 and cost about $175,000—say ten times that much in terms of today's currency. Whenever possible the workers who drilled the holes into which the support timbers nestled were suspended in rope slings from the rims above. Often, though, this procedure would not work because of overhangs. In such cases the men swung into place by a long crane attached to a car that ran on rails laid along the finished portion of the flume.

Unhappily the gold that the operation was designed to recover proved to be too fine to be captured by the technologies then available. The operation collapsed, and the manager committed suicide.

Other strenuous mining activities were precipitated during the early 1900s by the discovery of yellow carnotite ores from which compounds of uranium could be extracted. At first uranium was used as a source of radium. During World War II it became desirable again as a producer of atomic power. Carnotite also contains vanadium, valuable in making durable steel alloys. Again prospectors swarmed through the rough desert canyons and the strangely shaped basins that lie on the mesas between Paradox Valley and the rivers that twine nearby, the Dolores and the San Miguel.

One center for processing the carnotite ores produced by the new stampede was a gaunt, discolored mill that crawled up the steep slope bordering the south side of the San Miguel 2 miles above its junction with the Dolores—almost exactly opposite the point where the old hanging flume received its load of water. This mill brings us back to our starting point, because the reduction of carnotite ore requires quantities of sodium chloride. To get this vital salt, engineers from the mill drilled a well into the underground rivulets of brine oozing from East Paradox into the Dolores River. Some of the brine that the well produced was evaporated in nearby salt ponds; more was pumped through a pipeline down the Dolores and up the San Miguel to the mill.

The process impressed the engineers of the United States Bureau of Reclamation. They were facing a difficult assignment. The average salinity of water stored behind the Imperial Dam on the lower Colorado River near Yuma, Arizona, was found to be 850 milligrams of salt per liter. Moreover the salt content was rising. Predictions said that unless corrective measures were taken at once, the salt concentrations at Imperial might reach 1,200 milligrams per liter by the year 2000. Inasmuch as salt damage to crops in 1973 had amounted to $53 million, further increases could bring the toll to $124 million a year by the end of the century.

American and Mexican farmers in the Southwest raised such a stir that the Bureau of Reclamation was ordered to rid the Colorado River of 1.5 million tons of salt per year. A search for villains began, and at once baleful eyes riveted on Paradox Valley. *There* was the source of an annual 200,000 tons of the economically poisonous stuff.*

Experiments indicated that a fence of wells drilled on either side of the Dolores River where it crosses the valley would suck up 180,000 tons of brine before it reached the stream. As plans stood in the fall of 1974, this brine would be pumped by pipeline out of the valley to a desolate basin about 20 miles away. There it would be impounded in a solar evaporation facility to be called Radium Reservoir in honor of early-day carnotite mines located in the vicinity. Radium Reservoir might last, according to Bureau calculations, for one hundred years, at the end of which time it would be filled with what surely will be one of the world's largest artificial salt heaps, some 18 million tons in weight.

The effort will subtract from the Colorado River roughly 12 percent of the 1.5 million tons of salt that the Bureau hopes to eliminate each year. It will reduce the salinity of the water at Imperial Dam by 15 milligrams per liter, or 2 per cent of the 850 milligrams currently polluting the water there. Triv-

---

* Other saline springs, along with seeping irrigation water in the valleys near Grand Junction, add to the Colorado's unwanted load. Paradox, however, is the chief culprit.

ial? Not really, the Bureau says, because an annual reduction of 16 milligrams of salt per liter will benefit the water users of the Southwest by $3.68 million per year—assuming that the crops that are freed from salt retardation then escape bugs and market declines.

One element is not touched on in these studies. The flow of salt out of Paradox has been constant for several millennia, and probably will stay constant for as long as any considerable portion of the 3-mile-thick salt bed under the valley floor remains undissolved. Yet the concentration of salt in the lower Colorado River increases each year. Why?

The chief villain is not steady old Paradox but rather the Bureau of Reclamation's own proliferating dams, aided by the dams of all the other agencies that store water on the Colorado River drainage system. In the dry, hot, windy climate of the intermountain West, water evaporates rapidly from reservoirs, an action that concentrates the saline solutions present in every stream. Moreover, as Professor Thomas M. Griffiths of the University of Denver points out, the flushing action of spring floods vanishes whenever a stream is dammed. The mud with which most salts are associated no longer rolls turbulently into the Colorado River and on to the Gulf of California, but settles instead in the reservoirs. During the period of storage, the mud's burden of salt is thoroughly dissolved and dispersed throughout the accumulating water, adding still more to the concentrations caused by evaporation.

Once upon a time it was thought that gigantic reservoirs would be the economic saviors of the arid West. Bureaucratic momentum has kept that belief rolling for scores of years. But not all our tamperings with nature are serendipitous. Unanticipated salinity, in fact, is the reverse. The engineers of the Bureau of Reclamation are aware of this. They themselves predict that further "development" of the upper Colorado River system—that is, more dams—will lift the levels of salt at Yuma, Arizona, to at least 1,200 milligrams per liter by A.D. 2000. Yet the Bureau keeps on planning dams.

There is only one Paradox capable of serving as an engineering scapegoat. After the bulk of its salt has been eliminated, what then can be done? One obvious answer is simply to say "No!" to plans already in existence for imprisoning some of the last free streams in the mountain West. At least there would be no new reservoirs to add to the problems of salinity. And as a serendipitous side effect we would still be able to hear, in the valleys that survive, the sound of running water.

PART FOUR

*Byways*

# 13
# MARMOTS AND MARBLE

On a clear day you can see almost forever from a jeep, "jeep" in this case being a generic term still used throughout Colorado to mean any four-wheel-drive vehicle. The rugged byways that these metallic work horses are capable of traveling not only put their occupants into the middle of the high country's scenic drama of sky and peak, but also afford long glimpses back into the past and ahead toward an uncertain future. Scores of such roads could be described, but space and patience would run out. So this account will limit itself to two that are exciting because of the variety they offer along their twining courses.

The one that this chapter will follow begins where the pavement ends just beyond a clutter of blocky condominiums sprawling out from the bottom of the ski runs near Crested Butte. Except for dust and narrowness, the route offers no problems at first, and low-slung cars can follow it for several miles.

The way hangs on a terrace high above the meandering East River. The fields are massed with wild flowers. In July just outside the ski center the most conspicuous of them are tall yellow composites, a family whose relatives often look so much alike that amateur botanists, and I am one, are hard put to separate one member from another. Those lying like spilled sunshine on the slopes above East River are, I'll guess, gaillardia mixed with arrowleaf balsamroot. Anyway they are big and flashily rayed, overpowering even the showy columbine, scarlet gilia, and lupine that struggle for footing among them. Botanical uncertainty in these parts is embarrassing, like not being able to distinguish bordeaux wine from burgundy in Paris. For here, 7 miles from the ski resort, in the old mining camp of Gothic, elevation 9,500 feet, is one of the unique educational institutions of the world, the Rocky Mountain Biological Laboratory. Until a year or so ago one stern yellow sign told travelers, "No Hunting or Picnicking in the Townsite." Another warned, "School Zone, 20 miles per hour." The relationship implicit in the yellow signs is even closer than that between yellow composite flowers. The entire town of Gothic is a school—or, if you prefer, vice versa.

In the beginning, that is in 1879, Gothic was a rambunctious silver mining town, proud of its hell-raising. One legend avers that when former President Grant visited Colorado in 1880, he asked to see the wildest camp in the state. As a matter of course he was taken to Gothic. He arrived in July, personally driving the big stagecoach that carried his entourage along the narrow road. A group of horsemen galloped out to meet him, firing their pistols into the air. Whether or not this added up to toughness in the mind of the man who had witnessed the goriest battles of the Civil War is a matter on which the records stay silent.

Another legend says that the name of the town came from a loose-jointed syllogism. Goths were barbarians. The prospectors swarming into the valley were also barbarians. Ergo, the place where most of them congregated should be called Gothic.

The trouble with that tale is the magnificent gray mountain that rises across the stream from the town. The couloirs that furrow its broad cliffs have created rock forms reminiscent of the arched windows running along the side of a Gothic cathedral. So it would seem that some barbarian was cultured enough to propose, and his fellow barbarians were understanding enough to accept, Gothic as the name of their new home. Moreover not all their pleasures consisted of bloody fights and orgiastic revels. During the early years, so a counter-rumor says, the townspeople's favorite recreation was to build a fire in the middle of Main Street and sit around it, smoking and telling stories. Prosperity did not last. The mines either ran out of ore or were crippled by the sharp drop of silver prices that came during the 1890s. By the opening years of the new century only one inhabitant remained, Gatwood H. Judd.

Inasmuch as the neighboring town of Crested Butte was also collapsing, Judd was lonesome at times. His only visitors were an occasional fisherman or hunter, and, with increasing frequency during the 1920s, carloads of students on field trips from Western State College at Gunnison, 35 miles to the south. Their mentor was Professor John C. Johnson of the Biology Department, who was fascinated by the adaptations that plants, birds, and animals make to high altitudes. The valley of the East River from Gothic to its head in the Elk Mountains appealed to him because of the number and diversity of specimens available for study.

Gradually Johnson began to dream of a wholly independent institution where interested students and researchers could watch plants and animals emerge from winter and follow them without interruption throughout the summer. Heartened by the encouragement of colleagues at several of America's leading universities, he turned in 1928 to the empty town of Gothic as a logical site for an instant school, to be called the Rocky Mountain Biological Laboratory.

Gatwood Judd, who had never lost faith that Gothic would again amount to something someday, was overjoyed. He prevailed on the absentee owners of the town's twenty-two-room ghost hotel and adjoining ten-stall livery stable to donate the buildings for use as classrooms, offices, and research library. The total cost—for recording the deeds—was $3. Johnson spent another $200 paying the delinquent taxes on the rest of the town's buildings and in that way obtained control of the townsite. In terms of labor it was no bargain. Fortified by student help, he and Judd cannibalized many of the tottering cabins in order to transform the rest into usable living quarters. Meanwhile his wife and her friends launched a crash program to make curtains, draperies, and closet hangings.

Living was—and to an extent is—Spartan. For years Gothic's residents carried their own household water from the creek and studied by kerosene lamps. In the 1950s the Lab at last installed an electric generator. It is for lighting purpose only, however; heating and cooking are still done by wood stove. Privies remain outdoors. One central wash and shower house is provided with hot water. Laundry is either done on an old-fashioned, corrugated scrubboard and put through a hand wringer, or else is driven to the recently installed laundromats at Crested Butte. Electronic communication with the outside is by radio. Since the operators at either end of the system are likely to be away on errands, contact is erratic.

Only three of the town's original buildings remain. Of the others, one burned; another was knocked off its foundations by a snowslide. Most, including the transformed hotel, died of normal attrition and had to be replaced by newer cabins. There is no pattern to the re-created town—just lots of space between buildings. No one bothers with yards. The native grass is tall and spangled with blue flax, asters, and the brilliant little yellow flowers of cinquefoil, a ubiquitous mountain member of the rose family. (You see what these botanical influences do to one.) Birds are everywhere. When first I met Dr. John C. Johnson, Jr., who succeeded his father as director of the Laboratory, he was out in front of his house with a hose, making mud that swallows could carry off for building nests.

The growth of the ski resort at Crested Butte ended Gothic's isolation. During July and August the cars of fishermen, campers, and sight-seers rattle incessantly and dustily along the county road that bisects the town. A year or two ago Johnson for the first time felt he had to hire a young couple to spend a snowbound winter in Gothic to guard against vandalism.

About seventy-five students and staff, divided about equally between men and women, attend the summer classes. They come from colleges and universities scattered across the nation. Some are undergraduates; more are postgraduates. Often a professor from some institution will recruit a cadre of his better students to help him with a project. Evening seminars are conducted two or three times a week by visiting VIPs in the fields of botany and biology. Paul Ehrlich, whose scholarly discipline is butterflies (butterflies congregate where so many flowers blossom), is a regular lecturer. Field trips to the Gothic Natural Area, an untouched 900-acre reserve of forest and tundra near the head of East River, are a staple.

Most of the students have never been in the mountains before and consequently find the living experience as enthralling as their scientific work. Although they can easily drive to Crested Butte and Gunnison for recreation, they spend many of their weekends backpacking in the high country. A popular two-day, 20-mile hike is up Copper Creek and across the Snowmass-Maroon Bells Wilderness area to Aspen. There the walkers pick up a car that other students have brought around by road. They drive the automobile back to Gothic while the erstwhile motorists return afoot.

Occasionally there are dissents. Sometimes a resident who is not a biolo-

80. *The Palisades of the Gunnison Country, seen across the frozen surface of the Blue Mesa Reservoir.*

81. March lays a faint lemon-yellow glow across a Tomichi Valley ranch in the Gunnison country.

82. *The peaceful Rocky Mountain Biological Laboratory occupies the site of the raucous old mining town of Gothic.*

83. *Patches of scarlet gilia, which may grow anywhere from the foothills almost to timberline, glow like embers in dry, open places. This field is near Gothic.*

84. This tottering old powerhouse near the remote town of Crystal is one of the best-known relics of the mining stampede.

85. Sunlit spruce and shadowed waterfall, Crystal Canyon.

86. Silver mines were sometimes located almost on the tops of the peaks in the Mosquito Range. This decaying building stands at about 13,000 feet beside the four-wheel-drive road over Mosquito Pass.

87. Parry's primrose, an exuberant mingler, here joins forces with marsh marigold.

OVERLEAF:
88. In spite of the densely inhabited urban strip along the Front Range, where 80 per cent of Colorado's population resides, the state still boasts miles of relatively untouched land. This view is from the Ten-Mile Range back of Breckenridge and looks toward the Mount of the Holy Cross.

89. Ice clamps down on a waterfall in the Front Range near Georgetown.

gist will arrive with a spouse who is. For such people, who feel excluded from an esoteric society knit together by common purposes, the days can grow monotonous. "You get so you even go walking in the rain," one young woman from Michigan told me. "You could learn to identify the flowers," I suggested. "Even the composites." She looked shocked. "Oh no! I want to enjoy them. They're all I have." She quoted Thoreau, rebelliously, as if she had been saving the ammunition for just this shot. " 'What sort of science is that which enriches the understanding but robs the imagination?' "

To the layman, some of the projects carried on at the Laboratory do sound arcane. One scientist from the University of Kansas is involved in a twelve-year study of yellow-bellied marmots. He captures them in live traps, marks them in certain ways, and turns them loose, painstakingly tracing what he calls their spatial distribution and population dynamics. Another investigates "the tactics of high-altitude dragonflies." A group from the University of Arizona spent considerable time studying the bioenergetics of hummingbirds. The tiny creatures burn up food so fast that at these altitudes they have trouble living overnight and often become torpid at dark, until the sun revives them. Yet the profusion of blossoms tempts them to follow the riot of nectar up the slopes toward extinction. Which flowers nourish them most? Why?

What about human beings? I asked Dr. Johnson. Did the Laboratory study their responses to altitude? He shook his head. "Our approach is academic, not utilitarian." He fixed me with a look that reminded me of the bored young wife. "But whatever knowledge we acquire about any kind of life is also relevant to human life."

Above Gothic the road follows the meandering East River through one of the loveliest of all high valleys. Every mountain color is here—blue pools of water, varied hues of grass and willows and aspen, dark tongues of fir, the intense green of tundra setting off snow-streaked summits of gray and maroon rocks. Where the valley forks, the ascending road swings left. It narrows, hanging high above aptly named Emerald Lake, but remains feasible for ordinary cars on over Schofield Pass (10,700 feet) to more wild-flower gardens at Schofield Park beside Crystal River. There a sign warns that the next 2 miles pitch through Crystal River Gorge on a 27 per cent grade. "Travel at Your Own Risk." You'd better believe it.

The first problem is the bridgeless ford across the Crystal River. It's a bright, hard-flowing stream quite different from the more indolent East River. (Its name, incidentally, comes from a locally common translucent quartz called crystallite.) Indeed, the whole aspect of the country has changed. It is shaggy, convulsed, and sliced by narrow canyons. As you pause to examine the main gorge, you hear from somewhere below the deep roar of what evidently is a giant waterfall.

The actual crossing of the river is not difficult. Potential trouble comes from the wetting that the jeep's brakes receive. The linings turn treacherous. Of the several fatalities that have occurred on this stretch of road, most are attributed, in surmise, to brake failures. It is better simply to gear your four-wheel-drive vehicle into compound low—don't ever try a normal car here—and inch your way down across the transverse ribs of sharp rock that roughen the road's surface.

Although the road drops steeply, the canyon plunges faster. A pair of waterfalls thunder one after the other into two foam-fretted turquoise pools named the Devil's Punchbowls. Seen over the edges of your hubcaps, they are dramatic, awesome—and somehow disappointing, constricted as they are in the tight V of a dull yellow canyon. Snowslides sweep the slopes each winter. One avalanche annually deposits in the lower gorge a discolored, debris-littered mass of snow that hangs there all summer long; the river flows underneath it through blue-gleaming caverns that I for one have no desire to explore. On some summers rockslides crash down the cliffs. Because of so much scouring, little vegetation clings to the sides of the gorge. Starkness and power—those are the impressions, and you are astounded to learn that this "impossible" road was used for years by long pack trains of donkeys carrying supplies and ore between the heavily mineralized Crystal Canyon area and the railroad terminus at Crested Butte.

At the little town of Crystal, the tight bands of rock relax into a wide, aspen-filled bowl where the main river and its north fork unite. Openings in the canyon walls give glimpses of chiseled peak fronts. On a sunny flat in the middle of this green haven are a handful of cabins. Most are in good repair, for Crystal, which is generally approached from below, is a ghost town only in winters, which are severe. As is happening throughout most of the Colorado mining country, urban folk are buying homesites in the old camps and transforming them into summer residences.

What has not been adequately renovated is a far-famed relic of the mining stampedes that lies a short distance below Crystal. It is a long wooden structure built atop a stone hogback at whose feet the river scolds and frets. At the western extremity of the hogback, the stream bends sharply and drops over a low waterfall. At that point the clifftop building drops a long, ladder-adorned penstock down the rock into the gleaming pool at the base of the falls. Though the structure is called a mill—its full name is the Sheep Mountain Tunnel Mill—it was not used for grinding ore. Rather, it was an early-day hydroelectric plant, furnishing power to Sheep Mountain Tunnel and other nearby mines—an ally of inestimable aid in man's long struggle to master the mountains.

Eyeing the mill's weather-tormented boards, you wonder how they can possibly withstand next winter's heavy snowfall. Local people wonder, too, as do photographers who come from afar to record the relic. Occasionally they collect funds for shoring up the weakest spots. Patches, however, will not suffice much longer, and there are those who believe, I among them, that for the sake of restoration and preservation, the structure should be designated a National Historic Site.

Eight miles farther downstream are the even more amazing ruins of Marble, named for extensive deposits of pure white, close-grained marble found in Yule Canyon to the south. The stuff was too ponderous to be dragged far by wagon, however, and so Marble began life as one more metal mining town. Then, about 1906, a railroad built originally for tapping coal beds farther down the Crystal River extended its tracks to the quarries. The town boomed then. Marble from Yule Canyon, the stone shaped in a cutting mill 1,700 feet long, was used for building the Lincoln Memorial and scores of neoclassic structures from New York to San Francisco. In the early 1930s hundreds of workmen spent a year removing from the mountainside perhaps the biggest chunk of stone ever quarried—a 100-ton piece for the Tomb of the Unknown Soldier. Alas for records. The block was too big for the railroad to handle, and it had to be pared to 57 tons before it could be transported to Washington.

By that time fashions were changing. Architects no longer designed pseudo-Roman temples for banks and government offices. Marble veneer replaced solid blocks. During World War II the quarries closed, and the railroad was torn up for scrap. During those same years mudslides battered the town, and soon it looked more decrepit than the silver mining camps it had outlived for decades.

Lately, like other ghost towns, Marble has been undergoing a summer revival. You forget that, however, the moment you walk through the trees to the old workings. Sepulchral marble foundations, the support once of company houses, gleam palely in the forest gloom. Though the roof has gone from the mill, its white walls and the white pedestals that once supported heavy machinery still stand. Scattered everywhere are fragments of marble ranging in size from pebbles to massive blocks. Walking about in that white, dead silence, brushing aside tendrils of greenery, you feel as Muriel Wolle says she felt in her *Stampede to Timberline,* that you have stumbled onto the ruins of a forgotten Mayan temple.

Oddly, there at the end of this long road back among projects that failed because of changes in economics and style, you recall the young vitality at Gothic. For here, too, is a laboratory that in its own way speaks eloquently about the population dynamics and bioenergetics of human beings who in their own time followed their temptations, as hummingbirds do, toward the limits of existence.

# 14
# THE ARKANSAS MIXING BOWL

Leadville, Colorado, nestled 10,152 feet high near the headwaters of the Arkansas River and nicknamed the Cloud City, claims to be the loftiest incorporated municipality in the United States. Her residents like to boast that if they look west they see Colorado's two highest peaks, Mounts Elbert and Massive, culminating points of the Sawatch Range, the tallest mountain chain in the United States. If they turn around and look east, they see the Mosquito Range, a smaller but still mighty uplift that contains five peaks rising more than 14,000 feet in elevation.

The byway that we will shortly follow from east to west crosses both ranges. In surmounting the Mosquitos it produces still another geographic superlative: Mosquito Pass, 13,188 feet in elevation, the highest automobile crossing of a mountain range anywhere in North America.

Economic superlatives match geographic ones. During the past hundred years the mines of the Leadville district have turned out well over $1 billion worth of gold, silver, lead, zinc, and molybdenum. Most of the first two minerals were produced at a time when gold was worth a meager $20.67 an ounce—compare today's prices!—and silver averaged less than $1.00. Yet even those values will be eclipsed by the worth of the water being funneled toward the insatiable cities and farms at the edge of the plains.

These outpourings came in waves. First was a short-lived gold rush that began in 1860 and revolved around an ephemeral town called Oro City. Oro was succeeded by Leadville, child of a frenzied search for carbonate ores of lead and silver, plus incidental gold, that began in 1878 and continued until the end of the century. During that time the Cloud City's population approached 40,000 as compared to today's 7,000.

Molybdenum mining, whose output has exceeded the other efforts in value (but which has had no appreciable effect on our byway), surged into prominence during World War II; the great Climax Mine atop Fremont Pass 13 miles north of Leadville is said to be the largest underground mining operation in the world. And now there is water. It is not exactly a Johnny-come-lately. Storage for the Colorado Fuel & Iron Company's mills in Pueblo and for the farms at Rocky Ford on the plains began in 1902 in a diminutive predecessor of today's mammoth Turquoise Reservoir, 4 miles west of Leadville. A sizable transmontane tunnel began whisking Western Slope water into Twin Lakes Reservoir, 16 miles south of Leadville, during the 1930s. But the big rush to mine the snow melt of the high country did not come until the 1960s. As we shall see, it is still continuing full force.

Each outburst of activity created an instantaneous demand for mail, passenger, and freight transportation. The easy way to reach Oro City and afterward Leadville from the supply centers to the east was to cross South Park, circle the southern end of Mosquito Range at Trout Creek Pass, a modest 9,346 feet high, and then turn north up the Arkansas River. This was not the short way, however. From the transportation hub of Fairplay in South Park, the distance to Leadville by way of Trout Creek was 72 miles. Via Mosquito Pass it was 21 miles. When travel was by foot, horseback, or freight wagon, that 50-mile spread could amount to days in time. Inevitably, therefore, reckless entrepreneurs repeatedly defied the heights in an effort to speed communication. Their first efforts, which came during the early 1860s, involved a trail for mail and express couriers. No identifiable traces of the trail remain, however, and so our journey to the top necessarily follows the wagon road that supplanted it in 1878.

The byway begins just short of little Alma, 6 miles north of Fairplay on State Highway 9. Like the road out of Crested Butte up the East River, this one at first presents no difficulties for standard automobiles. Farther on, when altitude and grades increase, it is comforting to be able to draw on the extra traction of a four-wheel-drive vehicle.

The initial stretch of the journey follows Mosquito Creek past the site of the old log cabin mining camp of Mosquito. As the Mosquito Mountains close in around the road, one can't help wondering about the repetitious name. Why mosquito, of all things, for such enormous geologic pachyderms? Legend answers that when the first miners in the area were setting up rules for their yet unnamed district, a mosquito landed on a space that had been left blank in the documents until the anonymity could be resolved. *Voilà!* District, creek, and the entire range promptly became Mosquito.

A few miles up Mosquito Creek the road reaches the remnants of a mill which once crushed ore from the fabulously rich North London Mine, located well above timberline on the northern side of London Mountain, a spur that runs eastward from the main range. Because of the mine's situation its operators could not obtain as much water as the ore reduction processes required. Accordingly the company placed its mill 1,000 feet down the slope beside Mosquito Creek. Ore was transported there in buckets carried by moving cables suspended between wooden towers, much after the fashion of modern ski lifts. This was the first aerial tramway in Colorado. It worked so well that a shortline railroad was built up the canyon to handle the mill's rapidly expanding production.

Another ingenious innovation proved less successful. This was an attempt to generate power for the mill's machinery by means of an enormous windmill with vanes 60 feet tall. The breezes that swept through the gulch were regular enough, but too strong. Shortly after the contraption had been installed, a winter gale blew it over.

A short distance above the site of the mill, the road doubles back on itself and slants steeply up the mountainside. Side roads branch off into enormous basins dotted here and there with abandoned cabins and eroding mine dumps, targets of Sunday souvenir hunters. Green wedges of grass, sedge, and tiny dwarfed willows push stubbornly up against slopes of sharp-edged slide-rock marvelously painted with variegated lichen. Those piles of precariously balanced stones are difficult to walk on. Sometimes a single step is enough to cause a heap of them as large as a dining room table to slip downward a foot or two with a grinding rumble. When such a mishap occurs, you experience an instant of panic, envisioning a landslide engulfing half the mountain. I have never known of so cataclysmic an outcome—just twisted ankles caused by the unexpected shift in footing. Still, some of those giant tongues of slide-rock are in truth always moving, not visibly, but inexorably enough to be classified as rock glaciers, one more element in the constant attrition that has worn these once skyscraping ranges down to the rounded humps we see today.

The road tops out amid entrancing patches of miniature flowers—tiny hummocks of pink moss campion, white phlox, brilliant blue-and-white forget-me-nots. Where streamlets sparkle there are taller clumps of marsh marigolds and scarlet Parry's primrose. In sharp contrast to the dainty blossoms are the austere vistas. The long flatlands of South Park appear through notches framed by London Mountain and its parallel spurs. Beyond the Park's far rim rises the great massif of Pikes Peak, as commanding from this direction as it must have appeared to the pioneers who approached it across the plains from Kansas.

Westward, the snow-streaked sides of Mount Massive rise strongly above heavy black skirts of spruce and fir. To the right of Massive and directly behind the blue shimmer of Turquoise Reservoir, the land sags to Hagerman Pass, our ultimate destination, 12,050 feet high. Beyond Hagerman you can glimpse the far end of the Elk Mountains northwest of Aspen. Still farther away in the blueness are the flat lines of Battlement Mesa. Unless you climb to a peaktop, there is no other spot from which you can see so far east and west across the prevailing north-south alignment of the Colorado Rockies.

The nearer view is even more intriguing. The road zigzags down into broad Evans Gulch, passes two small reservoirs, and then, after skirting jumbled splotches of colored waste rock from abandoned mines, enters the town of Leadville, clearly visible 3,000 feet below. It was to link that town's predecessor, Oro City, with the new mining camps of South Park that this pass came into being. Initially, as has been noted, the way was a trail only, traversed irregularly by miners and on more definite schedule by the carriers of mail and express.

By far the most famous of the early mailmen was John Dyer, a fifty-two-year-old Methodist circuit rider who, lacking a horse, journeyed from pulpit to pulpit on foot. He supported his religious work by prospecting, generally to little avail. In times of need he took whatever odd jobs offered. During the early months of 1864, when flour in South Park cost $40 a sack, say $400 in terms of today's currency, he agreed to carry letters and gold dust once a week each way between the town of Mosquito and Cache Creek, 18 miles down the Arkansas from Oro City. His pay was $18 for each round trip.

Because the snow that winter varied from 3 feet to 20 feet deep, he traveled on what he called Norwegian snowshoes—skis 11 feet long. For help in balancing himself and braking his long descents he carried a single pole taller than he was. "The mail's weight," he wrote later, "was from twenty-three to twenty-six pounds, with from five to seven pounds of express matter," the latter mostly gold dust. During his weekly journeys he rescued several snowbound travelers. As the weather began to warm late in May he traveled at night when the soft surface of the snow froze hard enough to support him. Timid wayfarers sought his guidance but seldom gave him anything more than thanks. His work is commemorated by a small, slant-topped chunk of polished pink-purple granite placed like a tombstone on the very top of the pass. Its inscription reads,

>J. L. "Father" Dyer
>Methodist Preacher
>Author
>Carried Mail and Gold
>Over this Pass 1864
>"The Snowshoe Itinerant"

That marker now serves as a pylon in one of the world's most unusual contests, the annual Leadville burro race. Men and women compete. Each is accompanied by a donkey, called variously burro, jack, or jackass but never a simple biblical ass. Each burro is loaded with gold pan, pick, and other mining impedimenta covered with a canvas tarpaulin and lashed down with a pack rope. The idea is to drag or drive the donkey from Leadville's main street up the Mosquito road to the top of the 13,188-foot pass, circle Dyer's stone, and scramble back down as fast as possible.* Those who cover the ground in the shortest time receive generous money prizes and a certain amount of local fame. Both are well earned, for the climb is arduous and donkeys are given to fits of temperament. Going uphill the beasts sometimes balk and respond to pressure by trying to kick in their tormentor's ribs. Going downhill toward home they occasionally bolt, dragging their "masters" igno-

---

* Until recently the race course extended from Leadville to Fairplay. The towns fell into a squabble about management, however, and now the race goes up and down the west side of the mountain only.

miniously behind. In spite of these hazards people come from throughout the state each summer to compete—and in far greater numbers to watch.

The prospector with his burro was a symbol of uncomplicated times that faded quickly with the advent of the silver stampede of 1878. The carbonate ores that fueled the new rush were complex and had to be smelted in quantity. The smoke of industrialization filled the Arkansas's broad upper valley. Independent prospectors became wage earners who struggled bitterly for recognition through labor unions. As the mines that crowded each other up the slopes of the foothills east of town grew deeper and deeper, they encountered water that could be removed only with the most sophisticated of pumps. Trained engineers became the new elite of the mountain society. Their demands for equipment, like the demands of the townspeople for food, clothing, and drink, grew voracious.

When Leadville was incorporated as a city in January 1878, two railroads were within striking distance of its mines. The Denver & Rio Grande had reached the mouth of the Royal Gorge, the narrow chasm through which the Arkansas River bursts onto the plains. Unhappily, the D&RG had just locked horns with the Santa Fe in a struggle for the right-of-way through the constricted gateway. While the two companies carried their dispute to the courts, the Denver & South Park sought to outdistance them by hurrying up the canyon of the South Platte toward South Park and Trout Creek Pass. Unhappily, that railroad was inadequately financed for speedy construction—yet speed was what Leadville wanted above all else.

In the fall of 1878 a group of impatient Leadville businessmen decided that the only way to quicken the movement of freight was to build a wagon road across Mosquito Pass. They wouldn't have to go far—just 6 miles over the top to a road that already connected the North London Mine to Fairplay. But during the course of those 6 miles they would also have to go *up* more than half a mile into the teeth of winter.

With incredible optimism they chose November as the month to put crews to work on both sides of the pass. The recklessness paid off. The winter proved to be one of the mildest on record. Nearly every day the men were able to hack away at the rubble of slide-rock, and by the spring of 1879 the road was finished. It was 16 feet wide most of the way and contained only short stretches of grade exceeding 8 per cent.

For draft animals it was a fearful crossing. Long strings of horses and oxen could drag wagonloads of freight upward only a few score yards at a time before having to stop and gasp for breath. The ordeal produced a lung fever that killed them like flies. When teams going east met others coming west, they were able to pass only by means of intricate maneuvers well larded with luck and smoking profanity. One traveler reported that he was "rarely out of sight of dead horses and mules that have broken legs or are dead of overwork, and every precipice along the way shows the wrecks of wagons that have slipped over the edge into the gorge below."

The builders of the road collected tolls from the spring of 1879 until the summer of 1880, minus the snowy months of the intervening winter. In other words, the wagonway operated less than twelve months all told before the railroads arrived and put it out of business. But what months! An average of 150 outfits a day passed through the toll gates—stagecoaches, big freighters, prairie schooners, farm wagons loaded with produce. One load of chickens froze to death during the passage, a pioneering venture in refrigerated freight. Mingled with the wheeled vehicles were herds of cattle and sheep destined for Leadville's butcher shops. Of the riders and footmen who used the route there is no count. And then, almost overnight, the flow ended. Untended, the road disintegrated into a scratch buried under slide-rock that was impassable even for burros.

In 1949 it was reopened as a tourist attraction for jeep drivers who had learned to handle those powerful little vehicles during World War II. The move has proved popular. Good weather on summer Sundays will bring out from Denver and Colorado Springs two or three dozen vehicles full of wide-eyed sight-seers, plus more from Leadville. There is excitement and a strange sadness, too, in standing near the top of the pass, staring down the zigzags at their trailing plumes of dust, and imagining what the scene must have been like during one hectic year a century past.

During those same hectic months prospectors were streaming on west in search of more silver ore on the far side of the Sawatch Range. The most notable of their many discoveries were unearthed at what became the town of Aspen on the Roaring Fork of the Colorado River. Thousands of people flocked in, and again cries arose for better transportation.

The first response was a frightful wagon road that left the Arkansas Valley at Twin Lakes 16 miles south of Leadville and crossed to the Roaring Fork by way of Independence Pass, 12,095 feet high. Aspen lay 19 miles farther west—and 4,200 feet lower. Freight rates on those horse-killing grades were so astronomical, especially in winter when armies of shovelers had to be hired to keep the road open, that only the richest ore from mines filled with masses of low-grade ore could be shipped to the smelters at Leadville.

Certain capitalists who had moved to Colorado Springs for their health and while there had invested in Aspen properties determined to remedy the situation. One was James J. Hagerman, a Milwaukee banker who had made a fortune in Michigan iron mines. Another was Jerome Wheeler, part owner of Macy's department store in New York City. Modern visitors to Aspen's ski slopes will associate the latter's name with the town's refurbished Wheeler Opera House and the Jerome Hotel.

For the sake of their mines, Hagerman, Wheeler, and a handful of others agreed to underwrite plans already formed in Colorado Springs for a railroad, the Colorado Midland, that would cross the central part of the state to Grand Junction on the Colorado River near the Utah border. Because the upper stretches of the Roaring Fork presented grades impossible for a railroad to negotiate, the Midland's locating engineers decided to cross the Sawatch Range just north of Mount Massive. The gap they selected was renamed Hagerman Pass in honor of the line's new president. From Hagerman the tracks would wind down between the lovely red walls of the Fryingpan River to the Roaring Fork and thence to the Colorado. An 18-mile spur up the Roaring Fork would tap Aspen. The Midland's freight cars could then haul not just ore to the Leadville smelters but also coal from extensive beds along the Colorado River below Glenwood Springs. What was more, the cars would do it in quantity, for the Midland, unlike the other mountain railroads of early Colorado, would run on standard rather than narrow-gauge tracks— 4 feet 8½ inches between rails as compared to 3 feet.

The wide tracks reached Leadville in the summer of 1887. Graders meanwhile were slicing an ascending staircase of breathless hairpin curves up the forested northern flanks of Mount Massive. Fearful of the snow atop Hagerman Pass (12,050 feet in elevation), the engineers halted their spirals at 11,528 feet and punched a 2,200-foot bore under the crest—the highest standard-gauge tunnel in the land.

Alas for records! The snow at 11,500 feet also proved unmanageable, and the railroad had to acquire from outside speculators another, longer tunnel nearly 600 feet farther down the slope. Almost simultaneously silver prices collapsed. Hundreds of mines shut down. For the next twenty years the Midland floundered hopelessly in debt. Finally during the First World War it was abandoned, and its rails were torn up for scrap.

Automobiles promptly took over the grades as far as the lower tunnel, then called Carleton Tunnel in honor of its owner, A. E. Carleton of Colorado Springs. For another twenty years they crept through the 1.78-mile bore on alternating hourly schedules, east-west, west-east. Then, about 1940, the State Highway Commission decided that the Carleton Tunnel was no longer safe and closed it to traffic. At that the byway became a dead end, for the rest of the old railroad grade on up to Hagerman Tunnel had long since been rendered impassable by washouts and landslides.

During the 1960s it was reopened all the way over the top by engineers rushing across the Sawatches in search of Western Slope water. Grab while you can! Cities and farms along the South Platte River from Denver to the Nebraska border had assured their supplies with two monstrous diversions—the Colorado-Big Thompson Project, which carried water through a 13-mile tunnel under Rocky Mountain National Park, and a breathtaking reservoir-tunnel complex at Dillon on the Blue River. Now Aurora (a flourishing suburb east of Denver), Colorado Springs, Pueblo, and the agricultural communities scattered along the lower Arkansas as far as Kansas are seeking to emulate the others, although costs will almost surely exceed $300 million before the job is done.

Colorado Springs and Aurora moved first. Working jointly, they jumped the divide northwest of Leadville and dammed Homestake Creek, a principal tributary of the Eagle River branch of the Colorado. Since Homestake alone could not provide all the water the two cities wanted, construction workers sent out pipelines like giant tentacles to pull more water out of half a dozen small streams flowing off the sides of Holy Cross Ridge. These gleanings were then taken under the Sawatches by tunnel and dumped into a giant reservoir named Turquoise Lake, successor to the smaller storage pond of the same name that had occupied the site since 1902.

Turquoise Reservoir also serves as a gathering point for Western Slope water destined for Pueblo and the farms of the lower Arkansas River. The complexity of the work, officially known as the Fryingpan-Arkansas Project, boggles the imagination. A key element is a tunnel 5.5 miles long under the divide near the site of the old Carleton Tunnel. (Carleton couldn't be revamped and pressed into service because it tips the wrong way, from east to west.) From the western portal of the water tunnel, more bores, not all of them completed at this writing, reach out like splayed fingers to tap not only the headwater streams of the Fryingpan but also some of the Roaring Fork. This water has to be replaced. Accordingly another storage tank, Ruedi Reservoir, has been built well down the Fryingpan. Snow melt from the river's lower tributaries will be captured and held in Ruedi until needed each fall in Arizona and Southern California.

From Turquoise the commingled waters are taken south to the Twin Lakes Reservoir at the eastern foot of Independence Pass and used for generating power. After fulfilling that function the waters are divided and sent their separate ways.

The distribution system furnishes an interesting commentary on the growth of Colorado's ecological awareness. Almost no effort was made to hide the ugly scrapings left by the first projects to be completed—Homestake Dam and the pipeline that scars the Buffalo Peaks south of and across the river from Twin Lakes. An even worse scar would have been dragged along the base of Mount Massive by the open canal from Turquoise to Twin Lakes called for in original plans. But between 1967, when Homestake was completed, and 1974 a remarkable shift in sentiment occurred. The citizens of Leadville, who for a hundred years had been chewing their environment to pieces without the least regard for appearances, suddenly decided they did not want their favorite mountain blighted. Aided by environmentalists from throughout the West, they won an expensive demand that a buried pipeline of titanic proportions be substituted for the open canal and that the earth above it be restored to its original condition.

To complete our journey through Leadville's past to its present, we turned our Jeep down the Mosquito Pass road through Evans Gulch. After a pause to examine the clutter of mine relics on Fryer Hill, we drove on through the town past Turquoise Reservoir to the easy grades created originally for the Colorado Midland Railroad. These carried us high along the slopes of Busk Creek to the vicinity of the closed Carleton Tunnel. There a sharp hairpin curve swung us back along the far side of Busk's deep valley. Then suddenly the road steepened. Water engineers, impatient with the slow toil of the railroad grade, had left it for a more direct route upward through the glade-spotted spruce.

By luck, our timing was perfect. Storm clouds were gathering, which meant that the sky tossed with drama. Puffs of chilly air sent shivers through the tall grass and bistort, each slender stalk capped with clusters of tiny white flowers that from a distance looked like tufts of cotton. The hillsides glowed with paintbrush. Where the ground was moist we found, to our joy, rank upon rank of the densely flowered spikes of pink elephant's-head. Back against the rocks, gleaming in the shafts of sunlight that managed to dodge through the boisterous clouds, were the funnel-shaped blossoms of blue sky pilot, their cupped interiors warm with orange anthers.

It was the kind of day one dreams of when far from the mountains. Yet now that we were there I found myself looking past the flowers to the broad valley that we had just traversed from one high rim to the other. A scarred valley. We could see the spidery legs of abandoned railroad trestles and the stark white line where trees had been removed from the reservoir basin, which was not yet full of water. Beyond the town were dumps of waste rock, and above those was the slant of the road leading to Mosquito Pass. North and south through the heart of the valley ran the black thread of railroad tracks and the grayer line of the paved highway, both of them skirting on their journeys terrible slag heaps left by vanished smelters.

And the thought came that here, in almost the exact geographic center of the state, was a giant mixing bowl continuously agitated by implacable energies. Decades ago the valley's magnet of exotic ores had tumbled together thousands upon thousands of hopeful people in a frenzied search for wealth, with almost incalculable effect on the young state's economy. Now water from the Pacific side of the mountains is being blended in the same great bowl and thrust through unnatural channels to cities on the Atlantic side, again with incalculable effect—except for this: we do know that Colorado's population during the first part of the 1970s expanded at something like 13 per cent each year largely because of drinking water drained from the high country.

A hundred years of reaching out, of taking: an undeviating insistence that the loftiest mountains in America yield to man's will. That, I thought, is indeed the region's truest, most sobering superlative.

# 15
# FADS IN MOUNTAINTOPS

At different periods throughout the past, throngs of people who lacked interest in mountaineering nevertheless have clambered up a handful of Colorado peaks that for one reason or another were deemed to be special. The trails that were built for pampering them can still be traced through the gray heaps of stone, curious byways that shed a wry light on some of the quirks that ambition can take. The trails also help us realize that many of our reactions to nature are not fundamental but are the products of fashion.

Historically the first of the fad peaks were a pair of now-obscure Fourteeners that punctuate the Continental Divide a few miles southwest of the old silver mining camp of Georgetown—Grays Peak, 14,270 feet in elevation, and Torreys Peak, exactly one yard lower. The men for whom the two mountains were named, botanists Asa Gray and John Torrey, were unknown at the time to most Coloradoans. But they were leaders in their field and had done magnificent work classifying the plants that explorer John Charles Frémont had brought back from his Western expeditions. Accordingly a younger botanist who did much of his work in Colorado, C. C. Parry, decided to perpetuate their names in the twin summits.* After a struggle with geographers he had the label accepted, and in 1872 the two scientists came West to see their mountains.

Along with his wife, the sixty-two-year-old Gray ascended the peak that

---

* Parry's own name is commemorated by several of the high country's showiest wild flowers: fragrant Parry's clover; white, ground-hugging Parry's vetch; blood-red Parry's primrose; blue-black, deep-chaliced Parry's gentian; and, not least, Parry's townsendia, a gorgeous aster. A campground at Twin Lakes near Leadville has also been named for him but is misspelled Perry.

90. *This sand pile, a thousand feet high, stands in the Great Sand Dunes National Monument at the western base of the Sangre de Cristo Mountains.*

91. *The wilderness movement gained much of its impetus from the work of Arthur Carhart at Trapper's Lake. Note the forest of beetle-killed spruce on the far shore.*

92. Columbine thrive in sheltered nooks among the rocks above timberline. This clump is nearly 12,000 feet up, on the flanks of North Maroon Peak near Aspen.

OVERLEAF:
93. Maroon Bells. Although the peaks stand inside the boundaries of the Maroon Bells-Snowmass Wilderness Area, they are the best-known and most-photographed mountains of western Colorado. The nearest town is Aspen.

94. The western end of the Sneffels Range in southwestern Colorado, as twilight nears.

95. This fence is held upright by double posts. Nearby aspen groves supplied the material.

96. *The sheer north face of Mt. Sneffels.*

bore his name. Torrey, who was seventy-six, left the honor to his daughter. Whether or not the dignitaries walked or rode horseback up the trail that had been built to the summits four years earlier is not clear from Gray's letters. A few weeks after the ascent he wrote Charles Darwin somewhat ambiguously that he had "ventured . . . to take her [Mrs. Gray] up to the summit of Gray's Peak, 14,300, or thereabouts, where she acquitted herself nobly. The day was perfect, the success complete."

Anyway, there was a trail, which helps account for some of the twins' popularity. Tourists who made the short trip from Denver to romantic Georgetown, deeply entrenched between the stupendous cliffs of the south fork of Clear Creek, were readily lured over 10 miles of good wagon road to the foot of the peaks. From there they could scamper energetically to the top and be back in Georgetown by evening. Less vigorous travelers broke the journey at Kelso's Cabin, a hostelry of sorts that stood near timberline.

The all-powerful magnet that prompted most of those outings was a notion, fostered by local patriots, that Grays was the highest peak in the United States outside of Alaska. (Actually Grays is the ninth highest peak in Colorado, Torreys the eleventh.) On top of that allure was rhetoric like this from a veteran newspaper editor, Samuel Bowles of the Springfield, Massachusetts, *Republican*. Bowles toured the Rockies and Sierra Nevada in 1866 and again in 1868 and afterward recounted his adventures in a popular book, *Our New West*, published in 1869.

"No Swiss mountain view," trumpeted the author about Grays Peak, "carries such majestic sweep of distance, such sublime combination of height and breadth and depth; such uplifting into the presence of God; such dwarfing of the mortal sense; such welcome to the immortal thought. It was not beauty, it was sublimity; it was not power, nor order, nor color, it was majesty; it was not a part, it was the whole; it was not man but God, that was about, before, in us."

In May of that same year, 1869, the transcontinental railroad was completed, which led the *Journal of the American Geographical Society* to suggest in less exalted but perhaps more influential prose than Bowles's, "If any of you visit the Rocky Mountains [on the new railroad], the best peak for the ladies to visit and the most magnificent peak, with the least labor, is Grays Peak." By 1875 the enthusiasm had reached such proportions, with several

Eastern magazines carrying accounts of the summits, that a member of the Hayden Survey spoke of Grays as "the mountain that, of all others in the land, we have heard most about."

But who hears now? The fad withered as rapidly as it had grown. The only people who still use the old trail, a most charming byway, do so not because of fashion, which can make almost any ordeal acceptable, but simply because they like the ambiance of the high country.

The trail up Grays was built entirely for tourists. Other summit trails, particularly in the Mosquito Range east of Leadville, were extensions from nearby mines. The principal goal in the Mosquitos, sought by local people rather than by outsiders, was a set of triplets, Mount Lincoln (14,286 feet), Mount Bross (14,172 feet), and Mount Democrat (14,148 feet).

Working mines dotted all three mountains almost to their summits. One lone man lived the year around in a cabin near the top of Mount Democrat. The roads that served the mines allowed families as well as bachelor prospectors to visit the mountains by wagon or horse on weekend outings. They recorded their passing by adding a loose stone or two to the cairns built atop their chosen summits. As early as 1867, less than a decade after the beginning of the Colorado gold rush, the monument on Mount Lincoln had acquired so many stones that it spread out to 12 feet in diameter and stood 15 feet high.

As was the case with Grays Peak, part of Mount Lincoln's lure was a local belief that it was the highest peak in America. The notion ended during the 1870s when official surveys showed that the mountain could do no better than claim eighth place in the roll of Colorado's Fourteeners, barely ahead of Grays. To be reduced that far was so grievous a blow to Lincoln's admirers that they felt there was no use protesting the humiliation. Other mountain celebrants have not been so meek. Even today some of them fume about the federal surveys that keep undercutting their pretensions.

California's Mount Whitney, which was officially declared to rise 14,495 feet above sea level, was too high to argue about. Not so the next five peaks— Elbert, Massive, and Harvard in Colorado's Sawatch Range (they, too, are easily approached by trails from high mines), Blanca farther south in the Sangre de Cristos, and Rainier in the state of Washington. Figures released by the United States Geologic Survey in 1969 (and survey figures have been amended before) allot the following altitudes to the contenders: Elbert, highest in Colorado and second in the contiguous states, 14,433 feet; Massive, 14,421; Harvard, 14,420; Rainier, 14,410; Blanca, 14,338. Thus only 23 feet separate Rainier from Elbert. Only 1 foot separates Harvard from Massive.

Rainier fans have vowed to pile enough stones on top of their snowy mountain to surpass both Harvard and Massive, if not Elbert. Supporters of Mount Massive have made the same threat about Elbert. According to Perry Eberhart's and Philip Schmuck's entertaining book *The Fourteeners*, Harvard students sought to settle the matter in favor of their mountain by erecting a 20-foot aluminum flagpole on its summit. (Mount Harvard was named in 1869 by graduates of Harvard's new mining school.) Unfortunately the students put the pole on a false summit, whereupon a party from Cornell rectified the error and dubbed the big round peak Mount Cornell, a name unlikely to win official recognition.

Strangely enough, the most determined campaign to alter heights has focused on Blanca Peak, which was officially declared in 1969 to be 95 feet lower than Elbert and apparently beyond hope. But Blanca's principal supporter, Donald Bennett, has money as well as strident lungs. In between agitating for new surveys, he has hired men to heap up a rock monument and erect on it a 50-foot flagpole whose tip, he swore, was the highest point in Colorado. Few people other than Bennett pay much attention.

Blanca needs no artificial boost to lend it majesty. The peak itself is the culmination of a grand massif that sprang nearly 7,000 feet out of the flat floor of the San Luis Valley on the west. Long ridges, their precipitous sides embracing giant cirques dotted with bright lakes, extend like warped spokes from Blanca's top to a rim of other imposing summits. Three of the neighbors (Little Bear, Ellingwood, and Mount Lindsey, formerly Old Baldy) exceed 14,000 feet in elevation. Two others, California Peak and the Iron Nipple, rise to within less than 200 feet of that magic number. Long after winter's scuffs of snow have gone from the valley, the giant massif, which certainly looks as if it ought to contain the highest peak in the land, remains shrouded in drifts. Hence its name, given it long ago by Spanish wayfarers from New Mexico—Sierra Blanca, the White Range.

Sierra Blanca is the southern end of the Colorado portion of the Sangre de Cristo Mountains—a narrow range that Bob Ormes, in his *Guide to the*

*Colorado Mountains,* likens to an exclamation mark, with Blanca forming a strong period beneath it.* The space between the mark and the period is a forested ridge breached by a pair of alliterative passes, Mosca and Medano.

The prevailing winds of the San Luis Valley blow out of the southwest and are funneled by the mountains through the Mosca and Medano gaps. The valley across which the ceaseless winds blow—a valley three times as big as the state of Delaware—receives, on the average, only 8 inches of rain a year. The sparse vegetation that results is unable to anchor the sandy soil. The wind swoops up the fine grains and carries them along until it begins to rise toward the passes. There the burden drops out, forming more than 50 square miles of sand dunes, the tallest of them nearly 1,000 feet high. The area is now set aside as Great Sand Dunes National Monument.

It is a place of constant, subtle change. The colors of the sand vary with the strike of the light from white to yellow to ruddy. Curves, marvelously textured, climb gently upward on the windward side, then fall abruptly to the lee, much as snowdrifts do. Skiers, indeed, find the sand an acceptable summer substitute for snow. Except for the downhill motion, however, the experience is totally different. Back in the shifting valleys the wind stirs strange rumbles. The sand hisses even when no one disturbs it. Moonlight is an eerie time, lending grim credibility to tales of lost travelers and vanished herds of sheep.

The Blanca massif begins its abrupt rise not far to the south of the dunes. That slope of the Sierra is privately owned. Although it is possible to gain permission to approach the peaks by way of the Como Lakes, you'll miss a delightful byway if you do. To absorb as much of the great mountain as you can, swing around its southern end almost as far as La Veta Pass on U. S. Highway 160 and then turn north along a graveled road through oak brush and pine trees to Huerfano Creek. Follow Huerfano west, southwest, and then due south over an increasingly bad road—eventually it is fit only for four-wheel-drive vehicles—into an increasingly massive mountain valley.

The road was built to serve a mine near timberline. For years after the mine failed, the byway gave fishermen and climbers a long leg forward on

---

* Close to the New Mexico border and well south of Sierra Blanca is the Culebra massif, introductory mountains to the Sangre de Cristo Range of New Mexico. Geologically the Sangre de Cristos of Colorado and those of New Mexico form a single range. Visually they do not.

their trips. When last we were there, however, in the summer of 1973, we found the way blocked by a deep mat of boulders and tangled, shattered trees brought crashing into the valley by a winter avalanche. The Forest Service not only decided against removing the barrier but, so I understand, has closed off the road 2 miles farther downstream. Now you have a fairly stiff walk ahead of you before you can even start climbing toward the peaktop or those bright, trout-filled lakes inside the glaciated cirques. It's worth it, though, especially if you start before dawn and can watch the day's new sunshine slide down the ice-polished north face, making the sheer cliff gleam as with an inner light.

As is true of the view from most high peaks, the one from Blanca reaches endlessly. But to me this one has a marked difference, occasioned by the knowledge that it overlooks a different culture from the one most of us are used to. Names indicate the division. Northward, the Colorado mountain ranges are called Elk, Tenmile, Flat Tops, Never Summer. Towns are called Fairplay, Leadville, Steamboat Springs; rivers are called Gunnison, Roaring Fork, White, Arkansas. From Blanca, by contrast, you see mountains named Sangre de Cristo, San Juan, Culebra. Towns are called Del Norte, Alamosa, Conejos. You can trace the green diagonal of a river named Rio Grande across the yellow-gray lower reaches of a valley known as San Luis. There are exceptions, of course. There is a town named Buena Vista in the Arkansas Valley. At the southern foot of Blanca is Fort Garland, offspring of a military post built by the United States Army in the 1850s. But you know that in spite of Fort Garland's Anglo name, the village is composed mostly of houses built of adobe bricks, with strings of red peppers often dangling from protruding roof beams called *vigas*.

With binoculars you can pick out from Blanca's top the green fields around little San Luis, the oldest continuously occupied town in Colorado. The future state's first water rights originated there. Land holdings based on Mexican grants lap both Blanca and Culebra peaks and severely limit access. Mexican farmers on all sides of the mountains still resist the seemingly all-pervasive Anglo mores that surround them. Thus, as is true of the Anasazi country of the Four Corners area, the view from Blanca reaches through the years as well as across space, an association that creates for me a brooding sense of timelessness that other peaks lack. There is no logic to the feeling,

I realize, but that is the way with mountains. They assume the characteristics that their viewers want them to have.

A peak that illustrates even better than Blanca what the imagination can do to simple geology is the Mount of the Holy Cross. Located on a northern spur of the Sawatch Range, Holy Cross is the most isolated of Colorado's fifty-three major peaks and seldom seen by most tourists. Yet there was a time when, with the possible exception of Pikes Peak, it was the most renowned mountain in North America.

Its first giant boost toward fame came from photographs made in 1873 by William Henry Jackson of the Hayden Survey and from an outsized painting, 7 feet 10 inches tall by 6 feet wide, completed the following year by Thomas Moran. Both men first glimpsed Holy Cross from Notch Mountain, which is only 300 feet lower than the main peak and is separated from it by the deep chasm of East Cross Creek.

The famed cross, which occupies most of the mountain's steep northeastern face, is formed by snow-filled couloirs about 50 feet deep and as many wide. The vertical gully is about 1,400 feet tall. The transverse bars, the left one more precisely formed than the right, are made by converging crevices about 450 feet long. It is difficult to view the geologic oddity for the first time without feeling reverential for at least a moment, though whether or not Jews, Utes, and Zen Buddhists would react similarly is something else. This mountain was built for Christians.

During the 1870s there were no trails in the area. Jackson and a year later Moran gained their vantage points only after arduous struggles with bad weather, down timber, boulders, and bogs. "Horror!!!" exclaimed Moran in a letter to his wife. "The way up the Valley [of East Cross Creek] was infinitely worse than anything we had yet encountered. A swamp, covered with the worst of fallen logs and projecting through which were the roches moutonnées, or sheep rocks, round and smooth and slippery, ranging from ten to forty feet high."

Jackson and three men climbed Notch Mountain twice in 1873, lugging with them the glass plates, big cameras, and orange developing tent that were necessary for picture-taking in those days. Because rain prevented photography the first day, they retreated to treeline, spent a wet, miserable night, and returned the next morning for another attempt, which worked. Moran, by contrast, never gained the top at all. He was so exhausted by the difficulties of the long approach that he halted as soon as he had a good view of Holy Cross, on a ledge some 600 feet below Notch Mountain's summit.

The oil that Moran painted afterward romanticizes Holy Cross by having it shine luminously through parted mists. The composition emphasizes the cross itself by having the tumbling waters of East Cross Creek lead straight back toward it, although in actuality the intersecting couloirs cannot be seen from the deep valley. Unwarranted liberties? Moran scoffed. His intent, he said, was not to convey topography but to give "a true impression of the region." Fair enough. Jackson also heightened the effect of subsequent pictures he took of the mount (though evidently not the first one) by retouching his negatives.

The public liked the results. Jackson's photographs and Moran's painting won top honors in their divisions when exhibited at the nation's first Centennial Exhibition in Philadelphia in 1876. Wide-scale reproduction followed, and the way was prepared for the religious excursions that eventually took place. In 1912 three Episcopal priests, helped upward by a local mining engineer and his twelve-year-old son, held services on the summit of Notch Mountain. A pilgrimage by a handful of devout Christians retraced the route in 1919, and it may have been this that gave O. W. Daggett, a newspaper editor in the small mining camp of Redcliff, an idea for a spectacular publicity gimmick, Shrine Pass.

A short-cut automobile highway to the Western Slope was to be built over the Continental Divide at Loveland Pass. After crossing Loveland the road would drop to the Blue River. From the Blue it would go up Tenmile Creek to—well, there was the rub. The State Highway Department favored crossing Vail Pass and winding down Gore Creek to the Eagle River, gateway to the Colorado. Daggett wanted the road to use an unnamed pass south of Vail and come down Turkey Creek, striking the Eagle at his home town of Redcliff.

Vail Pass is 700 feet lower than Daggett's and thus could be kept open more easily in winter. But Daggett's proposed road afforded one of the few places in Colorado other than Notch Mountain from which the snowy cross on Holy Cross could be glimpsed. Visited by a stroke of inspiration, he named his proposed crossing Shrine Pass and toured the state expatiating on its visual magnificence. In 1922 he persuaded the Acting Secretary of Agriculture, who also headed the Forest Service, to set aside 350 acres "near the source of said Turkey Creek" where "any denomination may be given the privilege of erecting shrines or other structures to be used in connection with devotional exercises." Daggett at once laid plans for a fifty thousand-seat stadium from which worshipers could watch the rising sun "tip the cross of snow and transmute it to a 'Cross of Gold.' Then sing Hosanna!"

The hard realities of winter outdid the Hosannas. Vail Pass was chosen; the stadium on Shrine Pass was never built. Nevertheless the publicity that attended the controversy helped stimulate the growth of pilgrimages to that most superlative of viewing points, Notch Mountain. Enthusiasm reached such a pitch that in 1929 President Hoover apotheosized the peak as Mount of the Holy Cross National Monument. At that the Denver *Post,* which recognized circulation-building causes when it saw them, helped finance an automobile road up Bishop Gulch 4 miles to Camp Tigiwon, elevation 10,000 feet. (Later the Forest Service pushed the road on another 2 miles to Half Moon, elevation 10,500 feet.) From road's end a graded trail was built to the top of Notch Mountain, 13,734 feet. In 1934 the trail was used by eight hundred people during a single gathering, no small number to struggle afoot in that rarefied air to an elevation of almost 14,000 feet.

Many that came to the annual assemblies were ill and hoping for faith cures. Those unable to attend in person mailed handkerchiefs. So much linen arrived in 1932 that two rangers had to help the officiating pastor carry the packs of it up the mountain.

Then the fad ran out and in 1935 attendance began dropping radically. At the outbreak of World War II it ended entirely. The army took over the area around the headwaters of the Eagle River and on west to the Holy Cross ridge as a training ground for mountain troops and forbade entry by civilians. There was no pickup in pilgrimages afterward, partly because by then oldtimers were saying that erosion had so ruined the right arm of the cross that it was no longer a suitable symbol.

Because of the downgrading, Holy Cross was removed from the list of National Monuments in 1950. Fourteen years later, as partial though unintended recompense, another branch of the government, the United States Geological Service, uplifted the mountain's elevation from a supposed 13,978 feet to 14,005. Thus, for the time being at least, Holy Cross stands fifty-second among Colorado's major peaks. It's hardly enough to induce new pilgrimages.

How much charm has the mountain really lost? The answer depends on what you are looking for. In the opinion of Robert Brown, a Denver schoolteacher who has climbed in the area and who has studied hundreds of old pictures of the cross, erosion damage to the right arm is not as severe as reported. The appearance of the cross changes, he believes, with the varying patterns of the wind that drifts spring snow into the couloirs. Some years the visual results are fine; some years they aren't—if you want a cross.

The trail from Half Moon still zigzags gently up the east side of Notch Mountain, and many people still take it. The difference now is that the view, heady though it remains, is not an end in itself but part of a broader quest. The travelers you encounter on the Notch Mountain trail today are generally backpackers rambling through what is still one of the wildest parts of the Colorado Rockies. Their goal is the inspiration they can draw from the whole of the mountain scene, not just from a particular symbol.

Are these informal excursions, which take more people into the back country than did horseback rides up Grays Peak or religious pilgrimages to the top of Notch Mountain, just another fad? Are they, in essence, a spin-off of the massive publicity that has attended the conservation movement? I do not know. For myself I am content to swing off Interstate 70 at Vail Pass and follow the little byway that leads across Shrine Pass to the spot where Daggett wanted to build his fifty thousand-seat stadium. There, as the distant cross shines out in the morning sun, I'll sing hosanna that a few places like these still remain where we can look and be rewarded according to our lights.

PART FIVE

*Wilderness*

# 16
# TRIUMPH IN THE FLAT TOPS

One of the advantages of the new (December 1975) Flat Tops Wilderness Area at the headwaters of the White River in northwestern Colorado is a dead forest. The destruction, which spread across 66,500 acres, was caused during World War II by billions of fat, dark red, house-hunting insects a quarter of an inch long—*Dendroctonus rufipennis,* the spruce beetle.

*Dendroctonus* means "tree killer," but that is a human designation. The beetles, which are monogamous, are simply intent on rearing their families in the most satisfactory way they know. Each pair drills a tunnel a foot or two long between the inner and outer bark layers of an Engelmann spruce. There the female lays her eggs in a protective packing of wood dust. The larvae produced by the eggs feed on the tree's inner bark until they are mature. They then bore a way outside, fly off to find mates of their own, and begin a new round of housekeeping. It is no concern to them that large colonies settling on the same tree will cause the host to lose its needles and die.

When such natural checks on beetle propagation as woodpeckers and extremely cold weather fail, a population explosion results and masses of trees are slain by the beetles' frenzy for living. That was what happened in the Flat Tops area during the early 1940s. Because of World War II, money and manpower were not available for battling the outbreak. The plague, which at one point covered the entire 313-acre surface of Trappers Lake on the north fork of the White River with a stinking mat of drowned beetles several inches thick, continued until it ran out of energy and halted of its own accord. Not every Engelmann spruce or alpine fir in the region died, but most did, leaving canyons and hillsides covered by a waste of bare uprights as unresponsive to wind and sun as sailless masts.

At the trees' dead feet, however, life romped on. Grass and flowers luxuriated in newly opened glades of sunlight. Fresh evergreen seedlings reached for the sun. Meanwhile the hundreds of thousands of dead spikes that remained untoppled by winter gales slowly weathered to a beautiful silvery gray. By 1966 the United States Forest Service thought well enough of the devastated section that it used it as a reason for elevating the Flat Tops Primitive Area to new status as a Wilderness under the terms of the Wilderness Act of 1964. That "extensive silver forest of beetle-killed Engelmann spruce," the Service's recommendation declared, ". . . provides a natural laboratory for ecological study on a massive scale."

Another outstanding feature of the proposed reserve, the report went on, would be "Trappers Lake, a symbol of the serenity that is wilderness. It is a grand body of water that invites communion."

Curiously the recommendation alluded only obliquely to the fact that Trappers Lake was the site where, in 1919, the Forest Service first committed itself to the then radical philosophy of maintaining chosen parts of the public domain in their natural state for the benefit of future generations. It did not name the Forest Service employee, Arthur H. Carhart, who first glimpsed from the shores of that lake a vision of the role the Forest Service could and in his mind should play in wilderness preservation. Nor did it indicate why Trappers Lake, seedbed of these concepts, was never included in the Flat Tops Primitive Area, precursor of the proposed Wilderness Area. It is the purpose of this account to fill, in part, some of those strange gaps.*

## Seedbed of the Wilderness Movement

The Flat Tops are the climax of the White River Plateau, which slopes gradually upward from west to east. During the ascent broad grasslands dotted with islands of timber give way reluctantly to tundra fields and boulders. Frequent small lakes enliven the broad expanses. Whalebacks of rock appear here and there, but no tall peaks interrupt the horizon lines. Variety comes

---

\* As a young man in Denver I had the good fortune to know Arthur Carhart and listen to some of his tales. Memory proved inadequate for what follows, however, and so to reinforce it I leaned on Donald N. Baldwin's *The Quiet Revolution* (Boulder, Colo., 1972).

from deep amphitheaters and canyons that the rivers draining the section have carved out of the flanks of the huge tableland. Lining the depressions are splendid, stratified precipices capped with lava and broken here and there by coves where small tributary streams sing and tumble.

The area receives between 30 and 40 inches of moisture a year, twice the average that falls on the state as a whole. To protect this watershed and the fine timber that grew on it, President Harrison in 1891 created the 1.2 million-acre White River Plateau Timberland Reserve, the first such reserve in Colorado and the second in the United States. In 1905 Forest Reserves became National Forests, and their administration was transferred from the Department of the Interior to the Department of Agriculture. During the shuffling the White River Reserve became White River National Forest. Through amalgamation with other National Forests its boundaries have expanded to embrace more than 2 million acres.

Initially the Forest Service was charged with managing timber and water only. During the decade of the 1910s, however, it found itself handling vacationists as well, most of them urban families drawn to its domain by the rapid spread of automobile ownership (Henry Ford introduced the world's first moving assembly line in 1914) and by the appearance of federally funded interstate highways.

Bemused by the trend, Service policy makers decided about 1916 to lease to the public summer homesites in attractive areas under its jurisdiction. One of the first regions chosen for development was Trappers Lake, but implementation of the plan was delayed by America's entry into the First World War.

Up to that time the Forest Service had had no experience in managing recreational activities. Accordingly when Edward Sherman, Assistant Forester of the United States, was visited in Washington by a job-hunting landscape architect named Arthur Carhart, he was intrigued. After some delay, he hired Carhart at a salary of $1,800 a year and ordered him to report for duty to the Denver office on March 1, 1919. Skeptical forest rangers promptly dubbed the new exotic as their "beauty engineer."

The epithet was ill chosen. Carhart turned out to be a powerfully muscled, supremely self-confident, abrasive, and unbelievably energetic young man. He had been graduated from Iowa State College with a degree in landscape architecture in June 1916, aged twenty-four. For a year he had held lowly positions in his field and then had enlisted in the army. He sweat out the war in Washington as a sanitary engineer and was discharged as a first lieutenant. On the strength of the background he straightaway set about telling the United States Forest Service what it should and should not do while creating facilities for outdoor recreation.

He spent the spring of 1919 preparing a regional plan for recreational developments in San Isabel National Forest west of Pueblo, Colorado. In July he hurried on to Trappers Lake to survey the area for summer homesites—a big backlog of applications was piling up—and to lay out a road around its shores.

The forest-circled cliff-shadowed lake fired Carhart's imagination. When he returned to Denver with the surveys he had been ordered to make, he appended an unsolicited statement that in his opinion the plan was outrageous. Trappers Lake was of such superlative beauty that it should be preserved in its natural state. Roads, cabins, and campgrounds, if any, should be kept out of sight of, and at least half a mile away from, the waterfront.

Having delivered himself of that dictum, unprecedented for any underling in the highly utilitarian Forest Service of the day, he hurried on to Minnesota to draw up a recreational plan for what is now the Boundary Waters Canoe Area of Superior National Forest. He went back to Denver more convinced than ever that certain forms of outdoor recreation required "wilderness" for their fullest enjoyment. Moreover, so he declared to his superiors, it was the duty of the National Forests to provide the necessary tracts of unspoiled nature.

*Arthur Carhart's Private Revolution*

The notion that wilderness is essential to man's spiritual health was not a Carhart discovery, of course. Henry Thoreau of Massachusetts and John Muir of California, among others, had been expounding the doctrine for years. Carhart was simply underscoring their views, in his own pedestrian cadences, when he coined such lines as these: "The individual with any soul cannot live in the presence of towering mountains or sweeping plains without getting a little of the high moral standard of Nature infused into his being."

97. Streamlets plunging downward from the American Flats into Cow Creek near Ouray have sheared away the hillsides into cliffs hundreds of feet high.

98. Canyon Creek gouged this slit through the core rock of the mountains to escape from the high country back of Ouray. The walkway, upper right, lets sightseers penetrate the recess of Box Canyon, thundering with the noise of a waterfall almost totally encased in rock.

99. A snow-covered meadow resists encroaching evergreens.

100. *Ouray is blessed with one of the loveliest settings in the mountains.*

101. Alpenglow, the fading day's last radiance, suffuses slopes of Red Mountain, halfway between the towns of Ouray and Silverton.

102. Heartened by minerals revealed in their prospect holes, miners managed to perch this mine building atop a cliff near Ouray.

103. *This reduction mill, also near Ouray, processed ore from mines higher in the mountains.*

104. An abandoned powerhouse still clings to the brink of Bridal Veil Falls near Telluride.

105. The miners who swept across Colorado a hundred or more years ago looked first for veins, which often were revealed where steep streams had removed overburden from "outcrops." Blasted rock from the "prospect holes" that were dug for testing the outcrops left variegated "dumps" on the mountainside. If prospects seemed promising, mine buildings appeared, often in difficult spots. Ore from these mines was transported by donkey, wagon, or aerial tram to processing mills in valley bottoms where water was available. As the workings grew in size, hydroelectric power was often pressed into service. This picture shows waste dumps from prospect holes in the San Miguel Mountains. Rising mineral prices have led to the refurbishing of old mines like this one.

fluffed up the mummy bag. Preparing dinner, such as it was, kept me occupied for a while, but after that the loneliness came, as I suppose it does to anyone spending his first night by himself in so vast and remote a spot.

Because of the high western ridge behind me, cold shadows descended early. To keep warm I crawled into the sleeping bag, tightened the drawstrings around my neck, and sat there watching the light fade from the highest points. Then the stars winked on until the sky was frantic with the dazzle of them. Snuggling down, I invited sleep, but it would not come. I kept thinking I heard steps. At times, scorning myself while doing it, I sat up to listen better. There was nothing—just stream chatter and wind sighs. But I'd stay sitting for a few minutes, looking at that fantastic canopy of icy glitter and at the brooding silhouettes of the mountains, cutting raggedly across the horizon.

Eventually, of course, I did drop off, to wake with the sun full in my face. No dawdling that day. Mildred would be waiting at Maroon Lake. I slogged back through the willows to the long, slanting trail, so much more open than are many mountain paths. Grassy hillsides rioted with flowers; wet spots gleamed with crimson shooting stars and yellow snow lilies, their petals swept back like crowns. I saw the blue gleam of Crater Lake through the trees and then came out onto boulder fields where columbine basked in the sun. I was close now.

*The Crowded Wildlands*

The side trail to Crater Lake swarmed with people, many of them ill-clad for the walk. I was amazed until I realized that this was Sunday, one of the most beautiful Sundays of the year, and that the end of the Maroon Lake auto road was only 2 miles away. I was amazed, too, at seeing a sign almost as large as a billboard warning wayfarers not to try climbing the Maroon Bells or Pyramid Peak without proper equipment and guidance. The very fact that the Forest Service had felt compelled to erect such a traffic signal suggested much about the invasion of the back country.

While I was looking at the sign, I was approached by a middle-aged couple who supposed from my backpack that I was a ranger. The woman, very small, wore oxfords that she undoubtedly called walking shoes. The man, heavy-set and balding, carried a long stick that he had picked up beside the trail and used as a walking staff. He asked how much farther it was to Crater Lake.

I made a guess. He smiled happily. "We can make that!" He confided that they were vacationing from Chicago and one of their hopes was to venture into a wilderness.

As they walked off, I reflected that the girl at Snowmass Lake had been right. Wilderness is an idea. From this spot on the Chicagoans would see no signs, no motorcycles, no picnic tables, no conveniences. They would return buoyed by the thought that they had hiked in the wilds.

And then I thought of the pilgrimage I had taken to the edge of the Needle Mountains, during the trip on which we had beaten the train. We had ridden from Vallecito Creek across Columbine Pass into Chicago Basin, where a titanic horseshoe of 14,000-foot peaks and weather-shattered ridges curves around the headwaters of Needle Creek.

Years before, five of us, dragging rented donkeys, had camped on almost the same spot so that we could climb those peaks and traverse those ridges. On the second trip I had simply wanted to remember. So I walked through the upper basin past the long snowbank that drops off the northeastern shoulder of Mount Eolus, where, braced on our ice axes, we had once glissaded 1,000 feet downward in little more than a minute. Then, after scrambling up a taxing talus slope, I reached a never-forgotten col in the rooster-crested ridge that runs toward Sunlight Peak.

Northward spread a wild disarray of peaks whose very names are delicious—Arrow, Vestal with its magnificent Wham Ridge, Storm King, Leviathan, Monitor, Turret. There are so many peaks that the surveyors had run out of names and had substituted numbers, Peak One on through Peak Thirteen, plus a stream called Noname Creek. The wonderful thing is that in all that jumble between Vallecito Creek and the chasm of the Animas River and from Needle Creek north to Elk Creek, there is not one artificial trail. Climbers go in from the railroad stops in the canyon—I had always dreamed that one day I would go with some of them—and the only aids they have are dim game trails. Aldo Leopold would have loved it, though I don't think he'd have gotten very far with his pack horses.

The isolated Needle-Grenadier section is one end of the wilderness spectrum. Crowded Crater Lake is the other. In between in an infinite spread of terrains meeting a wide variety of demands: the weekend magnet of Snowmass Lake, the "pack trail" over Buckskin Pass, the half-lost tumble of boulders and sapphire lakes under the southern cliffs of Capitol Peak. Not one place is deserted for very long except in winter, and even that bastion is falling. In December 1966 Philip Schmuck, Don Monk, and Kenneth Ross climbed two of the Fourteeners at the head of Chicago Basin, and every year now snow campers travel on skis all the way up West Maroon Creek and over the pass to Crystal River, emerging eventually at Crested Butte.

There is no wilderness. There is only the idea of wilderness. There, I think, is the key—for backpackers, skiers, day hikers, climbers, and horsemen to forget their occasional hostilities and remember instead that wherever they go someone else is right behind, eager to absorb what he, too, calls wilderness. Then perhaps every one of us will act throughout in such a way that all will find what their hearts desire.

I hurried on. Mildred and I were going to have much to talk about, including this: in the kind of wilderness I like best there are no solo trips.

EPILOGUE

*A Different World*

# 18
# THE SNEFFELS RANGE: HALFWAY BETWEEN YESTERDAY AND TOMORROW

Late in the afternoon one superb winter day Mildred and I left the San Miguel River at Placerville and drove east over Dallas Divide toward Ouray. As we topped out, we slowed in anticipation of that storybook wall of mountains, the Sneffels Range, northern front of the San Juan Mountains.

Although the impact of the view was as great as ever, I probably would not have stopped except for the sight of two skiers, a man and a woman, moving across a gleaming little meadow toward the edge of a shallow valley that would soon take them out of sight. A fence of yellow aspen logs blocked their way. They removed their skis in order to climb over the obstruction—the snow was not quite knee-deep in spite of a fresh fall the day before—and after readjusting their gear on the other side, they moved steadily ahead, not even glancing, so far as I could tell, in our direction. Moments later they disappeared over the hill.

From long familiarity with the area I knew they must be taking the trip for satisfaction alone. Nothing beckoned out yonder except meadows winding among aspen groves until the evergreens closed in perhaps a mile away. If the skiers wished, they could roam for a considerable distance through those transecting glades—and for a considerable time under the light of the nearly full moon which was just clearing the horizon opposite the setting sun.

It was a gorgeous evening. Noon's harsh contrast between the white of the new snow and the blackness of the spruce had given way to a wash of pastel colors. The sky was baby blue. The tops of the peaks glowed golden. The dusk thrown into the cirques by the crenelated ridges was suffused with violet light. Here and there where the undulant surface of the meadow rolled in such a way as to catch the horizontal rays of the sun, light sparkled from myriad prisms. The only mark on the new snow was that straight line of ski tracks— over the fence and on.

A big oil truck ground laboriously up the macadam road toward us. I doubt that the skiers, sheltered in the valley, heard more than a faint rumble. Inured to such passages on the highway, we did not pay much attention either, although our car shook as the truck went by, trailing a stink of diesel exhaust. As soon as it was possible to be heard again, Mildred said, her eyes still on the ski marks, "It was like stepping into a different world when they went across that fence. And it was so easy."

*Mountaineering on Mount Sneffels*

The thought returned the next summer as we again approached the Sneffels Range, a friend riding in the car with us. This time we came from the north, up the broad Uncompahgre Valley. On that route excitement builds gradually. From 60 miles away we could see only a blueness beneath cloud puffs left over from last night's storm. It was hard to tell whether the line was mountains or just our expectation of mountains. Then as the car sped ahead solidity came, a long east-west wall studded with square-topped towers, pinnacles, and pyramids. Almost exactly in the center of the wall was the huge, spike-topped helmet of Sneffels, as nearly symmetrical as a peak can be.

"Sneffels!" the friend mused. "Sniffles, almost. Where did such a name come from?"

"I'll show you."

Although our destination for the night was Ouray, where the eastern part of the range bends around the headwaters of the Uncompahgre River, I turned west at minuscule Ridgway, climbing toward the divide where we had seen the skiers the previous winter. We did not go that far, however. After crossing the east fork of Dallas Creek, we pulled off to the side of the road where we could look across an emerald hay meadow at the swiftly rising slopes.

Every curve and line seemed to have been contrived to enhance the grandeur of Sneffels' sheer northern face. Between treeline and the ribbed cliffs of the peak, a broad patch of snow still lingered, even though summer had advanced into July. Three giant couloirs, also filled with snow, rise out of that white patch and continue up the frontal precipice like the claws of an eagle track, stamped angrily into the dark rock.

A dirt road follows East Dallas Creek toward the mountains for several miles. Because of the previous night's heavy rain I did not want to risk it, and instead tried using my finger to point out landmarks. It was a poor substitute. Nothing except your own eyes can apprehend how the peak and its satellites seem to grow steadily higher and wilder-looking as you near them. Raggeder, too. What looks from the Uncompahgre Valley like an almost ruler-straight wall of igneous rock has actually been carved by ancient ice into a series of deep, cliff-girt bays.

"About seven miles from here," I said, "the creek forks. The main stream swings around the west flank of the peak into Blue Lakes Basin, between Sneffels and those big cliffs on Dallas Peak—an absolutely stupendous place. The left fork goes up almost under the north face, into Blaine Basin. That's where the mountain got its name."

Blaine, too, is a stupendous hollow, surrounded by vaulting ridges. In 1874 two members of the Hayden Survey climbed high onto those ridges and then with awe looked back down the slopes as if into a gigantic crater. One of them remarked to his companion that the depression reminded him of the Icelandic abyss described by Jules Verne in his fantasy *Journey to the Center of the Earth* as opening a way into the interior of the globe. His companion agreed. "And that," he had added, indicating the towering peak with the broad snow patch at its base, "is Snaefell," so named in Verne's story from the snow fields guarding its approaches.

"Why the name went down on the maps as Sneffels instead of Snaefell I don't know," I finished. And then, caught by memory, I added, "Blaine is where the San Juan Mountaineers had one of their base camps."

"Who are they?"

"They aren't any more."

I set about explaining. The San Juan Mountaineers were a totally informal group formed many years ago by my brother Dwight, Mel Griffiths, now of the University of Denver, and a handful of their cronies who also lived in nearby towns. I was an occasional appendage. All of us were in our late teens or early twenties.

By pooling resources the group acquired from catalogues a common stock of climbing equipment—mountaineering gear was more unwieldy and harder to come by then than it is now—and simultaneously gleaned from avid reading in technical journals a collection of Alpine phrases that they rolled lovingly on their tongues. Thus fortified, they set out to conquer every needle-like gendarme and aiguille on every arête in the San Juans.

In the process they absorbed more natural history and mountain economics than they realized and kneaded it, along with their climbing, into a place-love that escaped chauvinism only by being utterly ingenuous. I can remember Dwight looking straight up at some impossible cliff or down on some old mill building weathered to the color of the dumps of waste rock around it and giving his hands a great clap as if the only possible way to react to such a world was to applaud.

He and Mel and three others made the first ascent of Sneffels' north face by working out a route up the left-hand (eastern) claw mark of the eagle's track to the summit, then accounted to be 14,143 feet high. Dwight was so enthusiastic about the climb that a little later he led a young companion and me, roped together, up approximately the same route, taking advantage on the way of lessons learned during the first ascent. We crept along the flanks of weather-crazed pinnacles, teetered on loose boulders, chipped steps out of ice gleaming bluely under steep tongues of granulated snow, endured a battering of hail, crouched behind the dubious shelter of a small ledge as falling stones crashed down beside us—and finally gained the top, which is now accounted to be 14,150 feet high. I swear that if the mountain had been 7 feet higher that day, I'd never have made it.

"How about this!" Dwight exulted, pointing to all the nearby pinnacles he planned to climb, most of them named by the San Juan Mountaineers—Kismet, the Hand, the Penguin, the Thumb, murderous spires, every one of them. It is part of the irony of things that he died at Stanford University of polio at the age of twenty-three, while preparing a dissertation on the geology of the northern San Juan Mountains of Colorado.

## *A Woman in Marlboro Country*

I turned the car back across East Dallas Creek toward Ridgway and then, seeing a tiny, familiar figure outside a small ranch house of white clapboards, stopped abruptly. It was Marie Scott, a legend in her own time. She is very old now, about 5 feet tall and no heavier, her cowboys say, than a cake of soap after Monday's wash. Long before anyone in Colorado had thought of Women's Lib, Marie Scott, unencumbered by a husband, had set about carving a cattle ranch out of the slopes bordering Dallas Creek. Tales abound concerning her riding, roping, and cussing alongside the toughest hands of the district. So do stories of her outfoxing city investors arriving with lawyers to get the best of her in land deals. It is said that not long ago, when she was well over seventy, she snatched a pasture she wanted from under the nose of a competitor by crawling beneath the seller's pickup truck and clinching the deal while helping him repair a faulty transmission. By such methods this fragile senior citizen had made herself one of the biggest landholders in southwestern Colorado.

My stepfather, who once ran a small herd of pure-bred Herefords along with his other cattle near the Lone Cone, sometimes sold bulls to Marie. On the Western Slope such associations last through the generations, and so when Mildred and I and our friend appeared at her gate she asked us inside for a visit.

The door of the house opens onto a combination dining-living room Spartanly furnished, the floor covered with linoleum. Dominating the area is an enormous white refrigerator that would not fit into the cramped kitchen. There is a small dining table, a round-bellied heating stove, a few chairs, and a couch. All the furniture except the table is covered with Navajo blankets. Behind the couch a big picture window looks toward Sneffels.

Motivated partly by jealousy, I asked Marie whether many climbers went up East Dallas these days to tackle the north face. She grimaced. In her opinion mountain climbing is a waste of energy. "I quit noticing," she said, which probably meant that the ventures were becoming common. If only a few people went, she'd have kept track of them.

She was much more interested in showing us a present from actress Debbie Reynolds. Debbie, as Marie called her, had been in the region during the filming of *The Unsinkable Molly Brown,* and the two had become friends.

Marie sat us on the couch with our backs to the picture window and turned a switch. An enlarged, magnificent photograph of the Sneffels Range, transferred to ground glass with a light behind it, sprang into view—the exact view to which our backs were turned. One of Debbie Reynolds' cameramen had taken the picture originally, and the actress had arranged to have it made into this gift. Nothing could have pleased Marie Scott more.

I suppose that having on your wall an illuminated picture of the view you see every day is no more incongruous than having a picture of your wife and children on your desk. What did seem incongruous to me was this easy melding of two contrasting backgrounds—the once-isolated, uncomplicated, rigorous cattle ranch milieu of Marie Scott and the technological, urban sophistication of Hollywood. For Debbie Reynolds, Marie's world must have been totally different from anything else she had experienced. Yet she had entered it as easily as those skiers had crossed the fence of aspen logs the winter before.

*The Changing San Juans*

We spent the rest of our time in the northern San Juans witnessing similar facile transitions, most of them made possible by the remnants of the intense mining activity that had swept across the area during the closing decades of the last century. That mining in turn had depended on a very distinctive geology.

Once upon a time the San Juan Mountains were a gigantic dome covered by thick, banded layers of sedimentary rock. How many times the dome was eroded by water and ice to a peneplain only to rise again is uncertain. During one of the later swellings volcanoes exploded all over the dome, "a brilliant pyrotechnic display of over 100,000 eruptions from hundreds of vents," wrote geologist Wallace Atwood in *The Rocky Mountains.* Mount Sneffels and many of its neighbors are giant plugs of lava that cooled in the throats of the dying volcanoes. In many places molten ores welled into cracks, generally called veins, in the congealing magma.

Lava, cinders, dust, and angular chunks of metamorphosed rock compacted into a conglomerate called breccia. Ash solidified into tuff. These layers of volcanic material are often more than 2,000 feet thick. During the ice ages they were scoured fiercely by glaciers gathering in huge catchment basins on the slopes of the tormented dome. The result, in places, has been a series of deep cirques separated by towering saw-toothed ridges. Hanging valleys drop spectacular waterfalls into deep canyons littered with the debris of snow avalanches and landslides. The constant weathering also revealed, in the form of outcrops, the veins that had been filled with ores of gold, silver, lead, and zinc.

As soon as prospectors brought back word of the mineral wealth, the Ute Indians were cleared out of the area by the Brunot Treaty of 1873, and miners swarmed in. Wherever major streams came together in pockets large enough to hold a street or two, towns took shape. At first the citizens obtained their supplies by paying outrageous tolls to the builders of wagon roads. As wealth increased, narrow-gauge railroads thrust with arrogant audacity up the howling canyons. Trails for pack mules and donkeys ran like the veins in a leaf out of the central canyons up the side hills and tributary gorges to mines that often stood high above treeline. If the mines proved profitable, trails grew to be wagon roads, clinging like plucked eyebrows to the frowning face of the mountain.

Although most of the mines closed about the beginning of the present century, the larger towns (generally they were county seats) and the sturdiest of the high-country roads survived. Both the towns and the roads were rediscovered after World War II by increasing numbers of tourists. Many of the newcomers were either equipped with or able to rent four-wheel-drive vehicles. The result has been an unprecedented invasion of the high country. The most unathletic of lowlanders can now visit in comparative comfort places never seen by the town dwellers of the mining stampede. Those oldtimers, ironically enough, had lacked the means and time to reach the pinnacles. Today all you need is the ability to shift gears on the brink of a cliff without losing your cool. Even that is growing easier as county road crews, eager for tourists, gradually widen and smooth the more popular of the jeep roads, as they are called.

Ouray and its environs furnish a case history. The town is slowly becoming a tourist center just by being beautiful. The slopes that surround it are too steep for skiing, and so it has lacked the wintertime stimulus that remade the old mining towns of Aspen and Crested Butte and created such brand-new centers as Vail and Snowmass. You come to Ouray primarily for the mountains themselves and for the relics they contain.

The northern approach to the town is through a canyon bordered by walls of sedimentary rock whose terraces are bright green with stubborn trees and brush. Some of the rock is sandstone; some, limestone. Most is red, but here and there are vivid streaks of yellow. At the head of the valley, neatly framed by the chromatic cliffs, is a pyramidal peak, Mount Abrams (12,800 feet high), that would be quite undistinguished except for the focus brought to bear on it by the converging lines of water and slanting strata.

The town occupies the bottom of a huge cup formed by an unexpected widening of the canyon walls. As usual on our arrival we deposited our luggage at a motel and then drove slowly through the upper streets to look at the fine old Victorian houses, ornate with pillared verandas, filigreed woodwork, cupolas, and dormer windows. Years ago, when I had been working in the area's last surviving mine, most of those houses had been empty and tumbling. Now all are occupied, all are neat—and prices are fantastic.

After our tour of inspection we repaired to a familiar flat roof from which we could watch the drama of evening. The curving walls of the basin lead eastward into a massive horseshoe filled with steep forests broken by occasional glades. In the evenings elk graze in those openings and can often be seen from town with the aid of binoculars. Above the timbered slope is a crown of compacted volcanic material carved by weather into spectacular turrets and buttresses. In some lights the rock looks dark gray, but it is underlain with a brown-red tinge. As the sun drops, this tinge brightens until at times the normal alpenglow of the mountain evening burns with an intense pink radiance. As one watches the ethereal sky, sensing how swiftly the light will die, it is hard to escape a moment of melancholy.

*A Mountain Dilemma*

Summer mornings are generally bright and joyous. On one such crystal blue and golden day we decided to drive up Canyon Creek to the famed Camp Bird Mine and then swing along the back (south) side of the Sneffels Range as far into Yankee Boy Basin as we could go. Except for a place or two where the thoroughfare hangs breathlessly over Canyon Creek's deep gorge, the route is well maintained as far as the Camp Bird, which is still operating and quite possibly has produced over the years more precious mineral than any other mine in Colorado. Beyond the Camp Bird, however, the "road" grows narrower, rougher, steeper—or at least that was how I recalled it from previous trips. Supposing that we might need a little extra power and sturdiness in the car we used, we rented a four-wheel-drive vehicle.

It's a zestful drive, furnishing both roller-coaster thrills and a continually shifting panorama of cascades, cliff, pinnacles, tall spruce, and unexpected little meadows spangled with wild flowers. Strewn throughout the entrancing landscape is the decaying trash of the mining stampede. Once there were even small towns up here; the main one, named Sneffels, was located at the base of a rugged, square-headed mountain unimaginatively called Stony Peak.

Only a few of the old industrial and residential buildings remain standing, either in the abandoned towns or on the steep slopes outside. Avalanches, common in the precipitous district, have swept away some, and a few have burned. The majority, however, have simply collapsed under the weight of three quarters of a century of snow into jackstraw piles of splintered boards. Mingled with the wreckage are hunks of rusting machinery, tangled cables, and twisted rails that once had supported ore cars. Gray tree stumps abound. Dumps of waste rock run like scabby tongues out from the mouths of prospect holes.

Because the rubbish tells of a bold and strenuous life and because it is associated with such glamorous words as *gold* and *silver,* it seems romantic. Souvenir hunters wander around, digging in midden heaps for oddly shaped old medicine and whisky bottles whose glass has sometimes been tinted by age and sunlight to a delicate purple. They collect the pointed, iron-shafted candleholders that miners once thrust into cracks in the rock to light their work, and they pounce with joy on such discarded household items as cracked sadirons and broken coffee grinders. I admit to having done my share of that kind of pawing, and I'll say this for it: it does set your imagination working. What strange quirks of hope and stubbornness led people to try to put down roots in this hard, demanding world, so different from anything the majority of them had ever known before?

We never reached the heart of Yankee Boy Basin. As we crawled through the last scattered stands of runted trees toward the lower lip of the bowl, with cataracts foaming noisily to our left and the great cliffs of Potosi, one of Sneffels' major satellites, rearing high to our right, we came upon what must be one of the most extraordinary fields of long-spurred, white-and-lavender columbine in all the land. Acres upon acres of them tilt upward from the stream to the reddish feet of the precipices. Massed clumps push with soft insistence through mats of scrub willow. They barricade boulders already colorful with lichen and ring the gaunt, dwarfed timberline spruce with loveliness. Purple king's-crown, sky-blue chiming bells, and crimson paintbrush struggle for recognition but are overpowered.

We left our vehicle and wandered through the miniature jungle of blossoms until we found a spot of sun-warmed grass where we could sit with our backs against a smooth rock and eat our picnic lunch while watching the flow and stir of a mountain day.

Wind was the magician. The merest puff stirred the blanket of blossoms to agitated flutterings. Harder gusts turned the silvery undersides of the willow leaves to the sun, sending shimmers of light across the hillocks. Every now and then a more sustained whoosh whisked away the brawling sound of the stream. A moment later the air would become motionless again and the noise of the cascades flooded back. Dragonflies darted. Swarms of tiny insects —where do they vanish at the least stir of a breeze?—rose and sank above the briefly immobile flowers. But whether we felt wind or not, the clouds were never free. Ragged yarn balls of them, gray-bottomed, silver-edged, stampeded across the ridges, giving promise of summer's usual lightning storm and slashing shower.

Several hikers went by at intervals, and two four-wheel-drive vehicles. Then while we were still relaxing beside the rock, stretching out the last sips of white wine, we saw in amazement a gray sedan of no more than normal sturdiness coming up the steep road. It moved slowly, heaving and groaning. For a while it was stuck in the soft gravel of a dry wash, but the two male occupants managed to pry it loose. They continued to the rim of the basin, found a place where they could turn around, and crawled back, waving amiably as they passed us.

If one ordinary automobile can reach Yankee Boy Basin on a sight-seeing trip—and for all I know this was not the first—then others can. The next step will be to ask the county supervisors to have the worst places smoothed out just a bit—it'll help keep the tourists around a little longer. You know, Bill, that soft spot by the old Ruby Trust. And another. And then one more.

Years ago, the Forest Service, recognizing that these columbine fields were a treasure worth protecting, closed Yankee Boy Basin to grazing by sheep. It's harder to pass laws excluding people, especially since a few people were already getting up there by means of specially powered cars. Shouldn't everyone who wishes to see this sight be privileged to do so?

As far as we could tell, not a person picked a single blossom that day. So perhaps we have progressed since the summers when the first railroads to penetrate the mountains behind Denver attracted tourist trade by running wild-flower specials from which excursionists returned with, quite literally, washtubs full of columbine. Perhaps that small sign beside the road, "Take Nothing But Pictures," means something now. I don't know. But anyway, like it or not, even places like Yankee Boy are opening up again, and that is certainly a development I'd not have predicted years ago when I was sweating out my first paying job at the old Camp Bird Mine, down the hill a ways.

### Over the Hill to Resurgent Telluride

The situation was no different in Telluride. We went there the back way, over the mountains, still in our rented vehicle. The first leg of the trip lies along the paved highway that leads eventually to Silverton and Durango—past the malodorous stains of the Ouray city dump, along the granite-plated east side of the Uncompahgre Gorge, beside the disintegrating mine relics on the flame-colored shoulder of Red Mountain. At the top of Red Mountain Pass is a weathered directional sign that reads approximately as follows: "Telluride, City of Gold, 12 miles—2 hours. You Don't Have to Be Crazy to Take This Road, But It Helps. Jeeps Only." The gimmick works. Having been intrigued by the words, many tourists sign up for a trip on sight-seeing 4-wheel-drive buses plying out of Ouray. Some find the experience more exciting than they had anticipated.

The wheel tracks climb through tundra and gray fell-fields to Black Bear Pass, about 13,000 feet high, with stupendous views southward of the craggy peaks of the Grenadier and Needle Mountain sections of the San Juans. After dipping over the pass, the road enters a long draw full of lichen-splotched gray slide-rock. Conical peaks hump up against the constricted horizon.

When finally the land falls away into the head of San Miguel Canyon, it does so with startling abruptness.

The San Miguel River is formed by a fan of three streams—Mill Creek, Ingram Creek, and Bridal Veil Creek—that plunge through 3,000 feet of cataracts and waterfalls into a U-shaped glacial trough of singular beauty. About 2 miles below the horseshoe head of the trough, the town of Telluride is clearly visible, but for the time being most sight-seers are too nervous to notice.

An abandoned building teeters beside the brink of Ingram Falls. The structure used to house the transfer station of the Black Bear tramway. This means that it received from the Black Bear Mine, situated in a high cirque some distance away, a steady sequence of ore buckets suspended from moving cables supported by tall wooden towers. When the buckets reached the transfer building, they were shifted to another cableway that carried them steeply down beside Ingram Falls and its lower cataracts to the first level space in the bottom of the glacial trough, down there half a mile under your teeth.

A thrill eagerly sought by boys who grew up in Telluride was a ride in an ore bucket as it swung and clattered along its aerial path. We had different preferences. Some argued vehemently in favor of the Black Bear tram. I thought the one that dropped down Mill Creek from the great Smuggler-Union workings was superior. To anyone who has had either experience, today's ski lifts seem like the most delicate of imitations—a sentiment quite possibly attributable to nostalgia.

The jeep road into the trough isn't as direct as the tramway and carries far more people in, I imagine, greater safety—though not all sight-seers will believe that. The wheel tracks descend via a ladder of zigzags whose V-shaped ends alternate between the chute of cascades into which Ingram Falls plunges and the gray-brown cliffs over which Bridal Veil plummets in a hissing lace of mist 365 feet high. The V's where the zigs break into zags are so sharp that the drivers of the vehicles have to back and fill to get around them. Since the passengers in the backing four-wheel-drive vehicles cannot see any road from their seats, just empty space, they must believe with blind faith that the driver really knows where his hind wheels are. The effort creates a certain amount of tension.

More decrepit buildings sit on the exact brink of the Bridal Veil cliffs.

Once they housed a power plant. I am aware that it was a desecration to slap industrial plants smack dab on top of two of the handsomest waterfalls in the Rocky Mountains, and I hope as earnestly as any environmentalist that such an act is never permitted again. Just the same I would not have these relics taken away, even if the removal were economically feasible. We need these sights to help us remember what kind of land it was across which we are now sweeping with, comparatively speaking, so little effort.

At the bottom of the cliffs you pass the grimy mill buildings and the enormous tailing dumps of the Idarado Mine. For years Idarado, which has acquired title to all the claims between the upper San Miguel and Red Mountain, kept Telluride alive, and local residents appreciate the salvation. But now Colorado's new mountain renaissance, which has nothing to do with minerals, is transforming this remote area, too. Once-deserted houses—there aren't as many classic Victorian models as in Ouray—are being patched and painted, sold and resold on a soaring market. Because there is a hopeful new ski development nearby, structures that are built from scratch tend to follow the fad for blocky, shingle-sided condominiums. Although I have no figures to prove it, I imagine that because of the skiing, the new citizens of Telluride are, on the average, younger than those in Ouray. Nor does their verve and dash end with winter. When summer winds are right, hang gliders soar off in lovely flight from the steep ridges that rise between the town and the ski area.

Summertime culture, a modern mountain necessity along with gourmet restaurants, has also reared its head in Telluride. Central City began the trend with its famed opera performances. Aspen followed with a superb music festival and a prestigious Institute for Humanistic Studies. Ouray holds an annual art fair. During the summer of 1974, Telluride joined the procession with a film festival featuring old classics and new experiments, each one minutely analyzed at seminars conducted by avant-garde experts. It's a far cry from the touring vaudeville and drama companies that used to regale the miners in what every one of the old towns called its opera house—houses where opera was seldom, if ever, heard.

## A Most Uncertain Prospect

There are various jeep paths back to Ouray. Because we wanted to make a full circle of the Sneffels Range, we chose the one that climbs out of the red canyon of the San Miguel onto broad benches where aspen groves alternate with meadows of shimmering bunch grass. Eventually the route leads across Hastings Mesa to Dallas Divide, where we had seen the two skiers cross the fence the previous winter. Well before we reached that point, while we were still high on the massive slope of Last Dollar Mountain, we halted the car, got out, and walked to the edge of a little terrace, just to discover how far we could see.

It's a long way. Beyond the deep red gash of San Miguel Canyon rise isolated massifs that are geologic echoes of the titanic forces that created the San Juan Mountains. There is the many-pointed cluster of the Wilson Peaks, three of them topping 14,000 feet in elevation. There are the brown whalebacks of the Dolores Peaks and the graceful symmetry of the Lone Cone. Girdling them are rolling mesas of bright grass and ruffle-edged aspen forests.

Beyond those mesas the land falls off through ponderosa pine, scrub oak, and juniper to the desert cliffs of Paradox. The La Sal and Abajo Mountains of Utah glimmer in the blue distance. Stretching out from the base of the latter are the broad sage plains across which the road to the land of the Anasazi, the Ancient Ones, spears its way.

It's a vast land and it has been a hard-used one. The Anasazi overstrained their part of it. So did the miners who recklessly slashed down the forest around their workings and who spewed such quantities of waste into the streams that they became rivers of gray sludge. Stockmen overgrazed the mesas. Dam builders drowned the canyons and are still drowning them.

Some of those abuses are being checked. The Forest Service controls, not to everyone's satisfaction, the cutting of timber and the utilization of grass. Mines must help keep the streams clear by diverting their tailings into settling ponds. New dams are being challenged. Bits of relatively uninjured land—one fine block lies yonder around the Wilson Peaks—are being set aside as Wilderness Areas into which no mechanization of any sort can legally intrude.

Those are heartening accomplishments. But when you see how easily so remote and rigorous an area as the Sneffels Range is being overrun, you can't help worrying about what tomorrow will be like. Can these mountain lands, rising high out of the aridities that surround them, be made available to all the people who want and need them and still escape being scarred the way they were scarred by our sanguine predecessors?

I like to think so. I think it because I believe an awareness of how little is left is reaching out beyond the confines of the mountains themselves to people who like to think about the freedoms that the mountains—and the plains and the plateaus—have symbolized throughout our short history. If it were otherwise, I'd not be writing this book, which in effect is asking still more people to come see these wonders—but see them, I hope, with no desire to reduce them.

# GLOSSARY OF TERMS

AIGUILLE—a rock pinnacle sharp enough to suggest a needle. Most of the relatively few aiguilles in the Colorado Rockies stand out boldly on arêtes (q.v.) leading to or from major peaks. Cf. *gendarme*.

ALLUVIAL FAN—an accumulation of the materials of erosion deposited by water at the mouth of a mountain canyon.

ALPINE—the highest life zone (q.v.) in the mountains. It extends from treeline (q.v.) as far upward as plants and lichens can find lodgment.

ANTICLINE—rock stratum or strata that have been folded upward into a dome or arch.

ARÊTE—a thin, rugged, rocky ridge crest.

BASIN—a bowl-shaped depression lying between mountain ranges or embraced within the ridges of a single mountain. Basins may be huge. The Great Basin covers most of Nevada and parts of its contiguous states. Basins on mountainsides are smaller depressions open at one side for drainage. They generally are the source of streams; often small lakes are impounded in their lower sections' glacial moraines (q.v.).

BIOME—a well-defined ecological region supporting more or less uniform plant growths. The High Plains country at the eastern foot of the Rockies is a short-grass biome.

BRECCIA—a conglomerate rock composed of angular fragments held together by well-cemented sand. Much breccia is volcanic in origin.

CIRQUE—an open-fronted basin (q.v.) or rock amphitheater high on the side of a mountain. The product generally of glacial action, cirques are characterized by steeper sides than those associated with ordinary basins.

COL—a depression or saddle in a mountain ridge. Most high mountain road and trail passes utilize cols.

COMPOSITES—the largest family of flowering plants in Colorado. The three main groups of the family are classified according to the structure of the flower heads—ray, disk, or both ray and disk. The structures are too complex to describe in a short glossary.

COULOIR—a deep gully in the side of a mountain. Most couloirs are vertical, although occasionally one will run horizontally, as on the Mount of the Holy Cross.

CUESTA—a long, asymmetrical ridge with a cliff on one side and a slowly rising slope opposite the cliff. Misnamed Mesa Verde (see text) is a classic example. A mesa is flat-topped and generally has cliffs on more than one side.

DESERT VARNISH—dark streaks and blotches on sandstone cliffs. The discoloration is often caused by manganese dioxide leached from the soil by seeping storm water and then deposited on the cliff faces by the oozing moisture.

FELL-FIELD—an area above timberline strewn with boulders among which alpine plants find refuge.

GENDARME—a blocky pinnacle on the side of a mountain ridge or mountain slope. Gendarmes (to be subjective) are sturdier than but not so independent-looking as aiguilles (q.v.). As the name suggests, they are policemen guarding the summit.

KRUMMHOLZ—a dense, twisted clump of dwarfed timberline evergreens.

LACCOLITH—a domed massif (q.v.) formed by a mass of igneous rock pushing upward against and warping overlying sedimentary beds. Such massifs are sometimes called "bubble" mountains.

LARAMIDE REVOLUTION (Laramide deformation)—a period of widespread crustal disturbances during the Mesozoic era, some 70 million years ago. The basic linear pattern of the Rockies was laid down at that time.

LIFE ZONES—an ascending series of geographic regions defined by the kinds of plants and trees that grow in them. The main feature controlling changing growth patterns is altitude. For the principal zones in Colorado, see text, page 65.

MAGMA—molten rock originating in the earth's interior.

MASSIF—a cluster of peaks rising from the same land bulk.

MONADNOCK—an isolated hill that has resisted being eroded to the level of the peneplain (q.v.) that surrounds it.

MORAINE—rock debris, produced by grinding ice, that is deposited along the margins of glaciers. Lateral moraines are ridges that once lined the sides of glaciers. Terminal moraines are the confused rubble dumped at the ends of glaciers.

PENEPLAIN—land left nearly flat by a long period of erosion.

RANGE—an extended, often linear group of associated mountains and valleys. Though more extensive than a massif (q.v.), a range is nevertheless a subordinate part of a larger mountain system. Thus the Sangre de Cristo Range, which embraces the Blanca massif, is a discrete part of the Colorado Rockies.

SCREE—talus (q.v.). Some mountaineers apply the word *scree* to talus slopes composed of stones smaller than fist size. The same mountaineers sometimes use the term *slide-rock* (q.v.) to describe pieces of talus larger than footballs.

SLICK ROCK—a Southwestern colloquialism for relatively smooth expanses of sandstone from which the soil has been stripped by erosion.

SLIDE-ROCK—heaps of broken rock at the foot of cliffs or the disintegrated remains of cliffs. The stuff is called "slide-rock" because of its instability underfoot. Cf. *talus*.

SOLIFLUCTION TERRACES—undulant surfaces created when alpine soil saturated with moisture and warmed by the sun slips gently downward over the harder layers of frozen ground beneath.

TALUS—sheets and tongues of fractured rock guarding the base of mountain peaks and cliffs. See *scree* and *slide-rock*.

TARN—a small, high-altitude lake. Generally speaking, tarns are fed by underground seepage rather than by surface streams.

TREELINE (also *timberline* and *tree limit*)—the point on a mountainside beyond which trees do not grow. The line's average elevation in Colorado is 11,500 feet above sea level. Deviations from this average, wrought by either protection or exposure, can range up to 500 feet higher or lower.

TUFF—solidified volcanic dust and ash.

TUNDRA—in strict usage, the area above treeline, underlain with perpetual frost and supporting only lichens, sedges, coarse grass, dwarfed wild flowers, and stunted shrubs. More commonly, "tundra" means this growth alone rather than the area where the growth occurs.

# BIBLIOGRAPHY

The following is a list of books and pamphlets that for the most part can be found in Colorado's larger libraries or at least in the regions with which they deal. It is not a complete list, but indicates merely those books I have brushed across and have remembered. It does not include magazine articles. However, there are four regional publications whose current and back issues afford rewarding browsing. Confusingly enough, two are called *Colorado:* a commercial venture, *Colorado,* which is appealing in large part because of its color photographs, and *The Colorado Magazine,* the official publication of the State Historical Society of Colorado. The third publication is *Trail and Timberline,* issued by the Colorado Mountain Club. Environmental issues are well covered by a bi-weekly tabloid, *High Country News.*

Atwood, Wallace W., *The Rocky Mountains.* New York, 1945.
Bailey, Florence M., *Handbook of Birds of the Western United States.* Cambridge, Mass., 1921.
Baldwin, Donald N., *The Quiet Revolution.* Boulder, Colo., 1972.
Bird, Isabella, *A Lady's Life in the Rocky Mountains,* reprint edition. Norman, Okla., 1960.
Blair, Edward, and E. Richard Churchill, *Everyone Came to Leadville,* pamphlet. Gunnison, Colo., 1972.
Borland, Hal, *High, Wide and Lonesome.* Philadelphia and New York, 1956.
Bowles, Samuel, *Our New West.* Hartford, Conn., 1869.
Brown, Robert L., *An Empire of Silver.* Caldwell, Idaho, 1965.
―――, *Holy Cross, the Mountain and the City.* Caldwell, Idaho, 1970.
*Colorado.* American Guide Series. New York, 1970.
"Colorado River Quality Improvement Program, Paradox Valley Unit, Colorado." U. S. Dept. of the Interior, Bureau of Reclamation, Durango, Colo., August 1974.
Craighead, John J.; Craighead, Frank, Jr.; and Ray J. Davis, *A Field Guide to Rocky Mountain Flowers.* Cambridge, Mass., 1963.
Dyer, John L., *The Snowshoe Itinerant.* Cincinnati, 1890.
Eberhart, Perry, and Philip Schmuck. *The Fourteeners, Colorado's Great Mountains.* Chicago, 1970.

Evans, Laura, and Buzz Belknap, *Dinosaur River Guide,* pamphlet. Boulder City, Nevada, 1973.

Fenneman, Nevin M., *Physiography of Western United States.* New York, 1931.

Griswold, Don, and Jean Harvey Griswold, *The Carbonate Camp Called Leadville.* Denver, 1951.

Hart, Jerome, and Elinor A. Kingery, *Fourteen Thousand Feet.* Denver, 1931.

Leopold, Aldo, *A Sand County Almanac,* paperback ed. New York, 1972.

McConnell, Virginia, *Bayou Salado, the Story of South Park.* Denver, 1966.

*The Magnificent Rockies,* by the editors of *The American West.* Palo Alto, Calif., 1973.

Moenke, Helen, *Ecology of Colorado Mountains to Arizona Deserts.* Denver, 1971.

Nash, Roderick, *Wilderness and the American Mind.* New Haven, 1967.

"The National Grasslands Story," pamphlet. U. S. Dept. of Agriculture, n.d.

*National Parkway Guide to Rocky Mountain and Mesa Verde National Parks.* Casper, Wyo., 1972.

"Natural Resources of Colorado." U. S. Dept. of the Interior, n.d.

Nelson, Ruth Ashton, *Plants of Rocky Mountain National Park.* Third edition, n.p., 1970.

Niedrach, Robert, and Robert B. Rockwell, *Birds of Denver and Mountain Parks.* Denver, 1959.

O'Rear, John, and Frankie O'Rear, *The Aspen Story.* New York, 1966.

Ormes, Robert, *Guide to the Colorado Mountains.* Chicago, 1972.

———, *Railroads and the Rockies.* Denver, 1963.

Page, Charles A., "Your Passport to the Gunnison Country," pamphlet. Gunnison, Colo., 1973.

Roberts, Rhoda, and Ruth Ashton Nelson, *Colorado Wildflowers.* Revised edition, Denver, 1971.

———, *Mountain Wildflowers of Colorado.* Denver, 1967.

Rockwell, Wilson, *Uncompahgre Country.* Denver, 1965.

Smith, Duane A., *Rocky Mountain Mining Camps,* paperback ed. Lincoln, Neb., 1974.

Sprague, Marshall, *The Great Gates, the Story of the Rocky Mountain Passes.* Boston, 1964.

———, *Newort in the Rockies: the Life and Good Times of Colorado Springs.* Denver, 1961.

Tilden, Freeman, *The National Parks.* Revised edition, New York, 1970.

Ubbelohde, Carl; Benson, Maxine; and Duane A. Smith, *A Colorado History.* Revised edition, Boulder, Colo., 1972.

Vandenbusche, Duane, and Rex Meyers, *Marble, Colorado.* Denver, 1970.

Walker, Bryce S., and the editors of Time-Life Books, *The Great Divide.* New York, 1973.

Wolle, Muriel S., *Stampede to Timberline.* Boulder, Colo., 1949.

Wood, Nancy, and Myron Wood, *Colorado: Big Mountain Country.* Revised edition, New York, 1972.

Zwinger, Ann H., *Beyond the Aspen Grove.* New York, 1970.

———, and Beatrice E. Willard, *Land Above the Trees: a Guide to American Alpine Tundra.* New York, 1972.

# INDEX

Abrams, Mount, 210
Agriculture. *See* Farming
Alfalfa, 96, 137
Alluvial fans, 50, 218
Alpine fir, 5, 29, 67–68, 177–78
Alpine life zone, 65n, 68, 69–71, 86, 218
Alpine (downhill) skiing, 9
Altitude (heights): ecology and, 61, 62–71; fad peaks and, 164–73; life zones, 65–71
Anasazi (the Ancient Ones), 101–14, 216
Animal life, 51–53, 54, 70 (*see also* Hunting; Livestock; specific kinds, places); exterminating programs and, 55, 117–24
Animas Canyon, 11, 31–36, 188
Animas River and country, 31–36, 91, 198
Antelopes, 52–53
Antero Peak, 96
Anticlines, 135, 136, 218
Arapaho County, Colorado, 53
Arctic-Alpine life zone, 65n
Arêtes, 82, 84, 218
Arkansas River, 17, 49, 53–54, 56, 76, 78, 79–80, 91, 153, 154, 158, 161–62, 169; pattern of, 79–80; Royal Gorge, 79–80; Valley, 53–54, 79–80, 159–63, 169
Aspen (trees), 28, 30, 37, 38, 39, 40, 42, 44, 65–66, 77, 90, 94, 95, 203
Aspen, Colorado, 7, 8, 87, 98, 159, 160, 186, 192, 210; Institute for Humanistic Studies, 215
Atchison, Topeka and Santa Fe, 80
Atomic power, 97, 139
Atwood, Wallace W., 208
Austral life zones, 65
Automobiles, 82–83, 153, 154, 161, 179. *See also* Four-wheel-drive vehicles; Jeeps; Roads

Avalanche, 10
Avocets, 54

Backpacking, 30, 43, 148, 186–99
Banner trees, 5
Basin(s), 139; defined, 218
Battlement Mesa, 156
Beans (bean farming), 101, 106, 107, 113
Bear Lake, 81–82
Beavers, 42, 43, 67
Bedrock, Colorado, 137, 138
Big Sandy Creek, 55
Big Thompson Canyon, 64
Big Thompson River, 81
Biomes, 53, 69, 218
Birds, 38, 51–52, 54, 70, 90, 112, 148. *See also* specific kinds, places
Bitterns, 54
Black Bear Mine, 214
Black Bear Pass, 213
Black Canyon (Gunnison National Monument), 125–34
Black spruce, 44
Blaine Basin, 205
Blanca Mount, 166, 167–70
Blue Jays, 95
Blue Lakes Basin, 205
Blue Mesa Dam, 126, 127; Reservoir, 42, 127
Blue spruce, 42, 65
Boats (boating), 16–25 (*see also* Rafting); permits and regulations, 19
Book Cliffs, 93, 120
Boreal life zones, 65
Boulder, Colorado, 60, 62
Bowles, Samuel, 165
Bridal Veil Creek, 214
Bristlecone pines, 68
Brown, Al, 20, 24, 25
Buckskin Pass, 196, 199
Buena Vista, Colorado, 17, 169
Buffalo, 54, 55, 57, 77

Buffalo brush, 51
Buffalo grass, 50
Buffalo Peaks, 162
Bureaus, government (national). *See* specific bureaus, by name, e.g., Land Management, Bureau of (BLM)
Burrowing owls, 122–23

Cache Creek, 156
Cache le Poudre, 54
Cactus, 51; barrel, 51; flat-leafed, 64; prickly-pear, 51
California Peak, 167
Camp Bird Mine, 210–11, 213
Canada jay, 90
Canadian life zone, 65–66
Canyon Creek, 210–11
Canyons, 3, 59, 60, 92–93 (*see also* Valleys; specific canyons, places); river patterns and, 78–80
Carbonate ores, 153–54, 158, 160. *See also* Minerals; Mining; specific kinds
Carhart, Arthur H., 178, 179–82, 185
Carleton Tunnel, 161, 162
Carnotite ores, 97, 139–40. *See also* specific kinds, places
Carson, Rachel, 121
Cashin Mine, 137–38
Castles, The, 42
Cattle (livestock), 8, 11, 43, 54, 55, 77, 96–97, 98, 105, 138, 216 (*see also* specific kinds); ecological ranching and, 57–58; ranges, 77, 105–6; and wildlife extermination programs, 120, 122
Chasm Lake, 85
Cheat grass, 25, 27
Chicago Basin, 189, 190, 199
Chickadees, 35, 38, 90
Christian Canyon, 61

223

Cimarron River and country, 89, 126, 129
Cinnamon Pass, 30, 33
Cinquefoil, 148
Cirques, 4, 11, 80, 81, 218
Clark, John, 5–6
Cliff dwellings, Anasazi, 110–14
Cliggitt, Chuck, 127–29, 130–31, 132
Cliggitt, Mary Jean, 128, 130–31, 133
Climate. *See* Weather (climate)
Coal Basin, 43
Coal Creek, 42, 43
Coal mining, 8, 73, 78, 97, 160
Colorado, University of, 62, 160
Colorado-Big Thompson Project, 161
Colorado Midland Railroad, 160–61, 162
Colorado Mountain Club, 84
Colorado River, 7, 17, 79, 87, 91, 92–93, 136, 160; country, 92–93; Roaring Fork, 17, 87–88, 91, 159–60, 162; salt removal and, 140–41
Colorado River Storage Project, 26, 126
Colorado Springs, Colorado, 39, 60, 61, 63, 68, 160, 161; as Colorado City, 60; Garden of the Gods, 63
Columbine, 35, 90, 212–13
Columbine Pass, 189, 198
Comanche National Grassland, 56, 58
Como Lakes, 168
Composites, 145, 146, 148, 218
Congress, United States, 26, 182, 185
Continental Divide, 4, 6, 7, 54, 72, 75, 77–78, 79, 81, 87, 95–96, 164, 171, 188, 191
Cortez, Colorado, 101, 102, 104, 112, 113
Cottonwood (trees), 10, 28, 49, 53, 54, 64
Cottonwood Creek, 30
Cottonwood Gorge, 33
Coyotes, 52, 57–58, 123; poisoning of, 98, 118, 120–21
Crater Lake, 197, 198
Crested Butte, Colorado, 8, 9, 145, 146, 147, 148, 150, 199, 210
Crystal Canyon, 132
Crystal Creek, 132
Crystal Dam, 127, 128, 132
Crystal River, 88, 149–52, 199; Gorge, 149–52
Cuesta, 112, 218
Culebra Mountain, 168n, 169
Cunningham Gulch, 30, 31–32, 35

Daggett, O. W., 171–72, 173
Dallas Creek, 204, 205, 207–8
Dams, 81, 105, 126–27, 141, 161, 182, 216. *See also* Reservoirs
Dead Men's Point, 130, 131, 134
Deer, 10, 70, 95, 102, 105, 106, 109, 120, 122
Denver, Colorado, 19, 20, 39, 60, 61, 62–63, 64, 78, 161, 213; Park of the Red Rocks, 62–63
Denver South Park & Pacific Railway, 72, 73, 158
Denver & Rio Grande Railway, 73, 80, 158
Desert, 50–51, 93, 168

Desert Varnish, 23, 219
Devil's Head, 61
Devil's Punchbowls, 150
Dinosaur National Monument, 17–27; history of, 25–26; rafting in, 17–25
Dolores Canyon, 18, 108
Dolores Peaks, 216
Dolores River, 91–92, 101, 107, 108, 121, 136, 137, 138–40
Douglas fir (trees), 65, 90
Downhill (Alpine) skiing, 9
Dry-land farming, 49, 54–57, 58, 167; Anasazi and, 101, 105, 107
Dude ranches, 30
Duststorms (1930s), 55–57
Dyer, John L., 156–57

Eagle Canyon, 73
Eagle River, 92, 161, 171, 172
Eagles, 23, 85, 120, 121
East Dallas Creek, 205, 207–8
East River, 145, 147, 148, 149, 150, 151
Echo Park, 25–27, 182
Ecology (conservation, environment), xii, 19, 26–27, 55, 61, 62ff., 121, 162, 185 (*see also* specific aspects, individuals, places); animal and plant life and, 51–58; 117–24; farming and ranching and, 54–58; life zones, 65–71; national programs, 56; plains and mountains and, 49–56, 61–62; and range improvement, 105–6; rivers and water and, 53–55, 58, 78 (*see also* Rivers; water); tourism and recreation and, xi, 19, 83, 190–99 (*see also* Recreation) and wildlife extermination, 98, 117–24
Ehrlich, Paul, 148
Elbert, Mount, 79, 80–81, 153, 166, 167
Electric power, dams and, 126, 127. *See also* Dams
Elk, 66, 67, 70, 105, 120, 210
Elk Basin, 42–43
Elk Creek, 188, 190, 196
Elk Mountains, 77, 87, 147, 156, 169
Elk Park, 188
Emerald Lake, 149
Emmons, Lloyd, 110, 111
Engelmann spruce, 5, 29, 35, 43, 67–68, 90; spruce beetle and destruction of, 177–78
Environment(alists). *See* Ecology
Equinoctial snow storms, 39, 40, 43
Erosion, 50, 56, duststorms and, 55–57; and gullies, 56; ice water), 80–82
Escalante, Sylvestre, 112
Evans, John, 20, 22, 24, 25
Evans, Laura (Loie), 20, 22, 23, 25
Evans, Mount, 60, 64, 74, 82
Evans Gulch, 156, 162
Evergreens, 6, 7, 66, 68–69. *See also* specific kinds

Fairplay, Colorado, 154, 157n, 158, 169
Farming (agriculture), 54–58, 78 (*see also* Irrigation: specific aspects, crops, kinds, places);
Anasazi and, 101, 103–4, 105, 106, 107; dry-land farming (*see* Dry-land farming); duststorms (1930s), 55–57
Fell-fields, 70, 82, 219
Fenneman, Nevin M., 74
Ferrets, 121, 123
Ferrier, Grant, 41, 42, 43, 44
Ferrier, Mamie, 41, 42
Finches, rosy, 38, 70
Fires, and Wilderness Areas, 194, 195
Firewood, 38–39, 43
Firstview, Colorado, 58
Fir trees, 65, 66, 67–68, 90. *See also* specific kinds
Fish and Wildlife Service, 117, 120
Fishing, 30–36, 77, 81, 126, 132, 182. *See also* specific kinds, places
Flat Tops Wilderness Area, 177–85
Flowers, 29, 35, 51, 66–67, 69, 112, 145–46, 148, 149, 156, 163. *See also* specific kinds
Forest Service, United States, xiv, 56, 72, 97, 105, 115, 123 169, 172, 178–85, 197, 213, 216
Forget-me-nots, 69, 156
Four Corners country, 102, 112, 120
"Fourteeners" (peaks), 84–85, 164–73, 199
*Fourteeners, The,* 167
Four-wheel-drive vehicles, 30, 72, 83, 145, 154–55, 209, 211, 213. *See also* Jeep; Roads
Foxes, 121, 123
Fremont's squirrels (chickarees), 90
Front Range, 4, 63, 75–76
Fryingpan-Arkansas Project, 162
Fryingpan River, 160, 162

Gaillardia, 145
Gambel oak (scrub oak, oak brush), 29, 44, 63, 90
Game animals, 77 (*see also* Animal life; Hunting; specific animals); extermination of, 55, 119ff.
Garden of the Gods, 63; "Kissing Camels," 63
Geese, 54
Geological Service, 84, 166–67, 172
George, Barbara, 20
Ghost towns (ghost farms, ghost mines) 58, 72–73, 150–53, 211. *See also* specific places
Gilia, scarlet, 89, 90
Gilsonite, 93
Glaciers (glaciation), 4, 50, 80–81, 84. *See also* Ice
Glenwood Springs, Colorado, 17, 92, 160
Glossary of terms, 218–20
Gold (gold mining), 8, 60, 73, 76, 153–54, 209, 211
Gophers, 44, 70
Gothic, Colorado, 146–52
Gothic Natural Area, 148–52
Grama grass, 51, 55, 105
Grand Junction, Colorado, 93, 140n, 160
Grand Mesa, 93–94
Granite, 63, 74, 75–78, 87, 91

224

Grass(es), 25, 27, 29, 51, 57, 67, 90, 105–6 (*see also* specific kinds; places); wildlife extermination and, 117, 118, 121–22
Grasslands, 51–58
Gray, Asa, 164–65
Grays Peak, 164–66, 173
Greeley, Colorado, 53, 54, 60
Green River, 18, 21, 25, 26, 91
Grenadier Mountains, 188, 198, 213
Griffiths, Mel, 4, 5, 6, 7, 10, 205–6
Grizzly bears, 55, 120
Ground squirrels, 30, 52, 82
Grouse, 70, 90, 116, 119
*Guide to the Colorado Mountains*, 42, 167–68
Gunnison, Colorado, 8, 10
Gunnison, John, 93
Gunnison National Monument, 125–34; Black Canyon, 125–34
Gunnison River and country, 7, 8, 30, 42, 73, 79, 91, 92, 125–34; Lake Fork, 30, 33
"Guzzlers," 56

Hagerman, James J., 160
Hagerman Pass, 156, 160, 161
Hagerman Peak, 195
Hagerman Tunnel, 161
Half Moon (peak), 172, 173
Hallett Peak, 6, 82
Harvard, Mount, 166, 167
Hawks, 52, 112, 121, 123
Hay, 11, 37–38, 77, 96, 137
Hayden Survey, 136, 166, 170, 205
Haystack Mountain, 43–44
Hecox, Lem, 137–38
Highland Mary Lake, 30, 33, 35
Holes, river, 22, 24
Hollenback, Jim, 115, 122, 123
Holy Cross Mount, 170–73
Homestake Creek, 161
Homestake Dam, 162
Homesteaders (settlers), 95, 96–98
Hopi Indians, 103, 105
Horned larks, 52, 70
Horses, 55, 94–95, 159; and trails, 191–92, 193; wild, 55, 119–20
Hovensweep National Monument, 109, 110–11, 114
Hunting (*see also* Game animals): Anasazi and, 102, 106, 109; and wildlife extermination, 119–20ff.
Hydroelectric power, 126, 127. *See also* Dams

Ice: ages, 80; erosion, 80–82; tundra, 70. *See also* Glaciers; Snow
Idarado Mine, 21
Imperial Dam, 140–41
Independence Pass, 7, 160, 162
Indian Affairs, Bureau of, 105
Indian Peak, 4, 75
Indians, 51, 54, 55, 56, 60, 66, 85, 94–96, 120. *See also* specific people, places
Industrialization, 61, 97, 158, 215
Ingram Falls, 214
Institute of Arctic and Alpine Research (INSTARR), 3, 4, 5
Irrigation, 54, 58, 137, 139. (*See also* Dams; Reservoirs; Water

Jackrabbits, 52, 116, 119
Jays: blue, 95; Canada, 90
Jeeps, 83, 145, 150, 159, 162, 213, 214, 215–16 (*see also* Four-wheel-drive vehicles); "Jeep roads," 209, 214, 215
Johnson, John C., 147, 148
Johnson, John C., Jr., 148, 149
Judd, Gatwood H., 146–47
Juniper (trees), 64, 90, 105, 106, 112

Kayaks (kayaking), 17–19
Kenosha Pass, 37
Kivas, Anasazi, 103, 110, 111, 113
Krummholz ("wind timber") evergreens, 68–69, 219

Laccoliths ("bubble" mountains), 135–36, 219
La Junta, Colorado, 53, 115
Lakes, 79, 81–82 (*see also* specific lakes, places); dams and, 126; high-altitude, 81–82; "paternoster," 81; tarns, 81–82, 220
Land (*see also* Soil): developers and speculators and, 55, 97, 183
Land Management, Bureau of (BLM), xiv, 105–6, 109, 110
Laramide revolution, 50, 74–75, 79, 219
Larkspur, 31, 90
La Sal Canyon, 136, 138
La Sal Creek, 137–38
La Sal (The Salt) Mountains, 136–37, 216
Lasater, Tom, 57–58, 121–22
Lavender, Dwight, 205–6
Leadville, Colorado (Cloud City), 80, 153–67, 169; annual burro race, 157–58
Leopold, Aldo, 25, 181, 190, 191–92, 193, 198
Life zones, 65–71, 86, 219
Lightning, 50, 88–89, 112; "dry," 112
Limber pines, 68
Limestone, 61, 87, 210
Lincoln, Mount, 84, 166
Lodgepole pines, 5, 66
London Mountain, 155, 156
Lone Cone Peak, 88–89, 96, 104, 207, 216
Longs Peak, 74, 84–85; climbing, 84–85; the Diamond, 85; Keyhole, 85
Lowry ridge, 106–11
Lowry Ruins, 101, 103, 104–11
Lupines, 35, 66, 112

McCabe, Bill, 20
McElmo Canyon, 111, 120
Mairani, Guglielmo, 41–42, 43, 44–45
Mancos River, 112
Marble, Colorado, 151–52
Marble quarries, 151–52
Mariposa (sego lily), 90–91, 95, 112
Marmots, 70, 149
Maroon Bells (peak), 87, 186, 196–97
Maroon Lake, 186, 196, 197
Marsh marigolds, 69, 156
Massive, Mount, 80–81, 153, 156, 160, 162, 166, 167

Matheson, Colorado, 57
Meadows, The, 183
Mertensia (chiming bell), 66–67
Mesa Verde, 91, 104, 109, 110, 112–14, 218; National Park, 112–14
Mexico, Gulf of, 35, 50, 78
Middle Park, 74, 77, 78, 87, 92
Minerals, 50, 73, 83, 97, 153–61, 208–9, 215. *See also* Mines (mining); specific kinds, places
Mines (mining), 8, 32, 35, 60, 72–73, 83, 93, 95, 96, 98, 137–38, 139, 146–47, 150–52, 153–61, 162, 166, 208–9, 210–15, 216. *See also* Ghost towns; specific kinds, mines, places
Mississippi River, 53
Molas Creek, 188
Molas Lake, 188
Molybdenum, 153, 154
Monadnocks, 74, 219
Monarch Pass, 7
Montane life zone, 65–66, 86
Montrose, Colorado, 10
Moraines, 81, 219; lateral, 81, 219; terminal, 81, 219
Morrow Point, 128; Dam, 126–27, 128, 129, 134
Mosquito, Colorado, 153–54, 156, 157
Mosquito Creek, 154–55
Mosquito Mountain Range, 53, 79, 84, 166
Mosquito Pass, 153, 157, 158–60, 162, 163
Moss campion, pink, 69, 156
Mountains, Colorado, 49–51, 59ff. (*see also* Peaks; Ranges; Rocky Mountains; specific peaks, places, ranges); altitude and, 61, 62–71, 164–73; canyons, 59, 60 (*see also* Canyons); climbing, 82–83, 84–85, 164–73, 206; life zones, 65–71; origin, formation, history of, 49–50, 61–62, 74–75, 79; and plains, ecology of, 49–50 (*see also* Ecology); ranges, 74–85 (*see also* Ranges); and rivers and water, 53–54 (*see also* Rivers; Water)
Mountain sheep, 70, 77
Mudslides, 32, 33
Mule deer, 67
Muskrats, 54

National Center for Atmospheric Research, 62
National Forests, 179–80
National Grasslands, 56
Natural gas, 27
Navajo Peak, 4
Needle Creek, 198
Needle Mountains, 199, 198, 213
Never Summer Range, 75, 169
Niwot Ridge, 4, 7, 11
Nordic (cross-country) skiing, 9
North London Mine, 155, 158
North Park, 74, 77, 78
North Platte River, 79
Notch Mountain, 170–73
Nuthatches, 38, 90

Oil shale, 97, 183–84, 185
Ormes, Robert (Bob), 42, 167–68
Oro City, Colorado, 153, 154, 156

225

Otero County, Colorado, 58
Ouray, Colorado, 96, 203, 204, 209–10, 213, 215–16
Outward Bound School, 19–25, 187

Paintbrush, 35, 67, 89, 163
Paonia, Colorado, 41
Paradox Valley, 135–41, 216
Park of the Red Rocks, 62–63
Parks (flatlands), 77. *See also* specific parks, places
Park Service, United States, xiv, 19, 85, 105, 181
Parry, C. C., 164
Parry's primroses, 69, 156, 164n
Pasqueflowers, 29
Pawnee National Grassland, 56
Peaks, 84–85, 88–89, 164–73, 198 (*see also* Mountains; Ranges; specific peaks); climbing, 82–83, 84–85, 164–73, 205–6; fad, 164–73; trails, 164ff., 186ff.
Peneplein 50, 74, 219
Penstemon, 89, 90
Pesticides. *See* Poisons (pesticides)
Phlox, white, 69, 156
Piceance Basin, 183–84, 185
Pikas, 70
Pikes Peak, 58, 63, 74, 75–76, 82, 156, 170
Piñon pines (trees), 63, 105, 106, 112
Pipits (birds), 70
Pit houses, Anasazi, 102–3, 109
Placer gold mines, 139. *See also* Gold
Plains, 49–58, 74 (*see also* specific places); animal and plant life, 51–58; climate, 60; farms, 54–57; mountains and ecology of, 49–56, 74; population centers, 60; ranching and, 57–58; rivers and water and, 53–54; soil, 47–57
Plant life, 51, 63 (*see also* Flowers; Trees; specific kinds, places); altitude and, 63–71; farming and (*see* Farming; specific kinds); life zones and, 65–71; plateaus and, 89–91
Plateaus, 87–98
Platte River, 56, 78
Pleasant View, Colorado, 101, 108, 109
Poisons (pesticides), 55, 98; of prairie dogs, 117–24; problems of, 120–22; and wildlife extermination, 117–24
Ponderosa pine (trees), 28–29, 38, 59, 64, 65, 108; described, 64
Ponds, creation of, 105
Powder snow, 7, 9
Prairie dogs, 52, 115–24; described, 123–24; poisoning of, 117–24
Precipitation, annual. *See under* Rain; Snow
Predators, poisoning of, 98, 117–24
Primitive Areas, 181–85, 187–99
Pronghorn antelopes, 52–53
Ptarmigan, 70
Pueblo, Colorado, 53, 60, 78, 161, 180
Pueblos, Anasazi, 103–4, 108–14
Pyramid Peak, 196, 197

Quartz Creek, 72

Rabbit Ear Mountain, 78
Rafting (rafts), 16–25, 125–34; permits, 19; running the rapids, 125–34
Railroads, 54, 72, 73, 80, 93, 151, 155, 158–9, 160–63, 165, 189–90, 213
Rain (rainfall), 31–36; annual precipitation, 50, 54, 107–8, 179
Rainier, Mount, 166, 167
Ranches (ranching), 56, 57–58 (*see also* Farming; Livestock); dude, 30; ecological, 57–58; and wildlife extermination, 117, 120
Range(s): defined, 219; main, 72–85
Rattlesnakes, 123
Rawah Range; Wilderness Area, 75
Reclamation, Bureau of, 26, 125, 127, 135, 136, 140–41, 181, 183
Recreation (sports, tourists, vacationists), xi, 19, 30, 60, 73, 83, 97, 190–99; climbing and hiking, 82–83, 84–85, 164–73; ecology and, 26 (*see also* Ecology); fishing (*see* Fishing); Forest Service and, 179–85; hunting (*see* Hunting); skiing (*see* Skiing); snowmobiling, 8; and tundra country, 82–85; vehicles, 72, 83 (*see also* Four-wheel-drive vehicles); and Wilderness Areas, 179, 190–99, 216 (*see also* specific places)
Red Mountain, 213, 215; Pass, 213
Red rocks, 62–63
Reservoirs, 26, 29, 54, 78, 105, 126, 127, 140, 141, 161–62, 182. *See also* Dams; specific places
Ridgway, Colorado, 88, 89, 204, 207
Rio Blanco County, Colorado, 184, 185
Rio Grande River, 35, 79, 87, 188
Rittenhouse, Susan, 20
River runners, 16–25
Rivers (streams), 3, 17–25, 53–54, 78–80 (*see also* Water; specific places, rivers); "braided," 53; dams and reservoirs, 126–27 (*see also* Dams; Reservoirs); patterns of, 78–80; rafting and (*see* Rafting); valleys and, 91–98 (*see also* Valleys); water sports and, 16–25; Western Slope, 91–92
Roads (highways), 54, 83, 84, 97, 145, 150, 153, 154–63, 178, 180, 209, 215–16; jeeps and (*see* Jeeps); and mining, 153, 154–56, 158–63, 209, 214; wagon, 83, 153–54, 158–60
Roaring Fork River, 17, 87–88, 91, 159–60, 162, 169
Robinson Creek, 42
Rock, 42, 61, 62, 210 (*see also* specific kinds, formations, places); moraines, 81, 219; volcanoes and (*see* Volcanoes)
Rock islands, 125
Rocky Mountain Biological Laboratory, 146
Rocky Mountain National Park, 4–11, 75, 194; Bear Lake, 81; Front Range, 4, 63, 75–76; life zones, 65–71; main ranges, 72–85; Trail Ridge, 66–67; Trail Ridge Road, 64, 65, 69, 71, 82, 94
Rocky Mountains, 4, 28ff., 54, 59–61ff. (*see also* Mountains; Rocky Mountain National Park; specific mountains, places); formation, origin of, 49, 50, 61–72, 74–75, 79; life zones, 65–71, 86; main ranges, 72–85; plateaus, 87–95
*Rocky Mountains, The* (Atwood), 208
Rooster's Comb, The, 42, 43
Royal Gorge, 3, 79–80, 158
Rue grass, 51

Sacred Mountain District, 105, 109
Sagebrush (sage), 51 56, 90
Sage grouse, 116, 119
St. Vrain, Marcellin, 52
Salida, Colorada, 17, 79
Salt (brine), and water supply, 135–36, 137, 140–41
Salt grass, 51
Sand Canyon, 109
*Sand Country Almanac, A,* 25
Sand dunes (San Luis Valley), 168
Sandstone, 49, 69, 62–63, 84, 87, 135, 210
Sangre de Cristo Mountain Range, 76, 166, 167–69, 219
San Isabel National Forest, 180
San Juan Mountaineers, 205–6
San Juan Mountain Range, 10–11, 35, 75, 77, 79, 80, 84, 87, 91, 104, 107, 169, 196, 203, 205–17; National Forest, 192; Primitive Area, 188–92
San Juan River, 91, 106–7, 108–9
San Luis, Colorado, 169
San Luis Valley, 74, 77, 79, 95, 96, 167–68
San Miguel Canyon, 214, 216
San Miguel Mountains, 84, 88, 215
San Miguel River, 87, 91–92, 138–40, 214
Sawatch Mountain Range, 79, 81, 95–96, 153, 159, 160, 161; peak heights, 166
Saxifrage, 69
Schmuck, Philip, 167, 199
Schofield Pass, 149
Scott, Marie, 207–8
Sedimentary rock, 74, 87, 210
Sego lily. *See* Mariposa
Shale, 61, 87, 97. *See also* Oil shale
Sheep, 34, 54, 55, 70, 77, 96–97, 98
Sheep Lake, 43
Shooting stars (flowers), 67
Shrine Pass, 171–72, 173
Sierra Blanca, 167–70
*Silent Spring* (Carson), 121
Silver (silver mining), 8, 32, 146, 153, 158, 159–61, 209, 211
Silverton, Colorado, 30–31, 32, 35, 188, 190, 213
Skiing, 7, 8–9, 98, 203–4, 209–10, 215; downhill (Alpine), 9; Nordic, 9
Sky pilot (flower), 69, 163
Slick Rock, Colorado, 121

Slick Rock Canyon, 137
Slide-rock, 155–56, 219
Smog, 58, 111
Sneffels Range, 203–17
Snow, 3, 4, 5–7, 10, 11, 28, 39 (*see also* Ice); annual precipitation, 50; avalanches, 60; kinds, 7; powder, 7, 9; sports, 8–9 (*see also* Skiing; Snowmobiling); and water supply, 154, 162; white-outs, 5–6, 11
Snowmass, Colorado, 8, 186, 210
Snowmass Creek, 186, 192–94
Snowmass Lake, 186, 192–96, 198, 199
Snowmass Mountain, 195–96
Snowmobiling, 8
Snow reservoirs, 7
Soap Creek, 43
Soil, 49–57, 63, 68; conservation programs, 105–6; duststorms (1930s), 55–57; erosion, 56 (*see also* Erosion); farming and, 54–57 (*see also* Farming); ranching and, 57–58, 105–6; rivers and water and, 53–54 (*see also* Irrigation)
Soliffluction terraces, 70, 219
Song sparrows, 54
Sonoran life zones, 65, 86
Sopris, Mount, 87
South Park, 37, 40–41, 45, 53, 74, 77, 154, 156, 158; Buffalo Peaks, 77
South Platte River, 37, 38, 49, 53–54, 55, 59, 75, 79, 158, 161; Valley, 53, 54, 158
Split Mountain, 25, 26
Sprague, Edna (Ejay), 38
Sprague, Marshall, 38, 40
Spruce (trees), 66, 67–68, 77, 81, 94 (*see also* specific kinds); spruce beetle and, 177–78
Spruce Tree House, 113
Square Tower, 110
Steamboat Rock, 18, 25, 27
Storms, 3, 4, 5–7, 39, 40, 55, 60, 80, 92. *See also* Lightning; Rain; Snow
Subalpine life zone, 65n, 66–69, 86
Sunflowers, 51
Switzer, Ronald, 113–14

Tabeguache Utes, 96
Tarns, 81–82, 220
Tarryall Creek, 38, 40
Tarryall Range, 38
Tavaputs Plateau, 92–94
Taylor River, 17
Telluride, Colorado, 8, 73, 98, 213–15
1080 (sodium fluoracetate), 118–19, 120–24
Thunderstorms, 92
Timberline (treeline), 68, 69–71, 220
Torrey, John, 164–65
Torreys Peak, 164, 165
Towers, Anasazi and, 109, 110–14
Towhees (birds), 112
Tractors, 101, 102, 107, 114
Trails, 209; Wilderness Areas, 186–99
Transition life zone, 65, 86
Trappers Lake, 177, 178, 179–85
Trees (forests), 28–29, 50–51, 59, 63, 65 (*see also* Plant life; specific kinds, places); altitude and life zones and, 63–71; autumn leaves, 39–40; wind and, 5, 6, 68
Trout, 29, 30, 77, 126; cutthroat, 182; rainbow, 36, 132
Trout Creek Pass, 154, 158
Tucker, Becky, 30, 32–33, 34, 37–38, 39, 41–42, 45
Tucker, Bert, 30, 32–33, 34
Tundra, 69–71, 82–85; defined, 220
Tunnels, 154, 160–61, 162
Turkey Creek, 171, 172
Turquoise Lake, 161; Reservoir, 154, 156, 161–62
Twin Lakes, 160, 162; Reservoir, 154, 162

Uncompahgre Peak, 84
Uncompahgre Plateau, 89, 91, 95, 96
Uncompahgre River, 11, 91, 92, 204; Gorge, 213
Underground streams and water, 11, 54
United States Air Force Academy, 61
Upper Sonoran life zone, 65
Uranium, 97, 139
Ute Indians, 66, 94–96, 105, 110, 114, 299; reservation, 110
Ute Mountain, 104, 111; Pass, 75, 94

Vail, Colorado, 8, 210
Vail Pass, 171–72, 173
Vallecito Creek, 91, 191–92, 198
Valleys, 91–98, 135–41. *See also* Canyons; specific places, valleys
Vandenbusche, Duane, 127–28, 129, 130–31, 132
Vehicles, recreational, 30, 72, 83. *See also* Four-wheel-drive vehicles; Jeeps
Viiding, Marianne, 128, 129, 131

Volcanoes (volcanic activity), 50, 61, 75, 208–9, 210

Warm Springs (Yampa River rapid), 23–25
Water (water supply), 11, 53–58, 60, 78–79, 96, 105, 154, 161–63, 181–82, 183–85; dams and reservoirs, 105, 126–27 (*see also* Dams; Reservoirs); erosion and, 80–82; irrigation and farming, 54–57, 58, 78, 137, 139; rivers and, 53–54, 78–79 (*see also* Rivers); salt removal and, 135–36, 137, 140–41; sports, 16–25
Water Power Sites, 181–82, 183–85
Waterton Canyon, 17
Weasels, 70
Weather (climate), 60, 94, 113, 141 (*see also* Rain; Snow; Storms; Wind; specific aspects); life zones and, 65–71
Wells, 54, 56, 58
West Elk Wilderness Area, 41–42, 43
Western meadowlark, 51
Western Slope, 7, 87–98 (*see also* specific places); plateaus, 87–98, 183–85
Wet (Greenhorn) Mountains, 76; Valley, 76
Wheat, 54–55, 102, 106; grass, 51, 106
White-outs, 5–6, 11
White River, 91, 95, 169, 177, 183
White River National Forest, 178–85
Wilderness Areas, 181–85, 186–99 (*see also* specific places); tourists and, 179, 191–99, 216
Wild Horse, Colorado, 55
Wildlife. *See* Animal life; Plant life; specific aspects, kinds, places
Wiliams Fork River, 185
Willows, 54, 64, 67, 70, 155
Wilson, Mount, 84, 187, 216; Primitive Area, 187
Wind, 5, 6–7, 28, 50, 60, 70, 212; effects of, 6–7, 68, 212
Wolves, 55, 120
Woodstock mining camp, 72–73

Yampa River, 18, 21–27, 58, 92, 95, 108; Valley, 91, 92
Yankee Boy Basin, 210, 211, 213
Yucca, 51, 56, 64, 115
Yule Canyon, 151